ADVANCE PRAISE FOR

Fighting in the Streets

"Herman develops a powerful theory of racial violence that is as applicable to the early as well as late 20th century, and will be essential to understanding any future outbreaks of racial violence. A must-read for anyone interested in the origins of American race riots in particular, and global racial and ethnic violence in general."

Albert J. Bergesen, Professor of Sociology, University of Arizona

"Using sophisticated mapping and statistical techniques to compare several cases of urban ethnic violence that took place in 20th century America, Herman unlocks the fundamental combination of circumstances that fostered urban unrest during three presumably distinct periods in American history. Applying a uniform method to cases from each cycle of collective violence, World War One through World War Two, the 1960s, and the 1980s through 1990s, Herman shows that while surface circumstances surrounding urban riots vary greatly, the root causes do not. Rich historical descriptions both supplement and confirm the quantitative analyses, providing context to explain how rapid changes in population combine with economic inequalities to produce episodes of racial/ethnic conflict. Herman's writing is fluid, and fully convincing. This book is a must-read for students of urban politics and collective violence."

Bert Useem, Professor of Sociology and Director of the Institute for Social Research at the University of New Mexico

Fighting in the Streets

PETER LANG
New York • Washington, D.C./Baltimore • Bern
Frankfurt am Main • Berlin • Brussels • Vienna • Oxford

Max Arthur Herman

Fighting in the Streets

Ethnic Succession and Urban Unrest in Twentieth-Century America

PETER LANG
New York • Washington, D.C./Baltimore • Bern
Frankfurt am Main • Berlin • Brussels • Vienna • Oxford

Library of Congress Cataloging-in-Publication Data

Names: Herman, Max Arthur, author.
Title: Fighting in the streets: ethnic succession and urban unrest
in twentieth-century America / Max Arthur Herman.
Description: New York: Peter Lang, 2005.
Includes bibliographical references and index.
Identifiers: LCCN 2004014123 | ISBN 978-0-8204-7455-7 (paperback: alk. paper)
Subjects: LCSH: Riots—United States. | Violence—United States.
Ethnic conflict—United States. | African Americans—Social conditions—20th century.
Classification: LCC HV6477.H57 2005 | DDC 303.6'23'09730904—dc22
LC record available at https://lccn.loc.gov/2004014123

Bibliographic information published by **Die Deutsche Nationalbibliothek**.
Die Deutsche Nationalbibliothek lists this publication in the "Deutsche
Nationalbibliografie"; detailed bibliographic data are available
on the Internet at http://dnb.d-nb.de/.

Cover design by Lisa Barfield

The paper in this book meets the guidelines for permanence and durability
of the Committee on Production Guidelines for Book Longevity
of the Council of Library Resources.

© 2005, 2018 Peter Lang Publishing, Inc., New York
29 Broadway, 18th floor, New York, NY 10006
www.peterlang.com

All rights reserved.
Reprint or reproduction, even partially, in all forms such as microfilm,
xerography, microfiche, microcard, and offset strictly prohibited.

Printed in the United States of America

*For my parents,
Ralph and Catharine Herman,
and my uncle Gerald Herman*

Contents

List of Tables and Figures ix
Acknowledgments........................... xi

CHAPTER ONE
    Introduction............................ 1

CHAPTER TWO
    Theoretical Explanations for
    Ethnic Violence 9

CHAPTER THREE
    Investigating Urban Unrest 23

CHAPTER FOUR
    Black Migration and White Backlash:
    Chicago (1919) and Detroit (1943) 39

CHAPTER FIVE
    White Flight and Black Power:
    Newark and Detroit (1967) 75

CHAPTER SIX
    New Immigrants and Black Resentment:
    Miami (1980) and Los Angeles (1992) 114

CHAPTER SEVEN
    Insights from the Past,
    Prescriptions for the Future 157

References 175
Index 000

Tables and Figures

Table 3.1 Summary of Independent Variables Used for Statistical Analyses. 33

Table 4.1 Demographic Measures for Census Tracts with and without Riot Fatalities by City, Chicago and Detroit 62

Table 4.2a Poisson Regression Estimates of the Number of Riot Fatalities in Chicago Census Tracts as a Function of Change in Racial/Ethnic Composition and Economic Characteristics, 1910-1920 65

Table 4.2b Poisson Regression Estimates of the Number of Riot Fatalities in Detroit SMSA Census Tracts as a Function of Change in Racial/Ethnic Composition and Economic Characteristics, 1940-1950 66

Table 4.3 Linear Regression Estimates of the Number of Riot Fatalities in Chicago and Detroit Census Tracts as a Function of Change in Racial/Ethnic Composition and Economic Characteristics (Controlling for Spatial Autocorrelation) 71

Table 5.1 Demographic Measures for Census Tracts with and without Riot Fatalities by City, Newark and Detroit 103

Table 5.2a Poisson Regression Estimates of the Number of Riot Fatalities in Newark Census Tracts as a Function of Change in Racial/Ethnic Composition and Economic Characteristics, 1950-1960 105

Table 5.2b Poisson Regression Estimates of the Number of Riot Fatalities in Detroit Census Tracts as a Function of Change in Racial/Ethnic Composition and Economic Characteristics, 1950-1960 106

Table 5.3 Linear Regression Estimates of the Number of Riot Fatalities in Newark and Detroit Census Tracts as a Function of Change in Racial/Ethnic Composition and Economic Characteristics (Controlling for Spatial Autocorrelation) 110

Table 6.1 Demographic Measures for Census Tracts with and without Riot Fatalities by City, Miami and Los Angeles 142

Table 6.2a Poisson Regression Estimates of the Number of Riot Fatalities in Dade County (Miami) Census Tracts as a Function of Change in Racial/Ethnic Composition and Economic Characteristics, 1970-1980. 146

Table 6.2b Poisson Regression Estimates of the Number of Riot Fatalities in Los Angeles County Census Tracts as a Function of Change in Racial/Ethnic Composition and Economic Characteristics, 1980-1990. 147

Table 6.3 Linear Regression Estimates of the Number of Riot Fatalities in Miami and Los Angeles Census Tracts as a Function of Change in Racial/Ethnic Composition and Economic Characteristics (Controlling for Spatial Autocorrelation) 152

TABLES AND FIGURES

Figure 4.1 1919 Chicago Riot Fatalities and Percent Black, 1910 51
Figure 4.2 1919 Chicago Riot Fatalities and Percent Black, 1920 52
Figure 4.3 1919 Chicago Riot Fatalities and Change in Percent Black, 1910-1920 53
Figure 4.4 1919 Chicago Riot Fatalities and Percent Males Unemployed, 1920 54
Figure 4.5 1943 Detroit Riot Fatalities and Percent Black, 1940 56
Figure 4.6 1943 Detroit Riot Fatalities and Percent Black, 1950 57
Figure 4.7 1943 Detroit Riot Fatalities and Change in Percent Black, 1940-1950 58
Figure 4.8 1943 Detroit Riot Fatalities and Percent Unemployed, 1950 59
Figure 4.9 1943 Detroit Riot Fatalities and Median Household Income, 1950 60
Figure 5.1 1967 Newark Riot Fatalities and Percent Black, 1950 91
Figure 5.2 1967 Newark Riot Fatalities and Percent Black, 1960 92
Figure 5.3 1967 Newark Riot Fatalities and Change in Percent Black, 1950-1960 93
Figure 5.4 1967 Newark Riot Fatalities and Percent Males Unemployed, 1960 95
Figure 5.5 1967 Newark Riot Fatalities and Median Household Income, 1960 96
Figure 5.6 1967 Detroit Riot Fatalities and Percent Black, 1950 97
Figure 5.7 1967 Detroit Riot Fatalities and Percent Black, 1960 98
Figure 5.8 1967 Detroit Riot Fatalities and Change in Percent Black, 1950-1960 99
Figure 5.9 1967 Detroit Riot Fatalities and Percent Males Unemployed, 1960 100
Figure 5.10 1967 Detroit Riot Fatalities and Median Household Income, 1960 101
Figure 6.1 1980 Miami Riot Fatalities and Ethnic Composition, 1970 129
Figure 6.2 1980 Miami Riot Fatalities and Ethnic Compostion, 1980 130
Figure 6.3 1980 Miami Riot Fatalities and Change in Percent Black, 1970-1980 131
Figure 6.4 1980 Miami Riot Fatalities and Percent Unemployed, 1980 133
Figure 6.5 1980 Miami Riot Fatalities and Median Household Income, 1980 134
Figure 6.6 1992 Los Angeles Riot Fatalities and Ethnic Composition, 1980 135
Figure 6.7 1992 Los Angeles Riot Fatalities and Ethic Composition, 1990 136
Figure 6.8 1992 Los Angeles Riot Fatalities and Change in Percent Black, 1980-1990 137
Figure 6.9 1992 Los Angeles Riot Fatalities and Change in Percent Hispanic, 1980-1990 138
Figure 6.10 1992 Los Angeles Riot Fatalities and Percent Unemployed, 1990 139
Figure 6.11 1992 Los Angeles Riot Fatalities and Median Household Income, 1990 140

ACKNOWL-
EDGMENTS

I began this project nearly ten years ago when I was a graduate student at the University of Arizona in Tucson. During the course of that time, I have benefited greatly from the advice of numerous academic colleagues and the support of several interested parties. First and foremost, I am thankful for the guidance of my doctoral thesis adviser, Albert Bergesen, who sparked my interest in the study of urban unrest and provided me with the theoretical tools I needed to begin studying this important topic.

I would also like to thank my fellow graduate students and professors in the Sociology Department at the University of Arizona who were a constant source of feedback as I worked my way toward the doctorate. This list, while not exhaustive, includes the late Bill Bunis, Pat Goldsmith, Liam Downey, Andrew Jones, Richard Hutchinson, Kris McIlwaine, Dave Richmond, and Mark Konty, as well as Doug McAdam, Paula England, Hector Delgado, Calvin Morrill, Alfonso Morales, Jim Shockey, Sarah Soule, David Snow, Michael Sobel, , and Kathleen Schwarztman who all contributed their thoughts and reflections toward the dissertation project. Sociology Department administrators Sherry Enderle, Bonnie Thompson, Beverly Jones, Barbara McIntosh, and Vienna Marum kept me organized both materially and emotionally during my graduate school days. I would also like to thank librarian Christine Collin for taking the time to give me a hands-on tutorial of ArcView GIS which was so vital to this project.

During the 1998–1999 academic year, I had the distinct privilege of serving as a visiting scholar at Rice University. With the strong encouragement of my colleagues Chad Gordon, Stephen Klineberg, Elizabeth Long, Bill Martin, and Chandler Davidson, I was able to complete my doctoral thesis. I am especially thankful to Chad Gordon for the many wonderful working lunches we shared throughout the Houston metropolitan area and to Elizabeth Long and her husband Bill for taking me out on their sailboat.

During the 1999–2000 academic year, I served as a visiting assistant professor at Oberlin College where I made numerous friends among the faculty and staff. Bill Norris and Clovis White were a constant presence whom I could always count on for good advice, as well as Daphne John and Velko Vujavich who were always there to offer a kind word. I am especially grateful for the input of my nonsociology colleagues, Peter Silberman, Lipika Mazumdar, and George and Laura Boulukos who despite their backgrounds in music theory, anthropology, and comparative literature, respectively, were always eager to hear more about my "riots project." I value their friendship highly. I thank Rabbi Shimon Brand for keeping me spiritually centered and I am also thankful to the department administrator, Judi Davidson, who was always there to cheer me up during the bleak Midwestern winter.

From 2000-the present, I have been based in Newark, New Jersey, a fascinating, but often overlooked city, where I presently serve as an assistant professor of sociology and anthropology. Here I have benefited greatly from the advice and support of my sociology and anthropology colleagues Clay Hartjen, Brian Ferguson, Ira Cohen, Kurt Schock, Sheri Ann Butterfield, and Alex Hinton. Although many of my colleagues study topics regarding collective violence, they are nonetheless a most congenial bunch. In addition to the aforementioned cast of characters, I have also benefited from the guidance of Clement Price, Rob Snyder, Charles Russell, Mara Sidney, Kimberly Decosta Holton, Jamie Lew, Mal Kiniry, Barbara Gross, and numerous unnamed others. I am deeply appreciative to Andrew Beveridge of Queens College and John Logan of Brown University for offering their sage advice and providing me with historical GIS data for Chicago. My thanks to Susan Olzak, Douglas Massey, Thomas Sugrue, and Bert Useem for their continuing encouragement.

I am especially grateful to Alan Sadovnik for taking me under his wing and putting me in touch with the publisher of this book. I am proud to have him as a mentor. I am also exceeding grateful to Nela Navarro and Gabriella Frisoli, without whom it is unlikely that the manuscript would have been completed. As my executive editor, Nela Navarro handled the task with great aplomb. She helped blend my doctoral thesis and the more recent chapters on Newark and Detroit into a coherent, clear, readable manuscript. She was able to read through every word of every chapter, when at times I was unable to do so. I could not ask for a better collaborator. Gabriella Frisoli was instrumental in keeping me focused on the big picture as I continued my research on the 1967 Newark and Detroit riots. She was instrumental in designing the project website www.67riots.rutgers.edu, helped me streamline my teaching with Blackboard, and provided moral support over the long haul. She too is a great friend and colleague.

Last, but certainly not least, I am eternally grateful for the continued love and affection of my partner Jennifer Oshiki, who has been with me every step of the way, from the west to the east, through good times and bad, in sickness and health. She has helped out in innumerable ways, doing archival research, camera work for videotaped interviews, debating ideas with me regarding this book and other sociological topics, keeping me and the cats well fed, tending to my elderly parents, and keeping the house from falling down. She is a multitalented woman, whose talents are matched by her generosity of spirit. I am thankful for her presence in my life. With her everything is possible.

CHAPTER ONE

Introduction

Throughout the twentieth century in urban America, tensions among members of different racial and ethnic groups were periodically manifested in episodes of widespread ethnic collective violence, commonly referred to as "race riots." In recent years, interethnic violence erupted on the streets of South Central Los Angeles (1992) and Miami (1980), leaving scores of people injured, over sixty people dead, and several hundred million dollars' worth of property damaged. These events, characterized by acts of extreme brutality, such as the bludgeoning of a truck driver with a heavy oxygen canister at the corner of Florence Boulevard and Normandie Avenue in Los Angeles, or the insertion of a thorny rose into the mouth of a man lying prostrate on the bloodied pavement in Liberty City, Miami, were reported in the press as if they were novel phenomena. Such violence was portrayed as an ugly emergent aspect of life in today's "multiethnic," "multicultural" cities where immigrants from Latin America and Asia clashed with white and black native-born Americans over access to jobs, housing, and political power.

Yet, looking at episodes of urban unrest that took place earlier in this century, in cities like Chicago (1919) and Detroit (1943), one can observe the same phenomena, as members of different racial and ethnic groups assaulted and brutally murdered one another in the streets. In Chicago and Detroit, black workers were pulled off trolley cars by white mobs and viciously beaten or stabbed as they attempted to return home from work in the factories. White motorists driving through predominantly black neighborhoods were often stopped, pulled from their cars by groups of blacks, and beaten as their vehicles were set afire. As a result of such mob actions, over thirty people in each city lost their lives. Chicago and Detroit, with their diverse populations of white ethnic immigrants and black migrants, could also have been considered multiethnic and multicultural at the time.

So too were Chicago and Detroit sites of competition among newer and older ethnic groups. During the wartime and postwar years (1916–1918 and 1941–1945) older white ethnic immigrants in these cities found themselves being challenged for jobs, space (both housing and social territory), and power by a new wave of African-American migrants from the rural South. Later in the century in cities like Miami and Los Angeles, rapid demographic change fostered similar competition. Such competition, in turn, generates the potential for ethnic collective violence.

These common dynamics of rapid population change and contention among racial/ethnic groups for jobs, space, and power could also be observed during the major riots that took place during the 1960s: Watts (1965), Newark (1967), and Detroit (1967). Although much of the violence that took place during these civil disturbances involved police officers and black residents of inner-city neighborhoods, the structural underpinnings of these events are familiar. Black migration coupled with "white flight" from inner-city neighborhoods set the stage for confrontations among new black majorities and the entrenched white power structure. Black workers competed with whites for the remaining positions in the declining industrial sector, while black residents clashed with the sons and daughters of white immigrants who owned and operated a majority of stores in the now majority black ghettos. White police officers and politicians acted as proxies for those left behind by the "great suburban migration," seeking to maintain white control over neighborhoods that were no longer predominantly Italian, Irish, Polish, or Jewish. In their efforts to "hold the line" against a black community seeking to flex its newly found political muscle, police officers and military troops sided with the white citizenry and engaged in acts of reactionary violence. As was true with the riots in Chicago and Detroit during the first half of the twentieth century, as well as the ones in Miami and Los Angeles during the century's last two decades, outbreaks of urban unrest in America's cities during the 1960s were also associated with rapid demographic change and ethnic competition.

Given the association of competitive ethnic group relations and collective violence with rapid population change in all of the aforementioned cases, it should be clear that the riots of recent years are not in fact novel phenomena. Rather, the dynamics of urban unrest that characterize these recent riot events in cities such as Los Angeles and Miami point back to the turn of the century, the two World Wars, and the turbulent decade of the 1960s. This book therefore focuses on the striking similarities among these seemingly disparate historical events. Employing a comparative case method, I will closely examine six cases of urban unrest from three distinct historical periods. Based on these comparative case studies I will then construct a general explanatory model for urban unrest that I believe will help assess the potential for future episodes of collective violence in our cities. I will now briefly describe the three main periods of urban unrest in twentieth-century America.

The Wartime and Postwar Years

Shortly after the turn of the century, African Americans took part in what became known as the Great Migration, moving from the towns and villages of the rural South to industrial cities of the North. With the onset of World War I, demand for unskilled labor in the factories and slaughterhouses of the North increased dramatically. At the same time, cotton crops, a staple of the Southern economy, were devastated by the boll weevil parasite. Black sharecroppers and field hands found it difficult to survive. Faced with daily humiliations and threats of violence at the hands of whites under Jim Crow segregation, as well as a decline in their agricultural livelihood, many Southern blacks found the relatively high wages of the North to be an irresistible draw.

Beginning around 1910 and continuing through the 1950s, thousands of Southern blacks embarked on the journey by rail from the segregated South to the "promised land" of the North. Most settled in the industrial cities of the Midwest, particularly Chicago and Detroit. But as the black population of these cities grew dramatically, relations between whites and blacks turned sour. White Chicagoans and Detroiters, many whom had immigrated from Europe to America just a decade or two earlier, in short time came to view blacks as a potential threat to their economic security, political power, and ethnically organized neighborhoods. As young white men were sent off to war, black migrants filled their place in the factories, which temporarily led to racial integration on the shop floor but also to greater racial tensions, fueled by the belief among white workers that blacks might be used to undercut their wages and job security.

Realizing that increased numbers of Southern migrants were now able to vote under Northern legal statutes, black political leaders found themselves for the first time able to assert a modicum of influence in city politics. In cities like Chicago and Detroit, blacks were beginning to flex their political muscle, becoming key partners in a Democratic party coalition that was poised to take power at the local, state, and national levels. This too threatened whites' sense of control.

Residentially, in cities like Chicago and Detroit, blacks had been confined by the socially constructed boundaries of the "black belt," but these areas of settlement were rapidly becoming overcrowded. Black families began to move into the surrounding neighborhoods that had once been occupied almost exclusively by whites. Despite white resistance, the black belt neighborhoods were expanding, threatening to overwhelm the old ethnic enclaves of the Irish, Italians, Poles, and Eastern European Jews. Finally, African-American soldiers, returning from the front in Europe demanded to be treated with the respect and dignity they had earned in on the battlefield. Taking their cue from these soldiers, blacks in Chicago and Detroit became more militant in asserting their claims for equal treatment. Whites, particularly those of the working class and/or whose families had immigrated only recently, reacted to these developments with trepidation and anger, fearing the loss of their relative privileges and status vis-à-vis blacks. On one hot summer day in 1919, a black teenager by the name of Eugene Williams swam across the informal line separating black space from white space in Lake Michigan and was stoned by a white mob, sparking five days of violence in Chicago. Twenty-four years later in Detroit, on another hot summer day, a black teenager known as "Willie T" was ejected from a whites-only amusement park. Seeking revenge, he and his companions roamed the public beach at Belle Isle, scuffling with groups of white youths, including a group of sailors on shore leave. When rumor circulated that a black woman and her baby had been thrown off the bridge connecting Belle Isle to the mainland, Detroit erupted in racial violence that lasted for three days. In both Chicago and Detroit the battles began at the beaches, underscoring the nascent competition for space among whites and blacks in the industrial cities.

THE SIXTIES

At first glance, the major civil disturbances of the 1960s—Watts (1965), Newark (1967), and Detroit (1967)—seem to deviate from the pattern of the unrest that took place during the wartime and immediate postwar years in the first half of the century. The incidents that sparked violent ethnic conflict in the cities during the 1960s did not take place at recreational areas between white and black youths. Rather the precipitating incidents for these episodes of unrest involved confrontations between white police officers and black citizens that occurred during "routine" traffic stops (Newark and Watts) and raids on illegal nightclubs (Detroit). In contrast to earlier episodes of violence, the black participants in these events seem to have shared a common political orientation characterized by grievances (widely held among African Americans) against the "white power structure" (Fogelson 1971). Motivated by this "riot ideology," they identified white police and white-owned businesses as the "appropriate" targets for retribution. In keeping with this ideological position, the vast majority of people wounded or killed during these events were black civilians, killed by police officers or military personnel defending white-owned businesses and government property. In contrast to previous episodes of unrest earlier in the century, when white and black civilians squared off against one another, hardly any white civilians were killed during the 1960s disturbances. Because of their ideological nature and their defining clashes between black citizens and the police, the 1960s civil disturbances are often described by those sympathetic to their aims as "rebellions," "uprisings," or "ghetto revolts."

Yet, upon closer inspection, the same conditions that set the stage for urban unrest during the 1960s were present in episodes of urban ethnic violence that took place both earlier and later in the century. The 1960s riots in Watts, Newark, and Detroit, like the earlier riots in Chicago and Detroit, as well as the later riots in Miami and Los Angeles, were in large part a product of vast demographic and economic changes that transformed these cities and their respective neighborhoods. During the decade preceding the 1967 riots, Newark and Detroit were swept by a mass movement of people entering and departing the metropolis. As Southern blacks continued to migrate northward during the final phase of the Great Migration, whites fled from the cities to the suburbs. For the first time in these cities, blacks were the residential majority; the political system and municipal agencies, however, were slow to adjust to the new demographic reality. While neighborhoods rapidly changed in their racial composition, political power remained in the hands of whites. Managerial jobs in the private sector also continued to be monopolized by whites despite growing numbers of college-educated blacks. Eventually African Americans would make headway into these bastions of white privilege, but not before tensions had reached a boiling point. The riots in Watts, Newark, and Detroit were therefore largely a result of incomplete ethnic succession, a mismatch between the new black residential majority and whites who continued to exert political and economic control of the cities. The rocky transition from white to black majority rule would not be completed until these cities elected their first black mayors a few years later. Without the riots, this transition might have taken even longer to occur. Once again, population change lay at the heart of urban unrest.

THE POSTINDUSTRIAL ERA

On the surface, the events that took place in Miami (1980) and Los Angeles (1992) bear little resemblance to the "race riots" of the wartime and postwar years. Rather, they appear to be more akin to the 1960s riots. Rioting in both cities directly followed the acquittal of white police officers accused of severely beating black motorists, not scuffles between white and black civilians vying for recreational space. Furthermore, most of the African Americans living in Miami and Los Angeles at the time of the riots were, unlike those in Chicago (1919) and Detroit (1943), long-time residents, not recent migrants. The black communities of both cities, although on average poorer than the white populace, appeared to be relatively stable.

Yet during the 1970s and 1980s "sunbelt" cities such as Miami and Los Angeles experienced dramatic demographic change as a result of intensified immigration from abroad. A new wave of immigrants from Latin America and Asia moved into these Southern and Western urban areas that already had well-established black populations. Latino and Asian immigration would profoundly alter the economic, political, and residential landscape of these cities and in such a manner as to engender hostility between the new arrivals and the established black residents.

Prior to the outbreak of hostilities, black workers in both Miami and Los Angeles expressed concern that they were being displaced from their jobs in the hospitality, construction, and janitorial industries by recent Latino immigrants. With the decline of manufacturing in these cities, semiskilled and unskilled workers clung to the relatively few service positions available in an increasingly postindustrial economy. They bitterly complained about Asian and Latino immigrants who established businesses in predominantly black neighborhoods, accusing them of overcharging customers and poisoning the community with cheap liquor. They remonstrated against the dwindling of black political power, marked by the election of Latino politicians to city council. Finally, blacks in both cities, particularly in Los Angeles, feared residential displacement by the new wave of immigrants. In parts of L.A., neighborhoods that had once been 80 to 90 percent black were now evenly split among black and Latino residents. Black and Latino gangs clashed in the schools, the prisons, and on the streets of South Central, Compton, and Watts for supremacy.

In Miami, the threat of residential displacement never fully materialized. Rather, blacks remained hyper segregated in the ghettos of Liberty City and the remains of Overtown while Cubans and Haitians built thriving enclaves in the formerly white neighborhoods bordering these black communities. Surrounded on all sides by economically successful new immigrants, black Miamians felt bypassed on the road to political and economic power. So did African Americans in Los Angeles. When Latino police officers, along with white patrolmen, were implicated in the beatings of black motorists Arthur McDuffie in Miami and Rodney King in Los Angeles, these incipient ethnic tensions came to the fore.

LOOKING BACKWARD TO MAKE SENSE OF THE FUTURE

During the first half of the twentieth century, urban white immigrants and black migrants clashed over access to jobs, space, and housing. During the 1960s, as second- and third-generation ethnic whites moved out of the declining industrial cities, blacks sought a place at the political table. This too led to violent conflict. By the end of the twentieth century, blacks in postindustrial cities such as Miami and Los Angeles found themselves concentrated in service occupations, fending off the incursion of recent Latino and Asian immigrants into their workplaces and neighborhoods. Ironically, African Americans had come full circle from disenfranchised rural migrants to defenders of their urban space and limited economic prerogatives.

The main thesis of this book is that while the principal adversaries in the struggle for jobs, space, and power have changed, the process of ethnic succession continues unabated with predictable results. Demographic flux continues to reshape the ethnic contours of cities and their neighborhoods, placing new groups in contact and competition with one another. This leads to overt violence among natives and newcomers when and where the aspirations of these diverse groups are not accommodated. Recent history indicates that African Americans have borne the brunt of competition from immigrants. They have been both the victims and initiators of violence, but by no means is their central place in future conflicts clear. Rather, the next wave of urban unrest may pit today's immigrants against tomorrow's immigrants. Increasing the pool of economic resources available to newcomers and natives is a step in the right direction, but programs aimed at fostering cultural awareness are also necessary to ameliorate ethnic conflicts in multicultural America. Without mutual understanding and respect, the ongoing movement of ethnic groups through urban space will continue to cause friction and spark deadly ethnic/racial conflicts. Until we get a grasp on the dynamics of ethnic competition and succession at the neighborhood level, we will continually bear witness to fighting in the streets.

THE PLAN OF STUDY

The first two chapters of this book focus on theoretical explanations for riot activity and methodological innovations in the study of riot violence. In chapter 1, I lay the theoretical foundation for this study, rooted in the tradition of human ecology and ethnic competition. In chapter 2, I explain how the present research employs new methodological techniques for the analysis of riot violence, which include shifting the level of analysis from cities to neighborhoods through the use of census tract data and employing geographic information systems (GIS) software to map demographic processes over time and space. Chapters 3 through 6 focus on the riot events themselves. Chapter 3 presents a comparative case analysis of the 1919 Chicago riot and the 1943 Detroit riot. Chapter 4 does the same for the Newark and Detroit riots of 1967. Chapter 5 presents a comparative analysis of the Miami riot of 1980 and the 1992 Los Angeles riot. Each of these chapters provides a brief historical background on developments leading up to the outbreak of violence, statistical tests of competing explanatory hypotheses, and maps illustrating the relationship between demographic change and riot violence. Chapter 6 synthesizes the results of the comparative analyses presented in chapters 3, 4, and 5. In that chapter I once again compare and contrast the recent riots in Miami and Los Angeles with episodes of urban unrest that took place earlier in the twentieth century in Chicago, Detroit, and Newark. I assess the case for a general model of riot violence and offer some policy recommendations based on the available historical and statistical data.

CHAPTER TWO

Theoretical Explanations for Ethnic Violence

Sociological explanations for ethnic collective violence typically fall into two camps, one focusing on competition among groups for limited resources, and the other emphasizing segregation and economic deprivation as key factors in generating hostilities between members of different racial/ethnic groups. Proponents of the former perspective argue that violence is a product of increasing intergroup contact that generates competitive pressures, thus leading to the outbreak of overt hostilities. Scholars in the latter camp argue that it is the isolation of ethnic/racial minorities from mainstream society and their concomitant exclusion from access to political and economic rewards that causes them to engage in violence. Although these explanations are not mutually exclusive and indeed may be complementary in some respects, for the moment I will treat them separately and discuss their implications for the study of urban riots. I begin with segregation and deprivation accounts for collective violence.

SEGREGATION AND ITS DISCONTENTS

Segregation involves the spatial separation of different racial/ethnic groups that limits the potential for interaction among members of these groups in social institutions. Segregation typically refers to an unequal distribution of group population in geographical space but also applies to labor markets where members of particular racial/ethnic groups are excluded from certain occupational locations. Often, geographic segregation, labor market exclusion, and educational disparities go hand in hand, reinforcing one another in a "web of urban racism" (Baron 1969). Despite the passage of the Civil Rights Act of 1964 (which removed official/legal support for racial discrimination in housing, employment, and public facilities), high levels of residential and occupation segregation have persisted in many

American cities. This sad fact has led demographers Massey and Denton (1993) to characterize the present situation as "American Apartheid."

Like Baron, Massey and Denton argue that segregation is the key factor that helps to perpetuate inequality between whites and blacks by attenuating African Americans' social network ties to the mainstream and hence limiting access to economic and cultural opportunities. Furthermore, these scholars argue, persistent residential and economic segregation may foster the development of racial subcultures forged in opposition to the culture of the dominant racial majority. Such subcultural formation may further engender a perception of difference among minority and majority groups, helping to foster conflict where and when members of these groups do interact. In *Internal Colonialism* (1975)—a study of the so-called Celtic Fringe in Great Britain—Michael Hechter refers to the interaction of economic segregation and geographic isolation as creating a "cultural division of labor" between Scots and Englishmen. He details how persistent geographic and economic isolation led Scots to assert a national identity in opposition to that of England, at one time leading to overt warfare between the Scots and the English.

Blauner (1972) suggests that blacks in America's cities lived in a colonial relationship to a white majority that maintained political and economic control of the inner city long after they had ceased to live there. Analogous to Hechter's depiction of the economic exploitation of Scots who had been "colonized" by the English, Blauner considers African Americans, who are concentrated in poor inner-city neighborhoods, to be a colonized people whose labor is exploited by white elites. He argues that the "rebellions" that occurred during the mid- to late 1960s represent a political response to such "internal colonialism." Blauner and others (Feagin and Hahn 1973; Fogelson 1971) suggest that such riots deliberately targeted institutions symbolizing white political and economic power, e.g., police outposts, courthouses, and white-owned businesses. Likewise, McAdam (1982) characterizes the 1960s civil disturbances as a form of political protest.

For decades, scholars like Kenneth Clark (1965) and Karl Taeuber (Taeuber and Taeuber 1965) had noted the profoundly negative impact of segregation on the socioeconomic well-being of African Americans, suggesting that segregation led to various forms of "ghetto pathologies" such as higher rates of violent crime. Writing in the late 1980s, William Julius Wilson (1987) updated this school of thought, arguing that a transformation of the economy from primarily manufacturing to service industries exacerbated the effects of racial segregation. This economic transformation, he noted, helped foster the growth of an "urban underclass," a category comprised of persons who are persistently undereducated, unemployed, and concentrated in America's inner cities. Because of the absence of strong community institutions (a product of structural decay), inner-city dwellers have, according to Wilson, become more likely to reject the values of mainstream society and engage in deviant or criminal behaviors. Applying this perspective to homicidal violence, Peterson and Krivo (1993) found segregation to be a significant predictor of black victimization rates in large American inner cities. Isolated from mainstream society, members of racial/ethnic minority groups who live in highly segregated areas may be more prone to violence and primed for rebellion than their less segregated counterparts.

DEPRIVATION AND COLLECTIVE VIOLENCE

While some theorists examine the association between segregation and crime/violence, others place greater emphasis on how economic deprivation acts as a causal factor in outbreaks of riot activity. Although economic indicators of deprivation such as low income levels tend to be correlated with segregation, these scholars argue that it is economic deprivation, or the perception thereof, which gives rise to frustrations later expressed in violence. Such anger can be a response to impoverished conditions (absolute deprivation) or a sense of unfairness fueled by comparing the group's circumstances to that of another group or to prior expectations of group success (relative deprivation).

Absolute deprivation is characterized by deficits in economic or social well being for a group residing in a particular locale, e.g., high levels of unemployment, low levels of income, or low levels of educational attainment. As such, absolute deprivation theorists (Lupsha 1968, Downes 1968) argue that urban rioting is a product of real grievances against a system that deprives a particular group(s) of the necessities of life, e.g., jobs, food, and shelter. Rioting is a response to dire conditions of poverty that government and/or private industry have failed to ameliorate.

Relative deprivation, on the other hand, involves a disjuncture between expectations and reality, a sense that members of one's group are not receiving what they properly deserve. Such an explanation for violence relies on the psychological mechanism of frustration-aggression. Anger generated by unfulfilled expectations or loss of status is displaced and acted out against diffuse targets. Applied historically to racial/ethnic conflict in the nineteenth-century American South, Dollard (1949) argued that working-class whites, reduced to wage labor after the Civil War, took out their frustration on blacks whom had recently been emancipated from slavery. Likewise, Tilly (1969) notes that when peasants in France and England were displaced from the land during the eighteenth century, they engaged in "reactive collective violence." In short, according to relative deprivation theorists, a perceived or actual loss of group status or unfairness relative to other groups generates frustrations that may be manifested in collective violence. Using measures of income inequality between blacks and whites as indicators of relative deprivation, several scholars have found a significant association between relative deprivation and homicide rates (Blau and Blau 1982; Balkwell 1990).

Given that scholars have found empirical support for effects of segregation and income inequality on rates of homicide in American cites, one is tempted to suggest that segregation and/or deprivation are also responsible for incidents of interethnic violence that characterize urban riots. Yet empirical studies that compare the frequency and severity of rioting among American cities have failed to produce conclusive evidence for an economic deprivation account. Some early studies comparing riot and nonriot cities found an association between rioting and absolute deprivation (as measured by income and unemployment levels) (Downes 1968; Lupsha 1968). Later studies, however, that examined riot frequency and severity among cities found that, controlling for population variables, there was no significant relationship between minority income or unemployment levels and riot activity (Jiobu 1971; Spilerman, 1970, 1971; Olzak and Shanahan 1996; Olzak, Shanahan, and McEneany 1996). Indeed, Spilerman (1970, 1971) found that the only statistically significant predictor of riot frequency and severity was the size of a city's African-American population. Yet Myers's (1997) reanalysis of Spilerman's data finds that, in addition to black population size, measures of ethnic competition are also predictive factors of riot frequency and severity.

Despite these contradictory findings, I will nonetheless examine the effects of segregation and deprivation on violence that occurred during the six twentieth-century riots that are the focus of my study. I do so in part because of the common sense appeal of segregation/deprivation accounts, but also for the contrast they provide with another set of explanations for riot violence, broadly classified as ecological/competition theories.

ECOLOGICAL EXPLANATIONS FOR ETHNIC CONFLICT

Beginning in the early twentieth century, with the increasing urbanization of American society and the rapid growth of multiethnic industrial cities, sociologists began to identify the factors responsible for generating conflict and tension among members of different racial/ethnic groups. Noting the diversity of ethnic groups, residential arrangements, and economic activities performed in these cities, American sociologists developed a new perspective on urban society, one with strong implications for the study of interethnic violence. Robert Park and his colleagues at the University of Chicago, emphasizing the connection between the urban environment and the spatial arrangements of human activity, labeled their new perspective "human ecology."

Human ecology, as it applies to the study of intergroup conflict, begins with the premise that people are essentially territorial creatures. According to ecological theorists, human groups, such as racial/ethnic groups, become adapted to and occupy particular "communal habitats" (Park 1952) or "niches" (Barth 1969) in the socially constructed environment. This portrayal of human groups is analogous to that of animals and plant species who occupy particular locations and perform certain "functions" in the "natural" world. Borrowing from Charles Darwin and Herbert Spencer, ecological theorists posit that, like relations in the animal and plant kingdoms, human group relations are characterized by two fundamental processes, called by Park "dominance" and "succession."

These processes of dominance and succession are a product of "competition" among groups for preservation and access to the resources of habitat or niche. Human groups attempt to establish dominance within a communal habitat and exploit the resources of their particular niche. Other groups, in search of resources for themselves may seek access to the niche established by another group. Over time they may "displace" the dominant group from its established niche and thus succeed them. In the interim, however, there is a heightened probability of conflict as groups compete for control of niche resources.

The application of this ecological perspective to racial/ethnic relations is fairly straightforward, giving rise to a new body of sociological theory that has come to be known as "ethnic competition theory" (Olzak 1992; Olzak and Nagel 1986). Simply put, ethnic competition theory states that when one ethnic/racial group has established dominance over a particular geographic area, economic location, or political regime and another ethnic/racial group seeks to enter that niche, conflict is likely to ensue. The dominant racial/ethnic group may perceive the arrival of others as an "invasion," and attempt to exclude them from the niche. The newcomers, alternatively, may also develop a heightened sense of group solidarity and purpose emerging from the competition with the "dominant" group. Such strong feelings of group solidarity on both sides may foment violence.

According to ecological theory, to the extent that different racial/ethnic groups occupy different ecological niches (e.g., neighborhoods and workplaces), conflict between groups will be minimized. By contrast, when two groups overlap in physical, economic, or political space, the potential for conflict is greatly enhanced. Ironically, from this perspective, segregation reduces the potential for interethnic strife. It is desegregation, not segregation, that is seen as generating the most potential for group antagonism, the likelihood of conflict increasing to its peak level where there is "niche overlap" and neither group retains dominance (Olzak 1992). Applying such a notion to the comparative study of race riots in America, Grimshaw (1969) suggested that riot activity was likely to occur in "contested areas," neighborhoods where two racial/ethnic groups share the same space but where neither has achieved supremacy of numbers or power. This point was reiterated by Janowitz (1969) in his study of "communal rioting," riots in which members of different racial/ethnic groups engage in interpersonal violence against one another as a means of asserting or reasserting group boundaries.

Ethnic Competition Theory: Blalock and Beyond

While these early comparative studies of rioting were firmly grounded in historical events, what they lacked was an empirical specification of hypotheses that could be generalized to a variety of situations and tested with quantitative data. Hubert Blalock sought to bridge this gap between the theoretical and empirical realms and develop a generalizable, testable theory of ethnic group contention. In his groundbreaking book, *Towards a Theory of Minority-Group Relations* (1967), Blalock brought together ecological notions of competition with an emphasis on group resources, topics that would later provide the foundations for a resource mobilization approach to social movements. Doing so, he derived mathematical formulae that specified intergroup conflict as a function of the relative size of racial/ethnic groups whom he saw as competing for political and economic power. Based on this work, Blalock can be considered one of the founders of modern ethnic competition theory.

Ethnic competition theory, as suggested above, is a fusion of human ecology and resource mobilization theory. Human ecologists posit that racial/ethnic groups contend for the ability to exploit the resources of a particular geographic or economic niche. Conflict typically results from the efforts of one group to overcome its exclusion at the hands of another group that seeks to maintain control of its established niche. Restating this loosely in resource mobilization terms, one group seeks to promote social change, while the other seeks to maintain the status quo that favors them. According to mobilization theory, the group best able to marshal its resources will ultimately prevail. One such resource is that of a mass of group members who can be motivated to act in concerted fashion, thereby generating pressure for or against change.

To the extent that one group controls the majority of political and economic resources, minority groups must often rely on their sheer numbers and the motivation of group members to challenge the power of the "dominant" group. A good example of this is the Civil Rights Movement, whose success was largely dependent on its ability to effectively mobilize its African-American constituency and challenge Jim Crow segregation through a strategy of mass protest (McAdam 1982).

According to Blalock, as the "subordinate" group mobilizes its members to challenge the prevailing system, members of the "dominant" group must also mobilize their resources if they are to effectively fend off the challenge to their privileged status. The ultimate resource typically monopolized by the majority or dominant group is that of arms, the ability to put down any rebellion against their authority through superior force. Accordingly, as more members of the minority group are mobilized to take action to alter the status quo, more repressive action is undertaken by the majority group to keep the minority group "in its place," increasing the probability that force will be employed. The mere perception that the minority is increasing its mobilization potential, e.g., size and motivation, may be enough to engender a violent response by members of the majority group. As the size of the minority group increases, the likelihood of violence escalates at an accelerating rate. Thus Blalock asserts that there is a positive, nonlinear relationship between the size of the minority group and the potential for collective violence. He calls this notion "power threat."

As this notion pertains to ethnic collective violence, if power threat is operative we can expect that an increase in minority population proportion will enhance the potential for riot violence. The relationship between riot violence and percent minority (i.e., the proportion of a given geographical area's population that is minority) will be positive and nonlinear, with an accelerating slope.

In recent years, a number of scholars have empirically tested Blalock's power threat proposition. These studies, looking at black population size and the rate of lynchings in the historical American South, have yielded mixed, and at times, contradictory results (Reed 1972; Corzine, Creech, and Huff-Corzine 1983; Corzine, Huff-Corzine, and Creech 1988; Creech, Corzine, and Huff-Corzine 1989; Tolnay, Beck, and Massey 1993; Beck and Tolnay 1990; Soule 1992; Tolnay and Beck 1995). Rather than finding an accelerating rate of lynchings with increasing percent black, Tolnay, Beck, and Massey (1989) and Soule (1992) found an initially positive relationship between percent black and lynchings but with a decelerating slope. The number of lynchings eventually tapered off where percent black reached its highest levels. The pattern found by these researchers was not consistent with Blalock's power threat formulation. It is consistent, however, with another of Blalock's formulations: "competition."

Blalock makes a distinction between "power threat," which he views as primarily a matter of contention for political resources allocated according to group, and "competition," which pits individual members of different groups against one another for economic resources. Whereas power threat involves the mobilization of minority group members to collectively take control of macro-level resources, e.g., political office, economic competition is based on actors engaging individually to secure their personal interests, e.g., jobs. As such, the character and quantity of intergroup conflicts that economic competition engenders presumably differs from those based in power threat.

For Blalock, individuals competing for personal rewards as opposed to members of groups pursuing collective rewards theoretically leads to different empirical outcomes. Such outcomes are distinguished by whether they are attributable to absolute levels of percent minority or to relative increases with respect to some prior level of minority population. Power threat, based on the ability of groups to mobilize their human resources, depends on an increasing absolute proportion of minority group members who can collectively challenge the dominant group for control of institutions. Competition, which depends on the ability of individuals to mobilize their personal resources to attain individual outcomes, is affected more by the rate of change in minority group population over time. As the proportion of minority group members increase in the labor market, so too will the degree of contact and competition among individual members of minority and majority groups in pursuit of jobs. This, not surprisingly, leads to an increase in discriminatory measures taken by the majority group to exclude members of the minority group from the labor market. But as more members of the minority group enter the local labor market, the increased level of discrimination is averaged across those individuals. Increasing levels of discrimination bear lesser returns for the majority group once a high level of discrimination is already in place:

> Put another way, a given increase in the minority percentage should produce a smaller increment in inter-group competition in situations where there is already a high degree of discrimination, i.e., where the minority percentage is already high. For example, an increase of 10 percent Negro should produce a greater increase in degree of competition when this involves a change in percent Negro from, say, 10 to 20 percent than would be the case with a change from 50 to 60 percent. (Blalock 1967:148)

Based on this scenario, Blalock proposes that like power threat, economic competition will produce increasing levels of discrimination as the proportion of minority group members in the population rises. But rather than accelerating levels of discrimination as the minority proportion increases (power threat), discrimination will taper off with further increases in relative minority population size. Thus the relationship between percent minority and economic competition will be nonlinear, but decelerating rather than accelerating. As this notion pertains to riot violence, if individual based economic competition is the driving force, the potential for violence should increase in proportion to the relative change in minority population. Riot violence should occur in areas where minority population has increased rapidly, and reached moderate levels, rather than areas with the largest concentration of minorities. The relationship between riot violence and percent minority should be positive and nonlinear with a decreasing slope.

For almost two decades, since Blalock's groundbreaking work, ethnic competition theory lay in a near-dormant state. Indeed, it had not yet been given its formal name. With the publication of Michael Banton's *Ethnic and Racial Competition* (1983) and Susan Olzak and Joane Nagel's *Competitive Ethnic Relations* (1986), the essential elements of such a theory were revived and codified. Based on the quality of exchange relations among members of different racial/ethnic groups, Banton examines the preconditions for conflict. He suggests that competition among individuals for personal rewards will engender less conflict and hostility than competition among member of different groups for what are perceived as collective goals. This is analogous to Blalock's "power threat" and "competition" formulations in that the former involves mobilizing collective resources to achieve group-based outcomes, e.g., political power, whereas the latter involves individuals pursuing their personal economic aims. As such group-based competition is likely to lead to escalating tensions and violence whereas individual-based competition may lead to conflict in the short run until a new equilibrium is attained.

Originally focusing on ethnic group identification, Banton and Olzak and Nagel argue that group identities and solidarity are heightened by competition among groups for political and economic resources. Central to Olzak and Nagel's theory, however, is not an exchange relationship, but rather, the fundamental ecological notion of niche overlap. Applying this concept to ethnic collective violence, Olzak (1992) notes that when different racial/ethnic groups seek to occupy the same labor market niche there is a heightened potential for hostilities to occur among them. This may be considered merely a restatement of claims asserted by the early human ecologists and Blalock. Unlike previous scholars, however, Olzak specifies concrete mechanisms by which labor market competition is generated. In place of abstract derivations leading to competitive outcomes, Olzak deals with real historical processes. While agreeing with earlier theorists that competition is a function of population dynamics, Olzak provides the connective tissue between population change and ethnic/racial conflict.

For Olzak, a key process in the generation of labor market competition and conflict is migration/immigration. She suggests that intensified waves of internal or international migration help generate competitive pressures between newcomers seeking employment and natives seeking to maintain their economic status. To the extent that immigrants and migrants come from countries/regions with lower wage levels, these newcomers are often willing to work for less than natives and thus pose a potential threat to the economic status of established racial/ethnic groups. To the extent that these new arrivals are culturally or racially distinct, they are more likely to be perceived as competitors and more easily discriminated against. Citing the classic work of Robert Park, Olzak posits a connection between the rate of immigration and the potential for ethnic collective action:

> Rapid increases in immigration, indicated by sharp jumps from the previous year, produce shocks in labor markets, over and above the effects of constant high levels of immigration. They do so because big waves of immigration affect perceptions of threats to jobs and wage levels. The impact of a sudden arrival of a distinctly different population can be expected to place burdens on existing

housing, labor, and other markets, sharpening perceptions of in and out-group relations (Park 1949). (Olzak 1992:35)

As the population of immigrants/migrants increases, members of the established racial/ethnic groups, including earlier immigrants, seek to exclude the newcomers from the labor market. Historically, this was one motivation for white workers to form labor unions. In several cases, they did so with the tacit support of employers, who, by paying one group a higher wage than the other for the same kind of work, fostered a sense of competition among ethnic/racial groups. In a complementary fashion, employers seeking to undermine union power often used black workers as strikebreakers. Such competitive pressures enabled employers to threaten the more privileged group with replacement by lower-wage workers and thus helped keep down wages in general. Bonacich (1972, 1976) calls this phenomenon a "split labor market."

With integration of the labor force, the position of natives vis-à-vis newcomers may be weakened; collective action by established ethnic groups to preserve the status quo is likely to ensue. The connection between ecology and resource mobilization is clear. As the mobilization potential of the newcomers rises and the exclusionary boundaries of the "majority" group are challenged, so too does the level of repression employed by the majority/native group increase, culminating in the most severe cases with the use of deadly force. Olzak (1992), like Blalock (1967), considered population change to be a suitable indicator of competitive economic and political processes. Using the increase in proportion of foreign-born residents of cities as an indicator of labor market integration, Olzak found that such change was associated with the frequency of riot activity in those metropolitan areas. She thus established an empirical link between immigration and riot violence. By extension, Olzak suggests that intensified waves of black migration from the rural South to the industrial Midwest generated similar labor market effects as did immigration from abroad. As a result, changes in the proportion of black residents may be associated with the outbreak of violence in those cities, e.g., Chicago (1919) and Detroit (1943).

While integration of labor markets is a key factor in generating competition among racial/ethnic groups, Olzak proposes that there may be an interaction effect between immigration that leads to labor market integration and the performance of the economy. During periods of economic recession, the available pool of jobs shrinks and the labor market slackens. Such economic change, which can produce an increased perception of competition for work among members of different groups, is most potent when combined with continued immigration. According to Olzak, the effects of immigration/migration and labor market contraction interact to produce high levels of ethnic competition and heighten the potential for ethnic conflict.

I argue that economic contraction in combination with high immigration flows raises level of ethnic competition, which in turn, increases rates of collective action, at least initially. (Olzak 1992:37)

On the other hand, Olzak suggests that economic prosperity can also play a role in fostering ethnic conflict. The argument is as follows: With a general economic expansion, members of formerly disadvantaged groups may rise in occupational status. As they do so, they come into increasing contact with those who are/were located just above them on the occupational ladder. Such contact may cause the latter group to mobilize so as to protect its occupational niche. Thus those in higher-status positions are likely to employ exclusionary tactics, which may include violence. This dynamic corresponds to that posited by split labor market proponents.

In short, Olzak proposes that demographic change may combine with economic measures to heighten the potential for intergroup conflict. By contrast, however, Olzak argues forcefully, ethnic group contention is not simply a product of economic deprivation. Addressing the claims of deprivation theorists, Olzak notes that in her statistical analysis of twentieth-century riots, cities with the greatest frequency of rioting display a decreasing, not increasing, gap between the income of blacks and whites. According to deprivation/segregation theories, we should expect the opposite. Riot activity should be association with an increasing differential between black and white economic well-being. Furthermore, Olzak (1996) finds that rioting is associated with decreasing segregation, not stable or increasing levels of racial separation. This too, runs counter to the claims of segregation/deprivation theorists who argue that segregation is at the root of racial/ethnic inequality and is a key contributor to violence.

Despite empirical findings that lend support for a competition explanation of racial/ethnic violence (Olzak 1996; Myers 1997), ethnic competition theory is nonetheless subject to criticism on several points. To begin with, competition theorists may have erred in their conclusions regarding the effects of integration on ethnic/racial violence by ignoring the process by which such "integration" occurs. What Olzak and other ethnic competition theorists consider to be evidence of desegregation or integration may instead represent a temporary moment, part of a larger cycle that eventually leads to the reestablishment of segregation after one group has fled and another group has taken its place. Such was the case in many American cities where African Americans moved into white neighborhoods, which shortly thereafter became almost exclusively black. Periods of rapid population change, such as those induced by massive waves of migration or immigration may bring members of different racial/ethnic groups into increased contact with one another, but such contact is not necessarily a harbinger of long-term integration.

A similar criticism applies to Blalock's formulation of ethnic competition, in which he proposes that discrimination tails off as percent minority increases due to the effectiveness of discriminatory measures that operate to reduce overall competition. On the contrary, reduced competition may be produced by the failure of discriminatory measures by the "dominant" group to exclude members of the "subordinate" group from their economic niche. The reason discrimination decreases is perhaps not be due to the effectiveness of exclusionary measures, but rather, can be attributed to the fact that the niche has been overrun by members of the former minority group. The few remaining members of the previous "majority" group occupying the niche are in little position to exert their claims in the face of a former minority group that has now become a majority. This too could account for a positive nonlinear relationship with a decelerating slope between percent black and discrimination. Although the curve remains as Blalock predicts, the underlying mechanism may differ.

In the interim, a temporary state of niche overlap may develop. During this phase when neither group retains control, violence may be more likely to ensue. After succession has been completed and segregation re-established, the potential for contact and competition among members of different racial/ethnic groups should be reduced and the likelihood of conflict and violence decrease. In focusing on niche overlap (Olzak) and discriminatory thresholds (Blalock), competition theorists have described only one step in a larger process that other scholars like Duncan (Duncan and Duncan 1957) refer to as "ethnic succession."

In addition to their failure to consider the full temporal cycle of population change, competition theorists may also be criticized for their lack of attention to the spatial aspects of ethnic competition. Focusing exclusively on political power and labor markets, modern ethnic competition theorists lose sight of how such competition is spatially situated. More importantly, they neglect the fundamental truth that geographical space itself can be an object of contention. By ignoring the spatial element of competition, modern ethnic competition theorists have overlooked the historical origins and theoretical foundations of their own research, thus missing a key element in the generation of tension and violence among members of different racial/ethnic groups. The early human ecologists (e.g., Ernest W. Burgess, Amos Hawley, Roderick D. McKenzie, Robert Park) were concerned above all with dynamic processes of social change occurring across time and space (Abbot 1997). It was these scholars and their intellectual disciples (e.g., Donald Bogue, Otis and Beverly Duncan, Morris Janowitz) who first documented the process of ethnic succession and suggested that it might be associated with interethnic violence.

Ethnic Succession Theory
Ethnic succession, as conceptualized by human ecologists (Park 1952, Barth 1969), involves the displacement of one ethnic/racial group by another from its "niche" or "communal habitat." Racial/ethnic groups, like

biological species, contend for dominion over the resources of ecological niches in the urban environment. Such resources include jobs and political power, but importantly, as the early human ecologists recognized, contention over these resources is often connected with struggles for control of space. Therefore, space in its own right must be considered an object of contention. Indeed, perhaps the most obvious source of conflict between different racial/ethnic groups is competition for control of geographic territory or "turf." To the extent that members of different racial/ethnic groups compete for political clout or jobs with good wages, it should be clear that members of these groups may also contend for control of geographical territory. Physical space may be the ground upon which economic/political conflict is played out as well as an object of conflict itself. When turf is controlled by members of a particular racial/ethnic group, the entrance of another group into this niche can generate a perception of threat and be seen as an "invasion." Eventually, according to Park (1952) and Barth (1969), as group boundaries are contested, either the challengers are repulsed, an accommodation develops between the two groups, or members of the formerly established group go elsewhere. The latter of these outcomes is what is referred to as ethnic succession.

Ethnic succession in residential space involves the geographic displacement of one group by another, a process by which "one racial category of the population replaces another as residents of an area" (Duncan 1957:11). In less neutral terms, ethnic succession may be seen the surrender of one's group's turf to another. As such it carries strong cultural and psychological implications. When it occurs rapidly, ethnic/racial transition may destabilize the social institutions and disrupt the culture of the local community. As members of one group move in and the other move out, social control may break down and social disorganization occur (Shaw and McKay, 1929; Hirschi, 1969; Suttles 1972; Kapsis 1976, 1978; Morenoff and Sampson 1997). In-migration by members of a different racial/ethnic group may alter the sense of familiarity and routine that another group had established in "their" neighborhood. Thus, rapid changes in the proportion of newcomers to natives may be associated with an increased probability for riot violence to occur (Kapsis 1976). Likewise, ethnic succession may be perceived as transforming once "safe" neighborhoods into "dangerous places" (Rieder 1985). Attempts by the members of the established group to repel the "invaders" may lead to overt violence both across and among members of each group. Combining competition and social control perspectives, one might argue that the areas with the highest potential for violence are those in which rapid demographic change is manifested in the loss of institutional control by a formerly majority group to a competing subordinate group of growing size and strength.

Recent empirical research on the Los Angeles riot of 1992 (Bergesen and Herman 1998) supports such a claim. We found that there was a greater probability for riot fatalities to occur in census tracts that had experienced the greatest change in racial/ethnic composition over a ten-year period. Areas where African Americans were moving out and Latinos moving in at rapid rates were more likely to be touched by violence than tracts where the proportion of racial/ethnic groups was changing less quickly. That research helped set the stage for the present study that investigates whether such a dynamic applies more generally to rioting that occurred in other American cities earlier in the century.

RACE, SPACE, AND RIOT VIOLENCE

To suggest that residential ethnic succession plays a key role in the genesis of riot violence does not mean that such processes occur in complete isolation from struggles for political power or labor market competition. What it does suggest is the importance of a spatial perspective in contributing to a broader understanding of ethnic collective violence. Such a perspective leads to an examination of riot violence as it occurs locally, thus allowing us to better specify where such violence is most likely to break out. This is the topic of the following chapter, which describes how a spatial perspective combined with a local level of analysis can capture the residential succession dynamic of riot violence that political and economic competition measures based at the county or city level often overlook.

CHAPTER THREE

Investigating Urban Unrest

Previous studies of urban unrest have usually involved either detailed case histories of riot events or empirical studies conducted at a relatively high level of aggregation, removed from the historical context that framed the events themselves (Abu-Lughod 1997). In the former camp, there are excellent historical accounts of urban ethnic violence such as William M. Tuttle's *Race Riot* (1975), on the Chicago riot of 1919, and Dominic Capeci and Martha Wilkerson's *Layered Violence* (1991), on the Detroit riot of 1943. There are also numerous reports produced by public investigatory committees such as the Chicago Commission on Race Relations (1922) and the National Commission on the Causes and Prevention of Violence (1969). In the latter camp, there are several empirical studies conducted by sociologists that compare cities that experienced riot activity to those that did not, e.g., Lieberson and Silverman (1965) and Downes (1968). There are also several studies that have employed large data sets and multiple regression or event history models to examine the frequency and/or severity of rioting across a national sample of cities over time, e.g., Spilerman (1970, 1971), Olzak (1996), and Myers (1997). Few studies, however, have attempted to make the link between empirical hypothesis testing and historical case analysis. In the following chapters, I will attempt to provide such linkage. Nonetheless, because my objective is to test theoretical explanations for riot violence, in this study the emphasis will fall more heavily on the empiricist side of the coin.

TOWARD A LOCAL-STRUCTURAL APPROACH

From an empirical standpoint, statistical studies of riot activity have yielded widely varying results. While some scholars such as Downes (1968) found support for an economic deprivation account, others such as Olzak

(1996) and Myers (1997) have found consistent support for an ethnic competition explanation. By contrast, perhaps the most influential empirical study of riot violence, Spilerman (1970, 1971), found that neither economic deprivation nor ethnic competition indicators per se were able to account for the frequency or severity of rioting in his multicity sample. Rather, Spilerman found that the only significant predictor of riot frequency and severity among cities was the size of a city's black population.

As noted above, these studies used city-level data to make descriptive comparisons among riot and nonriot cities or performed inferential statistical tests to retroactively predict the likelihood of riot activity across cities over time. I suggest that there is a problem inherent in such an approach, one that results from using too high a level of aggregation to study what are essentially localized events.

The main theme of these studies is that riot activity is a city-level phenomenon, and thus the implicit assumption is that riot activity is distributed randomly or uniformly within cities. For these scholars, the key question is whether certain kinds of cities are more prone to rioting. While I agree that this is an interesting and important question, one must also consider the local dynamics of riot activity. It is doubtful that rioting is randomly or evenly distributed within cities. Rather, numerous historical studies suggest that riot activity tends to cluster in particular areas/neighborhoods. Therefore, I ask, given that a city has experienced rioting, where (within the city) is violent conflict most likely to occur? What kinds of neighborhoods or local areas are most susceptible to riot violence? Studies that employ city- or metropolitan statistical area– (MSA) level data may obscure the conditions that generate riot violence at the neighborhood level where such activity originates. Indeed, the reason that Spilerman may have found no effects other than black population size on the frequency and severity of rioting is that he didn't look below the city level. Had he compared neighborhoods instead of cities, he may have found that black population size is not the best, let alone the only, predictor of riot activity. Ultimately, rioting begins at the local level, and that is where my investigation begins.

SHIFTING THE UNIT OF ANALYSIS

To examine the local dynamics of riot violence, I have shifted the unit of analysis from the city or MSA (formerly standard metropolitan statistical area, or SMSA) to the census tract. By doing so, I have sought to bring the investigation of riot violence closer to the level at which the violence actually occurred and thereby capture the local conditions underlying riot activity that previous studies based upon city level data may have missed. I am not suggesting that the sources of riot behavior are generated specifically at the census tract level. The census tract is merely the most convenient, established, and objective unit of measurement for which population data is compiled at a local level. It is smaller than the MSA and larger than the block group (which covers only a few streets). As such, the census tract is the best available approximation for neighborhood. Using the census tract as the unit of analysis should bring us closer to an understanding of where riots occur within cities and why.

Employing the census tract as the fundamental unit of analysis raises several questions regarding the operationalization of ethnic competition theory. Since competition is conceived in terms of groups vying for scarce resources, do individuals from different ethnic groups compete for jobs, housing, and political representation at the census tract level? Do census tract level measures effectively capture ethnic competition that crosses census tract boundaries?

Labor markets are not limited to census tracts. Many people commute to work, crossing both census tract and neighborhood boundaries en route to their jobs. Political representation is also not limited to census tracts but typically takes place at the ward or district level, units larger than the census tract. It is important to note, however, that political and economic conditions generated at the macro level (labor markets and political regimes) may be manifested locally. As Katznelson (1981) suggests, racial/ethnic and class conflict generated in the workplace may be displaced into the neighborhoods where workers reside. Indeed, in the following chapters, I will show how waves of immigration/migration into national regions and cities can help generate a sense of competition at the local level where people live, particularly if newcomers are moving into the neighborhood and natives are leaving. I focus on the specific location of riot-related fatalities and the characteristics of neighborhoods in which they occurred.

The Dependent Variable

The dependent variable for this study is the number of riot-related fatalities in a census tract. While there are several possible indictors of riot activity, including fatalities, injuries, and arrests, of these, riot fatality data provide the most geographical specificity and the least amount of selection bias. For all six cases, coroners' reports contain the name, age, race, location (street intersection), cause of death, and time of death for each victim. With the exception of Los Angeles (where the preponderance of fatalities were attributed to drive-by shootings), the race/ethnicity of the killers are also generally known. Since the victims are known, as are the specific cause of their deaths, there is little room for selection bias. By contrast, injury and arrest data are severely subject to selection bias. Injuries that occur during civil disturbances may go unreported when some individuals choose not to seek formal medical treatment. This may have been especially true for undocumented immigrants in Los Angeles, who risked deportation if discovered by civil authorities while seeking medical aid. Furthermore, during these disturbances, some injured persons were turned away from particular hospitals and redirected to others. In 1943 Detroit, for example, hospitals were segregated by race. Thus, medical facilities where injured persons were admitted do not necessarily correspond with the locations where the injuries were sustained, thereby reducing the geographic specificity of such data.

As for arrest data, police bias is evident in studies that document disparities in the arrest of minority youths for drug crimes and other minor felonies (Eisenman 1995). Pastor (1993) argues that during the Los Angeles riot Latinos experienced a disproportionately high arrest rate due largely to joint targeting by police and immigration authorities.

In short, riot fatality data are less susceptible to biased police reporting or hospital practices and have the advantage of being linked to specific locations that can readily be mapped. By looking at the number of riot fatalities in a tract I am able to specify the "hot spots" where riot violence was most intense. Such an approach resonates with recent crime mapping studies conducted under the aegis of the National Institute of Justice. If we can determine where certain types of crime occur, then civil authorities can more efficiently utilize their resources. For instance, if we can estimate where ethnic conflict might be most intense, preemptive action can be taken to avert the development of a full-fledged disturbance. Such efforts may involve targeting job development and/or cultural awareness programs for neighborhoods most at risk for interethnic conflict, including efforts by faith-based community agencies that cross racial/ethnic lines. If riot activity has already commenced, police can more effectively determine how to control its spread by focusing on the potential flash points.

Having acquired a published coroner's report of riot-related fatalities for each city containing the street addresses or intersections where the victims fell, I located each death in geographic space. Using ArcView Geographic Information Systems (GIS) software and the geocoding (address matching) feature, I obtained geographic (latitude and longitude) coordinates for each riot fatality. Importing Topologically Integrated Geographic Encoding and Referencing (TIGER) census tract boundary files into ArcView, I was able to overlay riot fatalities on a map of census tracts, thereby locating each death within a specific census tract. This enabled me to match up the location of deaths and the demographic characteristics of tracts in which they occurred.

Independent Variables
Using CD-ROM data (U.S. Census of Population and Housing 1990 STF 3a), data tapes (U.S. Census of Population and Housing 1980 STF 3a), and print volumes (for census years prior to 1980), I compiled demographic data for the entire population of census tracts in each MSA or city. Such data include indicators of ethnic/racial composition—percent black, per-

cent foreign born, and percent Latino (Miami and Los Angeles)—measures that will be used to evaluate Blalock and Olzak's formulations of ethnic competition theory as well as the ethnic succession hypothesis. To test and control for economic deprivation, I also included median household income and percent of males unemployed in each set data set. Chicago (1919) is the only exception. Due to the lack of income data available for that time, I substituted the ratio of homeowners to renters as a proxy for income and the ratio of persons to dwelling as an indicator of deprivation. These variables and the theoretical perspective they are associated with are listed in Table 3.1.

From this basic demographic data, I computed measures of population change for each of these population categories over the ten-year period preceding each riot event. This involved matching tracts from one census enumeration to the next, taking account of tracts that had merged or split. For Chicago (1919), I performed this task by utilizing ArcView shapefiles and corresponding data provided by the National Historical GIS (NHGIS) project, located at the University of Minnesota. For Detroit (1943 and 1967), Liam Downey of the University of Colorado kindly provided me with an ArcView shapefile and corresponding database that linked data from the 1950s and 1960s to 1970 census tracts boundaries. This facilitated comparisons of population across the three decades, 1940–1970. For Newark (1967) and Miami (1980), I used a spreadsheet program along with ArcView to compile the data sets. Finally, due to the large number of census tracts in the Los Angeles–Long Beach MSA (1,637 tracts), compiling a data set for the 1992 Los Angeles riot required the use of a separate program. This program, provided by the International Consortium for Political and Social Research (ICPSR), utilizes TIGER files to match tracts from different decennial censuses.

The Chicago riot of 1919 and the Detroit riot of 1943 are the only exceptions to this general practice of compiling data for the decade preceding each riot. In Chicago, where the riot took place just a few months before the end of the decade, I compared population changes that took place between 1910 and 1920 rather than 1900–1910. I did so in part because of the proximity of the riot to the end of the decade, but also because census tract data was not available to the 1900 census of population and housing. The first census tract data for U.S. cities was not compiled until the 1910 decennial census. Chicago was one of the first cities to be subdivided into census tracts at that time.

For the Detroit riot of 1943, I chose to compile data for the period 1940–1950, rather than 1930–1940. I did so for substantive reasons, based largely on the history of twentieth-century migration patterns. During the Depression of the 1930s, the migrant flow from the South to the North, which began during World War I, slowed considerably. This migration resumed again during World War II. Using the span from 1930 to 1940 as the base for comparison of demographic data would thus fail to capture the effect of the massive influx of black and white migrants to Detroit that took place during the period 1941–1943. It was this wave of migration, I hypothesize, that was related to the outbreak of urban unrest in Detroit. While it is possible that some of the population change that took place in Detroit census tracts during 1940–1950 was influenced by the riot itself, the population change that occurred between 1940 and 1950 in Detroit should be more reflective of patterns of black in-migration and white out-migration in that city than data compiled during 1930–1940.

GEOGRAPHIC INFORMATION SYSTEMS ANALYSIS

An innovative means for exploring the relationships among riot violence and demographic characteristics of census tracts involves the use of geographic information systems or computer mapping software. GIS has been utilized for several years by researchers working in natural resources and environmental geography. Only recently, however, have social scientists begun to use this technology for their own purposes. GIS presents a powerful tool for the visualization and spatial analysis of practically any kind of phenomena that can be linked to geographical reference points. This software enabled me to produce customized thematic maps that overlay riot fatalities and demographic data. By displaying the visual association between riot-related fatalities and demographics, these maps allow for visual assessment of the ethnic succession process as it pertains to riot violence.

For each city I generated a series of such maps. The first two maps display the location of riot-related deaths and black population share for the beginning and end of the decade closest to the riot event. A third map shows the change in percent black over the decade along with the location of riot fatalities. These maps are meant to assess the ethnic succession hypothesis. Based on this hypothesis, I expect that rioting that took place earlier in the century in Chicago (1919) and Detroit (1943) would be most likely to have occurred where African Americans were moving in and whites moving out. If the ethnic succession hypothesis is correct, fatalities that occurred during the Chicago and Detroit riots should be located in areas that experienced high levels of black in-migration and white out-migration. I expect to find similar results for Newark (1967) and Detroit (1967). By contrast, in Miami (1980) and Los Angeles (1992), due to recent immigration and migration patterns, I expect that riot deaths will most likely be found in areas where African Americans were moving out and Latinos were moving in. Thus, for Miami and Los Angeles, I have included additional maps to illustrate the relationship between Hispanic in-migration and the location of riot fatalities. If the ethnic succession hypothesis is correct, riot deaths should be seen to have taken place in areas that experienced high levels of Hispanic in-migration and black out-migration. Finally, to address the economic deprivation hypothesis, I present maps for each city that overlay the location of riot-related fatalities and economic indicators (median household income and male unemployment). According to his hypothesis, the preponderance of riot fatalities should have occurred in tracts characterized by low levels of household income and high male unemployment rates.

STATISTICAL TESTS OF ETHNIC SUCCESSION AND ECONOMIC DEPRIVATION HYPOTHESES

GIS maps are useful for visualizing relationships among the location of riot fatalities and demographic characteristics of tract. However, they cannot tell us whether these relationships are statistically significant. More powerful tests are needed. To test for statistically significant relationships between the dependent and independent variables, I employ two main techniques: a difference of means test and Poisson regression. I turn first to the more basic technique, a difference of means, or "T," test.

Difference of Means Test (T-Test)

The difference of means test is designed to ascertain whether there is a statistically significant difference among the mean scores of two groups on a particular variable. The difference of means test I employ thus divides census tracts into two classes—those in which riot fatalities took place and those in which riot fatalities did not occur. Using this test, I compare "death" tracts to "nondeath" tracts for each of the independent variables in my data set. If the ethnic succession hypothesis is correct, tracts where deaths occurred should display a greater magnitude of change in racial/ethnic composition variables on average than tracts where deaths did not occur. If economic deprivation accounts are correct, tracts where deaths occurred will have a significantly higher percent of unemployed males and significantly lower median household income on average than tracts without riot deaths. The main limitation of this technique is that it can examine only one variable at a time. The difference of means test is unable to control for the simultaneous effects of several independent variables on the dependent variable. To do so requires multiple regression analysis. For the purpose of the present study, I will utilize a particular type of regression analysis that is well suited for event counts such as the number of riot deaths in a census tract.

Poisson Regression Analysis

As noted above, the advantage of multiple regression is that one can simultaneously examine the effects of several variables on the dependent variable or outcome while holding the effects of the other variables constant. Several assumptions must be met, however, to perform a standard OLS (ordinary least squares) regression. An important assumption is homoskedasticity, which indicates that the residual error terms all have the same variance. But in cases where the dependent variable has a limited range of variations, this assumption is violated. Riot-related deaths were relatively rare events. The vast majority of census tracts in each city I studied had no deaths occur within their borders. Hence there was a preponderance of zeros for the dependent variable. Furthermore, of those tracts where riot deaths occurred, many were of a singular nature. Five deaths were the most fatalities that took place in any census tract. If one were to use OLS, also known as "linear" regression, to model these relatively rare events, the sampling variances or standard error for the effects of the independent variables would be increased, thereby invalidating the results obtained by such hypothesis tests (Aldritch and Nelson 1984).

As Moore and Probst (2002) state, "not all regressions are linear or logistic." For the analysis of count data, such as the number of riot-related fatalities within a census tract, nonlinear models such as Poisson regression offer less biased estimates than OLS regression. Nonlinear models are also preferable to logistic regression, which is designed for dichotomous dependent variables—variables that can take on only one of two values. In the case where the estimated outcome is a numerical count, Poisson regression provides a suitable alternative to OLS regression models. Rather than fitting a straight line to the values of the dependent variable, it employs a nonlinear logarithmic distribution and estimates the likelihood of a tract experiencing multiple riot fatalities. The formula is as follows:

> Log [=α +ßx where [is the expected value for the Poisson variate of Y (in this case the number of deaths in a tract), X represents an explanatory variable such as percent black, and ßx represents the effects associated with the explanatory variables on [, the log of the mean of the dependent variable—number of deaths in a tract (see Agresti 1996).

Poisson regression models may also be biased if there are an unexpectedly large number of zeros in the dependent variable, which results in a severely skewed distribution of outcomes. In such a circumstance it may be preferable to use a zero-inflated Poisson model or a zero-inflated negative binomial regression rather than a regular Poisson regression model. One can check for the presence of overdispersion by examining whether the mean value of the dependent variable is higher than would be expected given the presence of a large number of zeros. One can also run a negative binomial regression and compare the results with those obtained with a Poisson regression. Applying the latter technique to the Chicago data and Newark data, I found that the results of a negative binomial regression did not differ significantly from those little obtained from a regular Poisson regression. The −2 log linear estimates for model fit were nearly identical in both the Poisson and negative binomial models. Furthermore, the dispersion parameters (alpha) in the negative binomial models were not statistically significant. Based on this preliminary data analysis, I will continue to use Poisson regression to examine the effects of population change and economic characteristics on the number of riot-related deaths in a census tract.

Poisson Regression Tests for Ethnic Competition and Ethnic Succession

ETHNIC COMPETITION

For purposes of statistical hypothesis testing, I will use relative population sizes as proxies for political and economic competition. Restating Blalock's "power threat" hypothesis for the census tract level, we should expect a positive nonlinear association between the relative size of the in-migrant group in a census tract and the estimated number of deaths that occur in that tract. This function is marked by an accelerating slope. By contrast, according to Blalock's "competition" formulation, we should also expect a positive nonlinear association between the size of the newcomer group and the intensity of violence, but in this case the relationship should be marked by a decelerating slope. To distinguish between these two formulations, I will use a squared term for the percent of in-migrants in addition to the non-exponential measure. If the main term for percent in-migrant is positive and significant and the squared term is also positive and significant, then we consider this finding as supporting the power threat hypothesis. If the main term for percent in-migrant is positive and significant but the squared term is negative and significant. we may consider this as evidence for Blalock's competition hypothesis.

To test Olzak's variations on ethnic competition theory, I will employ a series of interaction terms (see Table 3.1) The first, based on her notion that immigration combines with slack labor markets to foster violence, will be comprised of the interaction of the change in percent size of the in-migrant group (black migrants in Chicago and Detroit, foreign-born persons in Miami and Los Angeles) multiplied by percent unemployed. The second, based on Olzak's claim that competition for wages occurs during periods of immigration, will be composed of the interaction of the change in percent black or foreign-born multiplied by log median household income. A third measure will look at housing competition by multiplying percentage size of the in-migrant group by housing density (ratio of persons to dwellings). To avoid potential colinearity between these interaction terms and their main effects, I will center the two variables comprising the interaction, subtracting the mean value on each variable for each case before multiplying them to create the interaction term (see Jaccard, Turrisi, and Wan 1990).

ETHNIC SUCCESSION

To test the ethnic succession hypothesis, I examine the percentage change in the size of the in-migrant group, controlling for the relative size of that group at the beginning of the ten-year period for the city that is being investigated. Percent minority at the end of the decade will be employed to test Spilerman's "collective behavior" claim that the size of the minority (black) population is the key predictor of riot activity when controlling for demographic change (Table 3.1)

Poisson Regression Tests for the Interaction of Economic Deprivation and Segregation

To test economic deprivation claims, I have included percent unemployed and median household income in my Poisson regression models. I have also included several interaction terms created by multiplying percent black with economic indicators—male unemployment and median household income (see Table 3.1). I employ the first of these interaction terms to ascertain whether the concentration of unemployment in black neighborhoods is associated with riot violence. Likewise, an interaction of percent black and median household income is used to test whether riot violence was more likely to occur in neighborhoods where people were both black and poor. If either of these segregation/deprivation perspectives are operative, I expect to find significant interaction effects on the presence of riot deaths: positive for percent black and unemployment, negative for percent black and income.

CONTROLLING FOR SPATIAL AUTOCORRELATION

A potentially serious statistical problem in research conducted with geographically compiled data, e.g., census tract data, is that of spatial autocorrelation. A key assumption of regression models is the independence of each observation, such that neither the error terms nor the coefficients of the dependent variable are correlated from one observation to the next. Yet in many cases where geographic data is concerned, this assumption is violated. As defined by Anselin (1995), "spatial autocorrelation is the situation where the dependent variable or error term at each location is correlated with observations on the dependent variable or values for the error term at other locations." Simply put, observational units that are arranged closely in geographic space may not be entirely independent of one another. For example, by virtue of their proximity, census tracts may share a similar propensity for riot violence. Violence can spill over to adjacent tracts from a central point. This effect may then diminish with increasing physical distance (spatial lag) from that central point. Riot violence may also spread across geographically proximate census tracts because of regular patterns of interaction among individuals who constantly cross these boundaries (Odland 1988). Whether the lack of independence among observations is a result of diffusion or social interaction, the process of spatial autocorrelation poses serious problems for standard regression analyses. These

Table 3.1 Summary of Independent Variables Used for Statistical Analyses

Riot Year and Decade of Observation	Collective Behavior (Spilerman)	Power Threat and Competition (Blalock)	Ethnic Succession (change in racial/ethnic composition)	Ethnic Competition (Olzak)	Economic Deprivation	Segregation and Economic Deprivation
Chicago 1919 (1910–1920)	% Black, 1920	% Black, 1920 % Black Squared, 1920	Change in % Black 1910–1920, controlling for % Black, 1910	Change in % Black, 1910–1920 * % Males Unemployed Change in % Black, 1910–1920 * Ratio of Persons to Dwellings, 1920	% Males Unemployed, 1920 Ratio of Persons to Dwellings, 1920	% Males Unemployed, 1920 * % Black, 1920 Ratio of Persons to Dwellings, 1920 * % Black, 1920
Detroit 1943 (1940–1950)	% Black, 1950	% Black, 1950 % Black Squared, 1950	Change in % Black, 1940–1950, controlling for % Black, 1940	Change in % Black 1940–1950 * % Males Unemployed, 1950 Change in % Black 1940–1950 * Median Household Income, 1950	% Males Unemployed, 1950 Median Household Income, 1950	% Males Unemployed, 1950 * % Black, 1950 Median Household Income, 1950 * % Black, 1950
Newark 1967 (1950–1960)	% Black, 1960	% Black, 1960 % Black Squared, 1960	Change in % Black, 1950–1960, controlling for % Black, 1950	Change in % Black 1950–1960 * % Males Unemployed, 1960 Change in % Black 1950–1960 * Median Household Income, 1960	% Males Unemployed, 1960 Median Household Income, 1960	% Males Unemployed, 1960 * % Black, 1960 Median Household Income, 1960 * % Black, 1960
Detroit 1967 (1950–1960)	% Black, 1960	% Black, 1960 % Black Squared, 1960	Change in % Black, 1950–1960, controlling for % Black, 1950	Change in % Black 1950–1960 * % Males Unemployed, 1960 Change in % Black 1950–1960 * Median Household Income, 1960	% Males Unemployed, 1960 Median Household Income, 1960	% Males Unemployed, 1960 * % Black, 1960 Median Household Income, 1960 * % Black, 1960

Table 3.1 Summary of Independent Variables Used for Statistical Analyses, continued

Riot Year and Decade of Observation	Collective Behavior (Spilerman)	Power Threat and Competition (Blalock)	Ethnic Succession (change in racial/ethnic composition)	Ethnic Competition (Olzak)	Economic Deprivation	Segregation and Economic Deprivation
Miami 1980 (1970–1980)	% Black, 1980	% Hispanic, 1980 % Hispanic Squared, 1980	Change in % Hispanic 1970–1980, controlling for % Hispanic, 1970 Change in % Black 1970–1980, controlling for % Black, 1970	Change in % Foreign-Born 1970–1980 * % Males Unemployed, 1980 Change in % Foreign-Born 1970–1980 * Median Household Income, 1980	% Males Unemployed, 1980 Median Household Income, 1980	% Males Unemployed, 1980 * % Black, 1980 Median Household Income, 1980 * % Black, 1980
Los Angeles 1992 (1980–1990)	% Black, 1990	% Black, 1990 % Black Squared, 1990	Change in % Hispanic 1980–1990, controlling for % Hispanic, 1980 Change in % Black 1980–1990, controlling for % Black, 1980	Change in % Foreign-Born 1980–1990 * % Males Unemployed, 1990 Change in % Foreign-Born 1980–1990 * Median Household Income, 1990	% Males Unemployed, 1990. Median Household Income, 1990	% Males Unemployed, 1990 * % Black, 1990 Median Household Income, 1990 * % Black, 1990

problems are similar to those posed by serial time dependence or proximity among individuals in social networks.

Anselin (1995) distinguishes between the effects of two types of spatial autocorrelation on the quality of regression models. The first, the "spatial error" case where the error terms among observations group closely in space are correlated is, in his opinion. not as problematic as the latter type, "spatial lag dependence." The first form, spatial error, is a lesser problem than spatial lag. As with heteroskedasticity, if it is ignored, the OLS estimators remain unbiased but are no longer efficient. But if correlation among the observations on the dependent variable exists (spatial lag dependence), ignoring them can have profound consequences, biasing the OLS estimates and invalidating all inferences derived from the regression model. As Anselin puts it, "In a sense, this is similar to the consequences of omitting a significant explanatory variable in the regression model" (Anselin 1995:11).

The way to deal with this problem is to compute a spatially lagged dependent variable that allows for the estimation of a spatial autoregressive coefficient (Roncek and Montgomery 1984; Odland 1988; Anselin 1995; Land and Deane 1992). Using the spatially weighted dependent variable, one can reestimate the regression model controlling for the spatial lag effect. The formula is as follows: $y = pWy + X\beta + \varepsilon$ where Wy is a spatially lagged dependent variable, and p is the spatial autoregressive coefficient.

The first step is to build a spatial weights matrix that contains the relationships among the areal units—in this case, census tracts. I have computed this matrix using the criteria of binary contiguity, whether one tract shares its border with another. This can be a very labor intensive process when there are large numbers of census tracts in a city or MSA.

The following is a brief illustration of what a contiguity or spatial weights matrix looks like for a small sample of four census tracts. The first row refers to the tract ID number and the number of tracts that border it and the second row refers to the ID numbers of the bordering tracts:

100 3
101 102 103
101 2
100 102
102 3
101 103 100
103 2
100 102

Building such matrices for each city, especially for the Los Angeles MSA, which has 1,637 census tracts, would create a potential for serious computational errors. Furthermore, to run a regression analysis that controls for spatial autocorrelation involves multiplying each variable in each original data set by its corresponding spatial weights matrix to create spatially lagged independent and dependent variables. Without computers, this would be an exceptionally daunting task. Fortunately, Anselin and his colleagues at the Regional Research Institute originally located at the University of West Virginia created a program called SpaceStat that works with ArcView GIS software to create spatial weights matrices from raster data. This program also allows for estimation of maximum likelihood regression models that control for spatial autocorrelation with a spatial autoregressive term. Currently, in addition to SpaceStat, the popular S-Plus statistical software package offers an ArcView interface. This allows for the estimation of linear regression models with spatially lagged independent and dependent variables. At this point in time, neither software package provides for the estimation of nonlinear regression models such as Poission or negative binomial regression. Because my dependent variable (number of deaths in a census tract) is a count variable with several zeros, the lack of a nonlinear regression function in these statistical packages is a serious drawback. Programs like SpaceStat and S-Plus that help control for spatial autocorrelation may introduce other statistical biases associated with the use of linear regression techniques to model nonlinear relationships. In the present study, I will use the S-Plus extension for ArcView to test for spatial autocorrelation and reestimate my Poisson regression models as spatial linear regression models. We can thus attempt to control for spatial autocorrelation using the available modeling tools but must be cautious in interpreting the results of such analysis.

PRECIPITATING INCIDENTS VERSUS STRUCTURAL CAUSES

After performing a bevy of statistical tests, I hope to present a clearer picture of the effects of ethnic competition, ethnic succession, and economic deprivation on the riot violence at the neighborhood (census tract) level. However, before I present the results of these tests for Chicago, Detroit (two times), Newark, Miami, and Los Angeles, I wish to state further the case for employing a local-structural approach to the study of riot violence.

In assessing where and why rioting occurs, it is tempting to conflate short-term trigger effects (precipitating incidents) with deeper structural causes leading up to a major outburst of violence. One might argue, for example, that the Los Angeles riot of 1992 represented a spontaneous reaction to the acquittal of white police officers accused of beating a black motorist. But, the court's verdict is only a partial explanation for what later transpired. As both Lieberson and Silverman (1965), and Hofstadter and Wallace (1970) imply, to understand the potential cause(s) of urban riots, one must go beyond the immediate precipitating incidents and examine the structural context in which these events occur. To focus exclusively on the nature of precipitating incidents neglects both long-term structural changes associated with the outbreak of riot activity and the cumulative breakdown of cultural order that is reflected in numerous interethnic disputes that typically precede a major riot episode. Upton, in a comparative study of race riots, makes a similar observation:

> The precipitating incident is more important in its context than in its content. The precipitating incident channels generalized beliefs into specific fears and antagonisms, it confirms the existence, sharpens the definition, or exaggerates the effect of the immediate conditions. The precipitating incident is often thought of as a single event, i.e., the arrest or beating of a drunk driver, the assault of a young black woman, the shooting of a black youth, which explodes into a riot. Recent evidence suggests that there is no such thing as a precipitating incident. Rather, there is a long chain of escalating incidences and rumors that finally peak in the outbreak of rioting. (Upton 1989:23)

Specific knowledge of the trigger that sets off hostilities does not tell us *why* violence occurred *where* it did. Research that uses large data sets to compare the characteristics of riot versus nonriot cities also fails in this regard. Instead of reducing riot violence to precipitating incidents or offering overly macrostructural accounts of the origins of urban unrest, the purpose of this research is to propose and test a general model for urban ethnic collective violence. Given the occurrence of unrest in the six sample cases, this study addresses the questions of where and why such violence took place from a local-structural perspective. By examining decades-long structural changes in the racial/ethnic composition and economic characteristics of city neighborhoods, I seek to pinpoint the locus of violence and explain its logic. Using historical, geographical, and statistical analysis I will build a case for a general theory of riot violence that is rooted in the effects of rapid migration on the racial/ethnic composition and economic characteristics of neighborhoods.

CHAPTER FOUR

Black Migration and White Backlash:
Chicago (1919) and Detroit (1943)

On a hot day in Chicago, July 17, 1919, a group of African-American bathers sought to integrate the "whites only" beach located at 28th Street and Lake Michigan. Met by a volley of rocks and racial epithets, they initially retreated but soon returned with reinforcements and reiterated their rights to occupy the contested space. Meanwhile, a small group of black youths, including fourteen-year-old Eugene Williams, set sail on a makeshift raft to ply the waters of Lake Michigan. Crossing the informal boundary of 29th Street that separated the black section of the beach from the white section to the north, these black teenagers encountered a white man standing on a jetty, who proceeded to throw rocks at them. After dodging a few of these missiles, Williams was struck in the head and soon thereafter, drowned.

Williams's companions found a black patrolman who was on duty at the time and together they walked from 25th street up to 29th street in hopes of locating the assailant. But when they reached 29th street, and identified the assailant, the white police officer who had jurisdiction over that section of the beach, refused to make the arrest. As the argument ensued between the two policemen, William's companions, fearing further violence, made a hasty retreat. When a black bystander intervened in support of the beleaguered black officer, the white officer promptly arrested him. African Americans from a nearby beach soon gathered to demand justice. By now, rumors began to spread throughout the black community, suggesting that the white officer had prevented a rescue effort, and had, in effect, allowed Eugene Williams to drown. Among whites, a rumor circulated that it was a white swimmer who had drowned after being hit by a rock thrown by a black assailant. Both whites and blacks flocked to 29th Street to see what was happening. When a police wagon arrived to transport the "prisoner," it was pelted with bricks and rocks. An African-

American man then fired a shot into the group of officers. In response the police returned fire, killing the man. Then more shots rang out from the crowd. The Chicago riot had begun.

Soon violence spilled over from the beach to other sections of the city. After seven days of violence, thirty-eight people had died and 537 persons had been injured. Sixty percent of the victims were black, most of them having been beaten, shot, or stabbed by white civilians (Chicago Commission on Race Relations 1922:4–5; Tuttle 1975:3–8).

On another hot summer day, almost twenty-four years later, this time in Detroit, similar events ensued. On June 14, 1943, a black teenager, Charles Lyons (aka Little Willy) and a group of companions sought entry to the Eastwood Amusement Park in the predominantly white community of East Detroit only to be assaulted and chased off the premises by a group of white youths. Six days later, on June 20, with temperatures in the nineties, Lyons and his friends headed to Belle Isle, a publicly operated park in the middle of the Detroit River. There, they entered into a game of dice with some white youths. When the white youths accused them of cheating, Lyons and his friends quickly fled the scene. Angered by these accusations of cheating and their previous ejection from Eastwood Amusement park a week earlier, Lyons and his friends soon began to pick fights with nearby white picnickers, physically assaulting them and stealing their money. White youths responded in kind, attacking isolated groups of black beachgoers as they streamed toward the bridge linking Belle Isle to mainland Detroit. Several fights broke out on the bridge and a contingent of naval sailors on shore leave soon entered the fray (Shogan and Craig 1964:34–43; Capeci and Wilkerson 1991:3–6).

Rumors quickly spread regarding the incidents at Belle Isle. In a downtown nightclub frequented by black patrons, a man impersonating a police officer jumped on stage and announced that a black woman and her baby had been thrown off the Belle Isle Bridge. In the adjoining white neighborhood, not far from the nightclub, a story circulated that a white woman had been raped and murdered by blacks, also at the Belle Isle Bridge (Shogan and Craig 1964:42–43, 54).

Barred from entering Belle Isle, groups of blacks and whites mobilized for confrontation along Woodward Avenue, the main thoroughfare that demarcated white neighborhoods to the west from black neighborhoods to the east. Black bystanders attacked passing cars driven by white motorists while a white mob pulled black commuters off streetcars and chased them back across Woodward Avenue (Capeci and Wilkerson 1991:9). Soon Detroit was engulfed in rioting, including the looting of several white-owned stores located in predominantly black neighborhoods (Shogan and Craig 1964:48–49; Capeci and Wilkerson 1991:8–9). At the conclusion of four days of rioting, thirty-four people were dead and over seven hundred people were injured. Of the thirty-four fatalities, twenty-six (76 percent) were black. As in Chicago, most victims of the 1943 Detroit riot (62 percent) died at the hands of other civilians.

From a historical perspective, there are strong parallels between the Chicago riot of 1919 and the Detroit riot of 1943. Despite the passage of more than two decades since the 1919 Chicago riot, the precipitating incidents that led to collective violence among white and black citizens of Detroit were strikingly similar. So too were the underlying structural conditions that gave rise to rioting in these cities. The wave of urban unrest that swept Chicago and several other American cities, including East St. Louis, Missouri, Washington, D.C., and Knoxville, Tennessee, during the turbulent summers of 1917–1919 had taken place against a backdrop of wartime mobilization that brought significant waves of black migrants from the rural South to centers of industrial production located in the Midwest and Northeast. In Chicago, black migrants clashed with white immigrants over access to jobs, space, and political power. Now, two decades later, in Detroit, wartime mobilization again brought forth a stream of Southern black migrants drawn by the promise of steady industrial employment. Once more, competition and conflict ensued among a new wave of black migrants and a previous generation of white immigrants. In the summer of 1943, rioting swept through several American cities, including Detroit, New York (Harlem), and Los Angeles, all which had experienced substantial increases in black population in the span of ten years or less. When placed in this context, the Chicago riot of 1919 and the Detroit riot of 1943 can both be seen as part of a larger cycle of industrial expansion, black migration, and white backlash that characterized the wartime and interbellum years.

The Great Migration, which began just prior to World War I and continued through the 1950s, involved the relocation of approximately two million African Americans from the rural South to the urban North within a mere span of merely four decades. This exodus of black population from the South would dramatically alter the racial/ethnic composition of neighborhoods in cities of the North. As migration intensified, it generated increased levels of contact among whites and black in both workplaces and in public spaces. Given these perceived cultural differences between whites and blacks, such contact fostered competition among these groups for control of the shop floor, street corners, and public facilities. It is not surprising, then, that both the Detroit and Chicago riots originated in skirmishes involving access to public facilities and spread to the borders of white and black neighborhoods undergoing demographic transition. Feeling threatened by the growing presence of blacks as coworkers and neighbors, whites sought to hold the line again this perceived racial incursion. Blacks, on the other hand, having already been subjected to lynchings and pogroms in the South, refused to be cowed by whites' efforts to intimidate them. Each group, seeking to promote or defend its uneasy foothold in the urban environment, fought with one another for jobs, housing, and political power. The competitive nature of race relations in these cities thus primed black and white citizens to engage in acts of collective violence.

LABOR FORCE COMPETITION

Wartime production intensified the demand for industrial labor at the same time as American soldiers were sent overseas and immigration from abroad declined. To meet their expanding labor needs, employers helped induce an internal migration of African Americans from the rural South. As the two main industrial centers of the Midwest, Chicago and Detroit, received a disproportionately large share of migrant laborers during the wartime years. Within a short period of time, these cities experienced a significant increase in the size of their black populations. From 1910 to 1920, the black population of Chicago increased by over sixty thousand, from 44,103 to 109,458, a gain of 148 percent, most of the gain coming during the years 1916–1919 (Chicago Commission on Race Relations 1921, 1968:2). According to sociologists Otis and Beverly Duncan, 94 percent of this increase in black population was due to migration (Duncan and Duncan 1957:34; Spear 1967:141). In Detroit, from 1940 to 1950, the black population nearly doubled, from 153,773 to 304,677, a gain of 98.1 percent.

Throughout the war years, black migrants poured into Chicago and Detroit, encouraged by the prospect of finding ready employment in the stockyards, steel mills, and armaments factories. Work was generally easy to come by, provided that one was willing to labor under dirty, dangerous, and degrading conditions in unskilled occupations that white workers often referred to as "nigger" jobs (Darden, Hill, Thomas and Thomas 1987). Most black migrants to Chicago found work in the meatpacking and steel industries, working on the killing floor or manning the blast furnaces. By 1920, the census counted 4,313 black Chicagoans working in the iron and steel industries, an increase of 4,093 in a decade (Grossman 1989:183–184).

Black migrants arriving in Detroit during the early to mid-1940s also found it relatively easy to secure employment. With a general shortage of labor and the implementation of Executive Order 8802, which banned discrimination in defense industries, blacks began to see their numbers in Detroit's factories increase. According to Widick (1972:93), over 75,000 black workers (male and female) were hired as a result of President Roosevelt's executive order.

> The cumulative effect of economic forces, activism, and government assistance was that blacks made significant gains in Detroit's industrial economy during the war.... A 1944 report found that "a 44% advance in wartime employment brought with it an advance of 103% in the total number of Negroes employed." As Chrysler worker James Boggs recalled, "You could get a job anywhere you

went."... The percent of black men working as factory operatives rose from 29 percent in 1940 to 45 percent in 1950. (Sugrue 1996:27–28)

Yet all was not well in the factories of Chicago and Detroit. White workers did not typically greet the new employees with open arms. Rather, black laborers were often met with hostility by whites uncomfortable with the notion of working alongside blacks. In both cities, these sentiments were reinforced by a long history of labor disputes in which black workers were used as strikebreakers by employers bent on undermining the power of unions.

Beginning with the stockyards strike of 1894, Chicago's meatpacking and industrial tycoons periodically employed black workers as strikebreakers, or in union parlance, "scabs." Although some black workers honored the pickets and refused to take scab jobs, many black migrants had little experience with or loyalty to labor unions and therefore did not see taking these jobs as a conflict of interest. Black migrants from the South proved more difficult to organize than their Northern counterparts (Halpern 1997:52). With little knowledge of unions, they often expressed hostility or ambivalence toward the labor movement (Halpern 1997:52; Grossman 1989:214; Spear 1967:160). Employers used blacks' lack of identification with organized labor to undercut workers' demands for higher wages and better working conditions. The widespread use of blacks as strikebreakers, particularly during the 1894 and 1904 stockyard strikes and the 1905 teamsters strike, influenced white workers' perceptions that blacks were a "scab race," that the terms black and "scab" were synonymous (Halpern 1997:31; Grossman 1989:218; Tuttle 1975:119). Such perceptions led white workers during the 1905 teamsters strike to attack African Americans residing in the so-called black belt adjacent to their neighborhoods. This violence was indiscriminate. Even black union members were victimized. Despite fledgling efforts by the labor unions to organize black workers, the continued migration of rural blacks fed the fears of white workers and put even more strain on this already contentious relationship. As Tuttle notes, the labor disputes and violence of 1905 were merely a rehearsal for the more widespread violence of 1919 (Tuttle 1975:121).

The return of soldiers, both black and white, from the European front fanned the flames of racial tension and labor unrest in Chicago. Many African-American soldiers returning from Europe found themselves unwilling to live under Jim Crow segregation in the South and decided to join other blacks in the journey northward. At the same time, white soldiers returned to their homes and sought to regain their prewar jobs. As the war ended, however, industrial production slowed and the demand for labor decreased. The result was a market flooded with surplus labor, ripe for conflict among black and white job seekers. Protesting against postwar layoffs and declining wages, "upwards of 250,000 workers in Chicago were on strike, threatening to strike, or locked out by late July 1919" (Tuttle

1975:141). With memories of former strikebreaking activities, white workers feared that the continued growth of the black labor force would lead to their displacement from the jobs they had clung to so tenaciously.

In Detroit, by 1943, blacks had also acquired a reputation as "scabs." As late as 1941, blacks were still being used as strikebreakers, most notably at Ford Motor Company. There, an estimated six hundred to one thousand black workers, on orders from management, attacked union picket lines with metal bars and knives (Shogan and Craig 1964:25; Widick 1972:84). After the 1941 Ford strike ended, bitter feelings toward black workers persisted, especially among Southern white migrants who were already predisposed to hate blacks. Despite the official egalitarian stance of union leadership, these feelings extended beyond the Ford factory into other workplaces where black unionized workers continued to face discrimination by their white brethren. During a strike at Packard, in June 1943, Walter White, an NAACP official reported hearing a loudspeaker blare over the picket lines, "I'd rather see Hitler and Hirohito win than work next to a nigger" (Shogan and Craig 1964:32).

For blacks in Detroit, World War II represented a period of new-found economic opportunity. For whites, accustomed to segregation and the sense of white supremacy that accompanied it, times were uncertain. Despite the availability of work, many whites perceived their status to be threatened by the recent gains made by blacks. White workers felt particularly threatened as blacks began to receive job training that would allow them to move up into skilled jobs formerly held by whites. "By November 1942, blacks in 185 defense plants jumped from 22,200 to 33,500 (or 6.6 percent of all workers) and began to replace whites in training classes" (Capeci 1984:32). As blacks took advantage of training classes, whites watched with trepidation. One white worker asked incredulously, "We've got to teach them our trades so they can grab our places?" Another exclaimed, "After the war is over Negroes will undercut our wage rates and take away our jobs" (Shogan and Craig 1964:32).

The traditional split labor market, an arrangement in which whites occupied higher paying, skilled jobs and blacks were relegated to lower paying, less skilled jobs (Bonacich 1973), was breaking down, which made many whites uncomfortable and brought out their worst prejudices. Efforts to "upgrade" black workers to skilled positions met with resistance. In 1941, metal polishers at Packard declared a sit-down strike to protest the hiring of two African Americans. Over 25,000 Packard workers walked out in sympathy (Shogan and Craig 1964:32; Darden, Hill, and Thomas 1987). Similar strikes occurred at Chrysler's Dodge plant and the Hudson Motor Car Company (Widick 1972:93–94). Despite a booming wartime economy, some white workers nonetheless felt threatened by the presence of blacks in their workplace, particularly if blacks were performing jobs of equivalent skill:

As long as blacks were in the hot, dirty, 'nigger jobs,' most white workers felt secure. But as soon as war production policies placed blacks in so-called white jobs all hell broke loose. (Darden, Hill, Thomas, and Thomas 1987:68)

To summarize these trends, in both Chicago (1916–1919) and Detroit (1940–1945), black migration was encouraged to fill wartime labor shortages. Yet, African-American workers were also traditionally employed as a means to weaken the power of nascent labor unions. Thus, while employers welcomed blacks with open arms, white workers for the most part tried to keep blacks at arm's length. Despite the occasional olive branch extended to black workers willing to join unions, neither in Detroit nor Chicago did white labor advocate equality for black laborers. When blacks received the opportunity to improve their skills and pay, whites feared they would lose their monopoly on the better paying positions or, worse, be displaced entirely from their workplaces. As a result, many whites came to define their labor market position as a zero-sum game, one in which gains for black workers inevitably would be accompanied by losses for whites. When combined with the movement of African Americans into formerly white neighborhoods, such sentiments helped fuel racial backlash. Unable to hold the line against integration of their workplaces, whites sought to defend the racial/ethnic "purity" of their neighborhoods.

CONTESTED SPACE

In pre–World War I Chicago, blacks lived in a few isolated pockets spread throughout the city, with one major area of concentration on the city's South Side. Although informally designated as the "black belt," this area between 29th and 47th Streets, bounded by Wentworth Avenue to the west and Cottage Grove Avenue to the east, was in actuality a "mixed" neighborhood (Spear 1967:150). As such, the "black belt" served as home to small numbers of working-class whites (who lived there due to their economic circumstances) and African Americans of all social classes whose housing choices were circumscribed by discriminatory real estate practices. Although blacks accounted for only 2 percent of Chicago's population in 1910, Chicago was, according to Richard Wright, the mostly highly segregated city in the North (as cited in Spear 1967 and Tuttle 1975).

Hemmed in by the hostility of surrounding white neighborhoods and restrictive real estate policies, blacks began to build their own social and economic infrastructure, in Spear's terminology, an "institutional ghetto." With black-owned businesses, churches, and even a hospital, a stable black enclave appeared to be forming. Within a decade, however, the character of the black belt would change dramatically. Southern migrants, looking for affordable housing close to their new places of employment, gravitated to the black belt, in part because it was the only neighborhood open to them. The massive influx of migrants in search of housing overwhelmed the existing residential market. According to a study conducted in 1917 by the Chicago Urban League:

> In a single day there were 664 Negro applicants for houses and only fifty houses available. In some cases, as many as ten persons were listed for a single house. At the same time rents increased from 5 to 30 and sometimes as much as 50 percent. (Chicago Commission on Race Relations 1922, 1968:93)

The *Chicago Defender*, the most widely circulated newspaper in the black community, labeled the emergent housing crisis a "home famine." According to Grossman (1989:138), this shortage of housing for African Americans was directly linked to the eruption of racial violence in the summer of 1919.

Continuing black migration increased the black belt's population density, which, combined with a lack of capital improvements, brought about dilapidation and disease. A study of black-occupied housing conducted by Alzada Comstock and Sophonisba Breckenridge revealed a common pattern of dilapidation:

> 'In no other part of the city', wrote S. P. Breckenridge of the University of Chicago, 'was there found a neighborhood so conspicuously dilapidated as the black belt on the South Side'. 'No other group she added, 'suffered so much from decaying buildings, leaking roofs, doors without hinges, broken windows, unsanitary plumbing, rotting floors and general lack of repairs'. (Tuttle 1975:162; see also Philpott 1978:156)

Such conditions, were obviously not conducive to good health:

> Chicago's blacks had a death rate which was twice that of whites. The stillbirth rate was also twice as high; the death rate from tuberculosis and syphilis was six times as high; and from pneumonia and nephritis it was well over three times as high. The statistics indicated that the death rate for Chicago's blacks was comparable to that of Bombay, India. (Tuttle 1975:162)

Despite unsanitary and overcrowded conditions, blacks in Chicago continued to pay high rents, having little choice in where to live. In Detroit, the experience of black residents was similar. In the early 1900s, Detroit was Chicago's closest competitor for the dubious distinction of the most segregated city in the North. Like Chicago, blacks living in Detroit found themselves confined to a narrow strip of territory, close to the city's central business district. As in Chicago, this black belt, known locally as Black Bottom and, ironically, as Paradise Valley, also housed a significant number of poor whites. Responding to their involuntary segregation, blacks in Detroit, like their brethren in Chicago, began to build their own community institutions. But, as in the case of Chicago during World War I, this institutional structure in Detroit was ill prepared to absorb the massive wave of migrants who arrived as the nation mobilized for another world war.

With the exception of a few middle-class blacks who resided in a small enclave on the West Side, most blacks in Detroit remained confined to black bottom. Perhaps at one time, prior to the full onslaught of migration, the neighborhood had indeed seemed like paradise. In close proximity to the factories, it offered its black residents easy access to their workplaces. Despite a sizable minority of working-class whites, the neighborhood acted as a center of black community and culture. Black-owned and -operated institutions reflected the promise of proud self-determination. The sizable black presence offered security for migrants in the face of a hostile white-dominated society. It is understandable why Paradise Valley served as a magnet for migrants.

Mass migration, however, would provoke some of the same problems experienced by the black population in Chicago. With little new housing being built, and migrants streaming into the city, Detroit's black belt, like that of Chicago, was destined to become a crowded, dirty, and dangerous place. The resumption of black migration increased the density of an already crowded neighborhood, accelerating the decay of the local housing stock and exacerbating already unsanitary conditions (Lee and Humphrey 1943:92–93).

> In 1941, the Detroit Housing Commission reported that 50.2 percent of all dwellings occupied by Negroes were substandard, and the situation had hardly improved since. Now Negroes were crammed into storefronts and lofts as well as dilapidated apartments. Roofs leaked, stairways crumbled, and sanitary facilities were inadequate. Some 3,500 houses in Paradise Valley had only outside toilets, placed in shacks over holes in sewer mains. (Shogan and Craig 1964:29)

Again the connection between overcrowded, dilapidated housing and poor health observed in Chicago presented itself in wartime Detroit. According to official health commission reports, black residents of Detroit experienced significantly higher rates of tuberculosis and infant and maternal mortality than whites. Rates of tuberculosis and infant mortality in Paradise Valley greatly exceeded that of the city as a whole (Capeci 1984:37). Nonetheless, blacks paid considerably higher rents for these substandard dwellings than did whites.

Even in normal times, a Detroit housing official estimated that rents in the Negro slums had been running about two or three times higher than in white districts. A five-room shanty, for which a white family might pay $25 a month would be rented to five Negro families, one room to a family, at $10 to $15 a month each. A rundown flat worth about $10 a month in a white neighborhood brought $25 a month in Paradise Valley. During the war, the exorbitant rents paid by Negroes had climbed even higher (Shogan and Craig 1964:29).

Given the crowded, unsanitary conditions in the black-belt neighborhoods of Chicago and Detroit, it is not surprising that some African Americans sought to escape from the confines of these areas. Middle-class blacks who had arrived a decade or two earlier found themselves in the midst of more recent migrants of lower social class. As more migrants moved in, the character of the black belt changed. Crime and vice increased hand in hand with crowding and real estate dilapidation (Tuttle 1975:165). The more "respectable" members of the black community attempted to relocate, but their options were limited. To leave the ghetto, they would have to move into adjacent areas inhabited by whites, and to do so was to risk violence at the hands of white mobs and youth gangs (Phillpot 1991:156). According to historian Alan Spear, in Chicago the search by blacks for better housing outside the ghetto provoked numerous clashes with white ethnics, which "led directly to the racial violence that terrorized Chicago in 1919" (Spear 1964:150).

Middle-class blacks seeking relief from the crowding and crime of Detroit's Paradise Valley neighborhood faced a similar dilemma. To move outside the ghetto involved relocation into "white" neighborhoods, which were often "defended" by their residents. As early as 1925, when Ossian Sweet, a black physician, attempted to move in to an all-white neighborhood, the stakes were made plain. Dr. Sweet and his family faced several nights of harassment and vandalism at the hands of a white mob until, fearing for their lives, they fired a shot into the crowd, killing one member of the unruly assembly. Although Dr. Sweet was later acquitted of murder, the message sent by the mob was clear: blacks purchasing or renting homes in white neighborhoods would not be welcome.

Nonetheless, the rapid influx of migrants into Detroit's black belt made it inevitable that the black population would spill over its tightly defined borders. The "container" was about to "burst" (Lee and Humphrey 1943:93). Whites in Chicago and Detroit who lived in neighborhoods adjacent to the black belts reacted with trepidation to the prospect of black residential mobility. Collectively they mobilized to hold the color line. In Chicago, residents of the Hyde Park–Kenwood neighborhood, which stood in the path of eastward black belt expansion, formed a property owners' association designed to keep blacks out. Other neighborhoods bordering the black belt followed suit. These property owners' associations held numerous protest meetings, punctuated by inflammatory rhetoric calling for "use of bombs and bullets" to drive out the black "invaders" (Tuttle 1975:172–174).

Such pronouncements were more than mere rhetoric. They were statements of strategy. If simple harassment and threats failed to dislodge black families, overt violence was considered an acceptable choice. Beginning in 1916 and continuing through the early 1920s, numerous bombing of black residences and real estate firms took place:

From March 1918 to the outbreak of the riot, twenty-five bombs rocked the homes of blacks and the offices of realtors of both races.... Moreover, mobs brandishing brickbats and other weapons and missiles stoned buildings, and intimidation and threats of further violence burgeoned as well. "Look out; you're next for hell" read a "black hand notice." Another was addressed to black tenants on Vincennes Avenue: "We are going to BLOW these FLATS TO HELL and if you don't want to go with them you had better move at once." (Tuttle 1975:175–176; see also Philpott 1978:166–169)

In Detroit, several so-called neighborhood improvement associations were formed, also with the purpose of restricting black homeownership and tenancy. As blacks began to move into "white" neighborhoods, whites responded through organized campaigns of intimidation and violence. "For those white Detroiters unwilling or unable to flee, black movement into their neighborhoods was the moral equivalent of war" (Sugrue 1996:246). Among white working- and middle-class Protestants, such change helped fuel the resurgence of the Ku Klux Klan in Detroit, where it became the "unquestioned center of Klan strength in Michigan" (Jackson 1967:128–129).

While there is some validity to the notion that these actions represented a general war of all whites against residentially mobile blacks, social class and ethnicity were key factors in distinguishing those who fled from those who fought. Rather than a battle of the haves and have-nots, violence in Chicago that resulted over contested space was largely an issue of the have-littles versus those who had nearly nothing, a struggle between working-class white homeowners and blacks aspiring to homeownership (Philpott 1978:151; Grossman 1989:175).

In Chicago and Detroit, the most heavily defended neighborhoods tended to be those occupied by foreign-born working-class whites, particularly Catholics of Irish, Italian, and Polish heritage (Sugrue 1996:240). In both cities, the combination of working-class white immigrants and recent black migrants would prove particularly deadly. For Catholic immigrants, homeownership, church, and community came together as a package. Catholic parishes were drawn along ethnic lines, with residents urged to purchase homes in proximity to their mother church. Owning a home was both a mark of status and a signifier of being centered in a moral universe constituted by the boundaries of one's parish (McGreavey 1996:18–22). Such a view is echoed by the character Studs Lonigan in James T. Farrell's (1938) semiautobiographical account of life in one of Chicago's Irish immigrant neighborhoods.

Local clergy realized the ethnic dimensions of the communities in which the churches were located. They tacitly, and at times overtly, supported residents' efforts to maintain racial/ethnic neighborhood boundaries. Despite the official rhetoric of the mother church and the work of integrationist-minded clergy, some of the most active proponents of segregation in Chicago and Detroit, e.g., Father Luigi Giambiastiani, Father Constantine Djiuk, and Father Charles Coughlin (who was also a noted anti-Semitic orator), were parish priests.

Supported by the institutional authority of clergy and business associations, white immigrants vigorously defended their claims to territory versus the newest wave of "immigrants," the blacks. Helping to carry out these actions were youth gangs, officially constituted as "athletic clubs." Members of these gangs acted as the vanguard against racial integration of white immigrant communities, assaulting blacks who strayed into their territory and vandalizing the homes of the newest blacks residents. At the behest of neighborhood improvement associations and ethnic politicians, these "athletic clubs" served as enforcers of the neighborhood's racial/ethnic purity, guarding against the threat of "racial contamination" (Grossman 1989:178). A significant portion of the violence that occurred during the first two days of rioting can be attributed to ethnic immigrant gangs such as Ragen's Colts and the Shielders (Halpern 1997:66; Philpott 1978:172–174).

In summary, historical accounts suggest that both the Chicago riot of 1919 and the Detroit riot of 1943 were fueled by competition between whites of recent immigrant stock and even more recent black migrants from the rural South over access to jobs and housing. Yet little has been done in the way of formal empirical testing of this thesis. It is to this task that I now turn. Using Geographic Information Systems (GIS) and regression analysis, I will examine the relationship between rapid demographic change, economic competition, and riot violence.

EMPIRICAL TESTS OF THEORETICAL PERSPECTIVES

Geographic Information Systems Analysis

Figures 4.1–4.4 display relationships among the changing demographic characteristics of Chicago census tracts from 1910 to 1920 and the location of fatalities that occurred during the 1919 Chicago riot.

Figures 4.1–4.3 lend support to an ethnic succession account for riot violence. Figure 4.1 shows the location of riot fatalities with respect to the distribution of black population in 1910 Chicago. Figure 4.2. examines the black population distribution in 1920, again displaying the geographic coordinates of riot fatalities. These two figures, taken together, reveal the expansion of Chicago's black belt into formerly white areas. They show an increase in the number of tracts containing a black population of 50 percent or more from five tracts in 1910 to sixteen tracts by 1920. Figure 4.3 displays the change in percent of black residents by census tract from 1910 to 1920, along with the location of riot fatalities, uncovering a pattern of ethnic succession and violence on Chicago's South Side. Within just ten years, twenty-three census tracts had experienced a 20 percent or greater

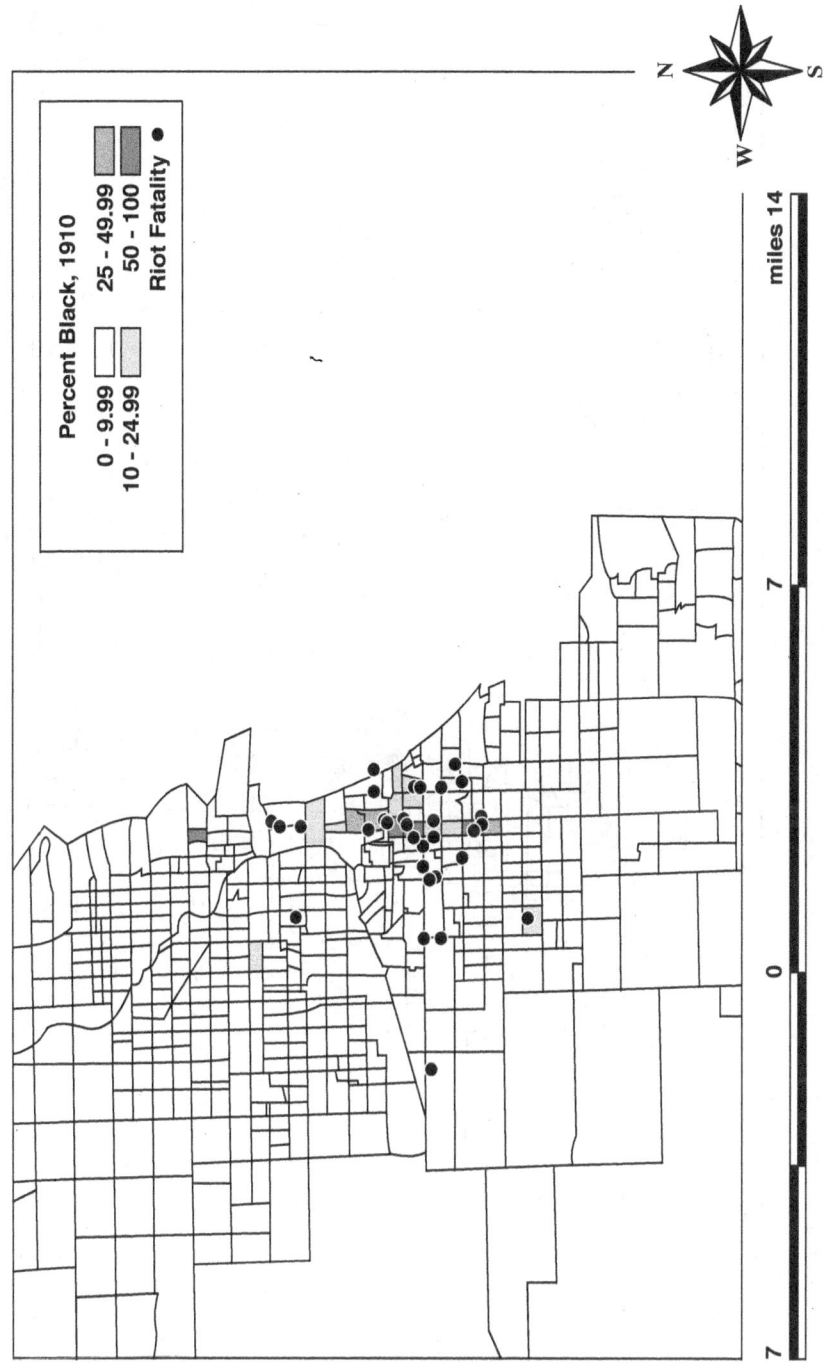

Figure 4.1 1919 Chicago Riot Fatalities and Percent Black, 1910

Figure 4.2 1919 Chicago Riot Fatalities and Percent Black, 1920

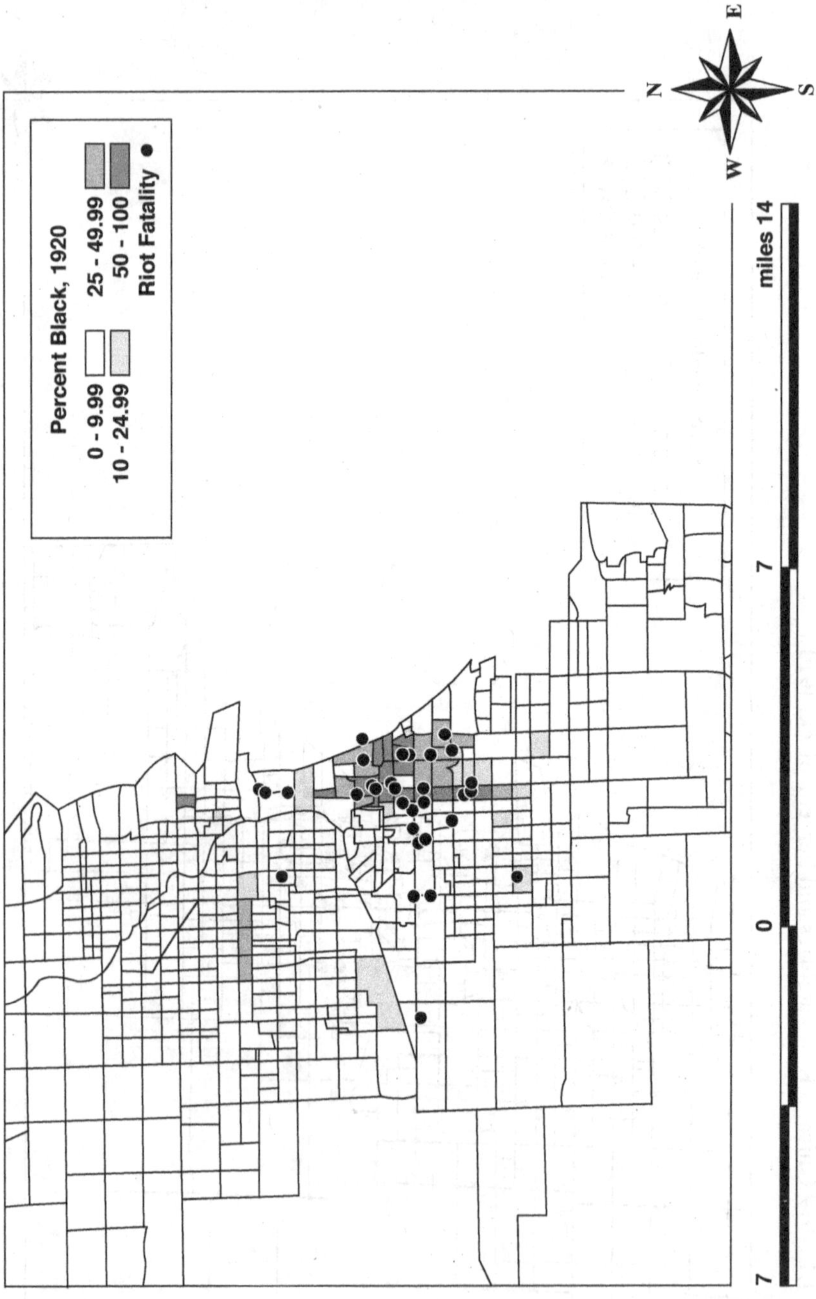

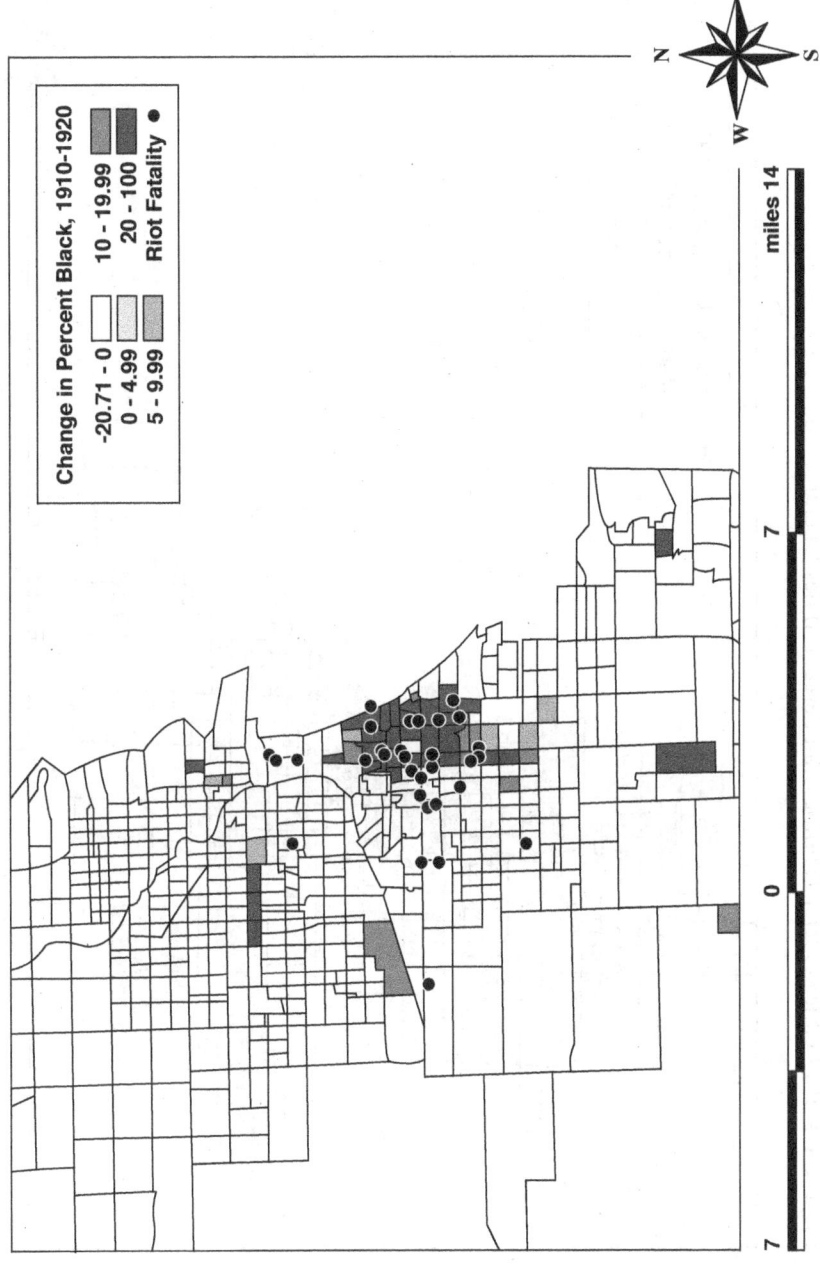

Figure 4.3 1919 Chicago Riot Fatalities and Change in Percent Black, 1910–1920

Figure 4.4 1919 Chicago Riot Fatalities and Percent Males Unemployed, 1920

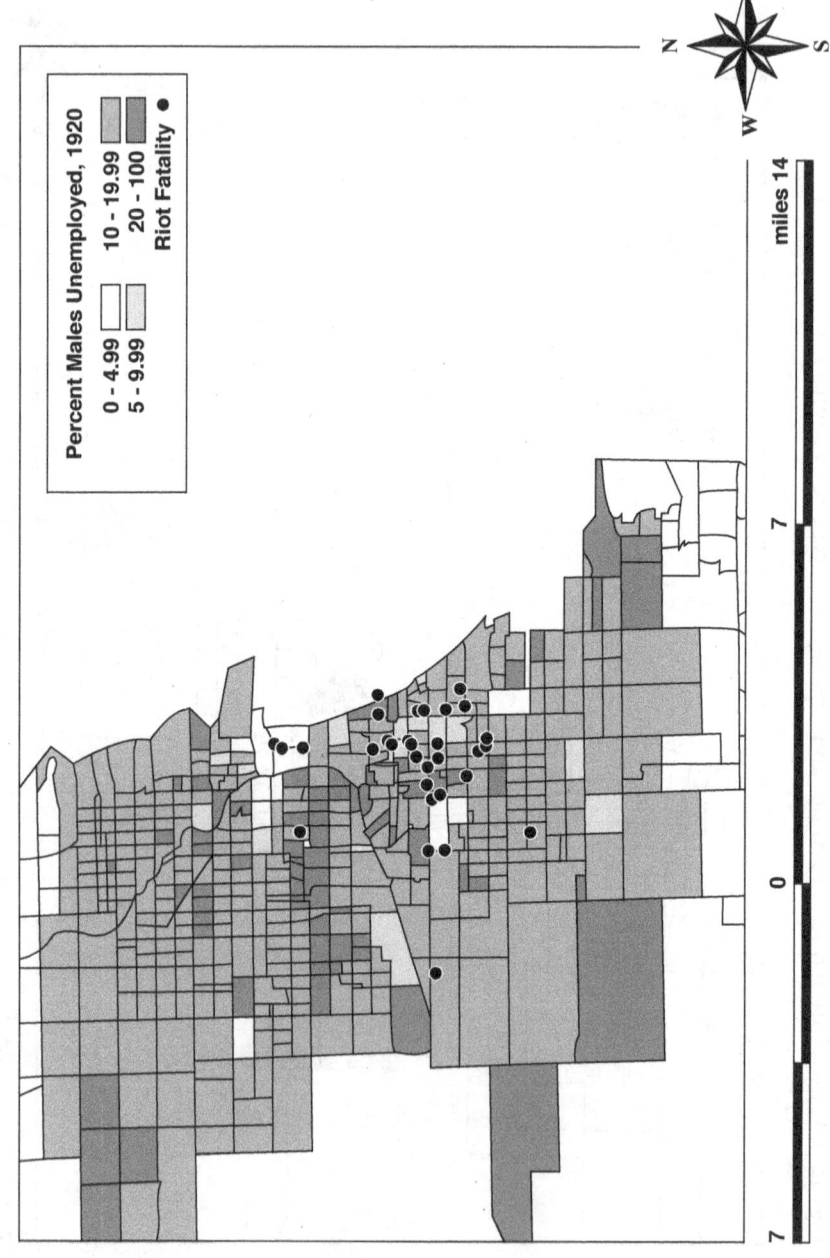

increase in black population. Of the twenty-nine reported deaths that resulted from rioting, fifteen occurred in these tracts where the black population increased by 20 percent or more over the decade. With the exception of a cluster of killings that took place west of Wentworth Avenue along the 47th Street streetcar line, most of the violence in Chicago took place in tracts located in or near the black belt. These are the neighborhoods that had experienced rapid black in-migration. By contrast, blacks who worked in the stockyards were dragged from the streetcars and brutally beaten as they attempted to return home. To get from the stockyards to the black belt, one had to pass through a predominantly working-class Irish neighborhood. With fists and knives, white youths expressed their fears of racial transition and their hatred of blacks. The majority of riot deaths took place within the zone of racial transition. GIS maps suggests that there is a relationship between ethnic succession and the location of deaths during the 1919 riot.

By contrast, GIS maps cast some doubt on the applicability of an economic deprivation account for the violence that took place in Chicago. There appears to be little association between the location of riot fatalities and percent males unemployed. Male unemployment is for the most part distributed randomly in relation to the location of riot deaths (Figure 4.4). Thus, GIS provides support for an ethnic succession interpretation of riot violence in Chicago. There appears to be no analogous relationship between economic deprivation (as measured by male unemployment) and the location of riot violence in that city.

Figures 4.5–4.9 present the results of a similar GIS analysis for Detroit. These maps explore the relationship between demographic change in Detroit census tracts from 1940 to 1950 and the location of fatalities that occurred during the 1943 Detroit riot.

The maps for Detroit lend similar support to an ethnic succession explanation for riot violence in that city. Figure 4.5 shows the location of 1943 riot fatalities with respect to the black population of Detroit in 1940. Figure 4.6 displays the same coordinates of riot-related death with respect to the distribution of Detroit's black population in 1950. Together, figures 4.5 and 4.6 show an increasing concentration of black population in the heart of downtown Detroit. The black population of the inner city was not expanding so much as "piling up" (Duncan and Duncan 1957). At the beginning of the 1940–1950 period, a sizable white population resided in downtown Detroit. By 1950, however, most of the white population had moved out of these formerly "mixed" neighborhoods. Like Chicago's South Side, Detroit's Paradise Valley was transformed by the ethnic succession process and touched by riot violence.

Figure 4.7 shows the extent of this population change and its correspondence with riot-related deaths. Of the twenty-three mapped fatalities, all but two are located in or border upon census tracts where the black

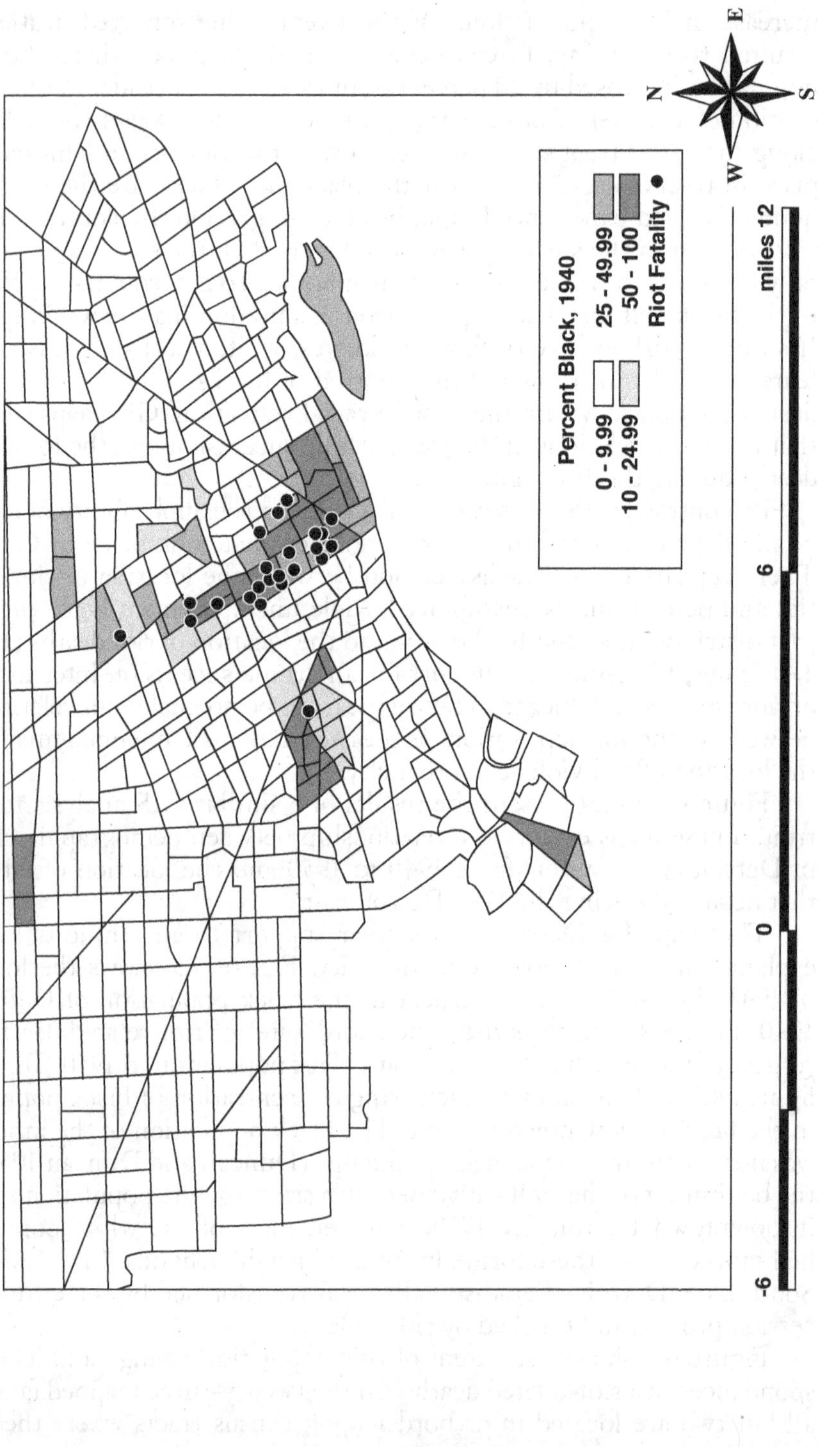

Figure 4.5 1943 Detroit Riot Fatalities and Percent Black, 1940

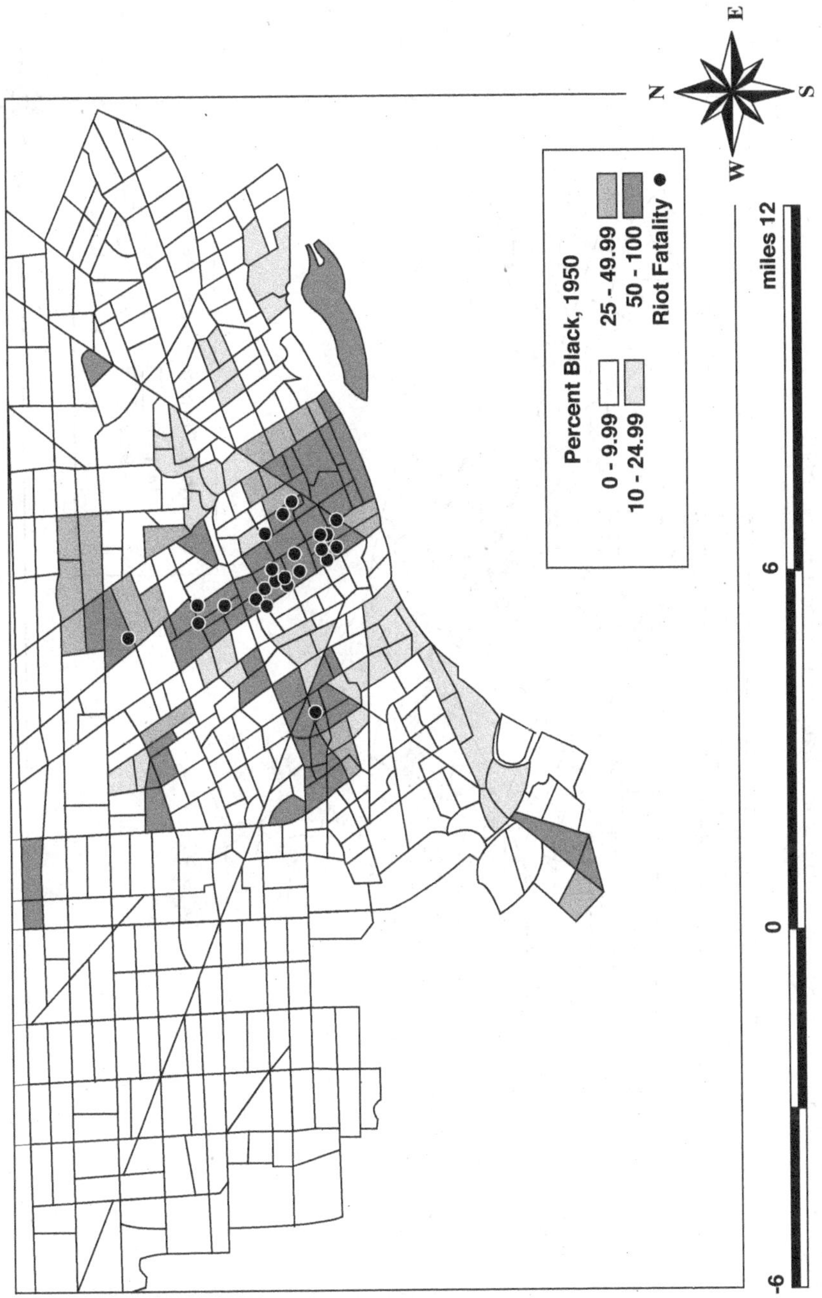

Figure 4.6 1943 Detroit Riot Fatalities and Percent Black, 1950

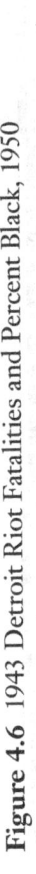

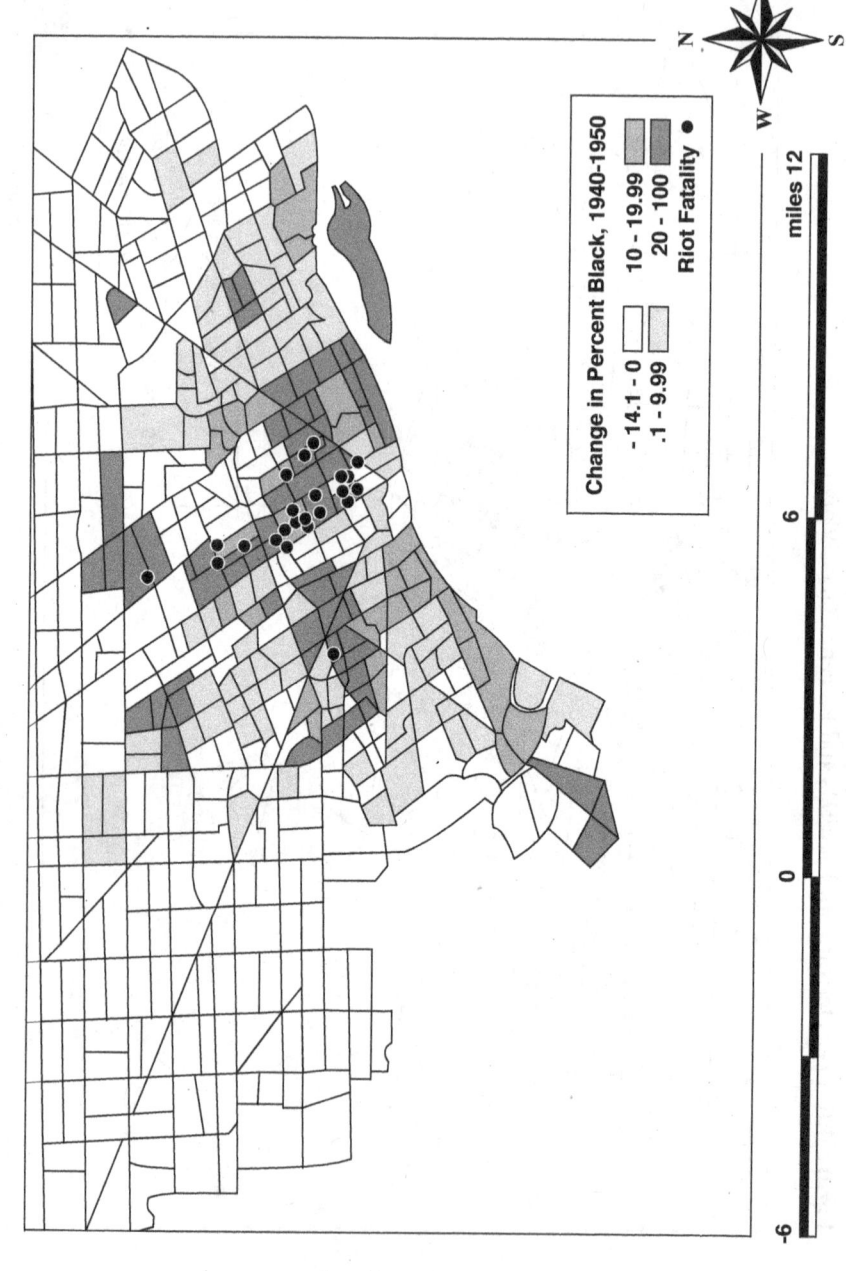

Figure 4.7 1943 Detroit Riot Fatalities and Change in Percent Black, 1940–1950

Figure 4.8 1943 Detroit Riot Fatalities and Percent Unemployed, 1950

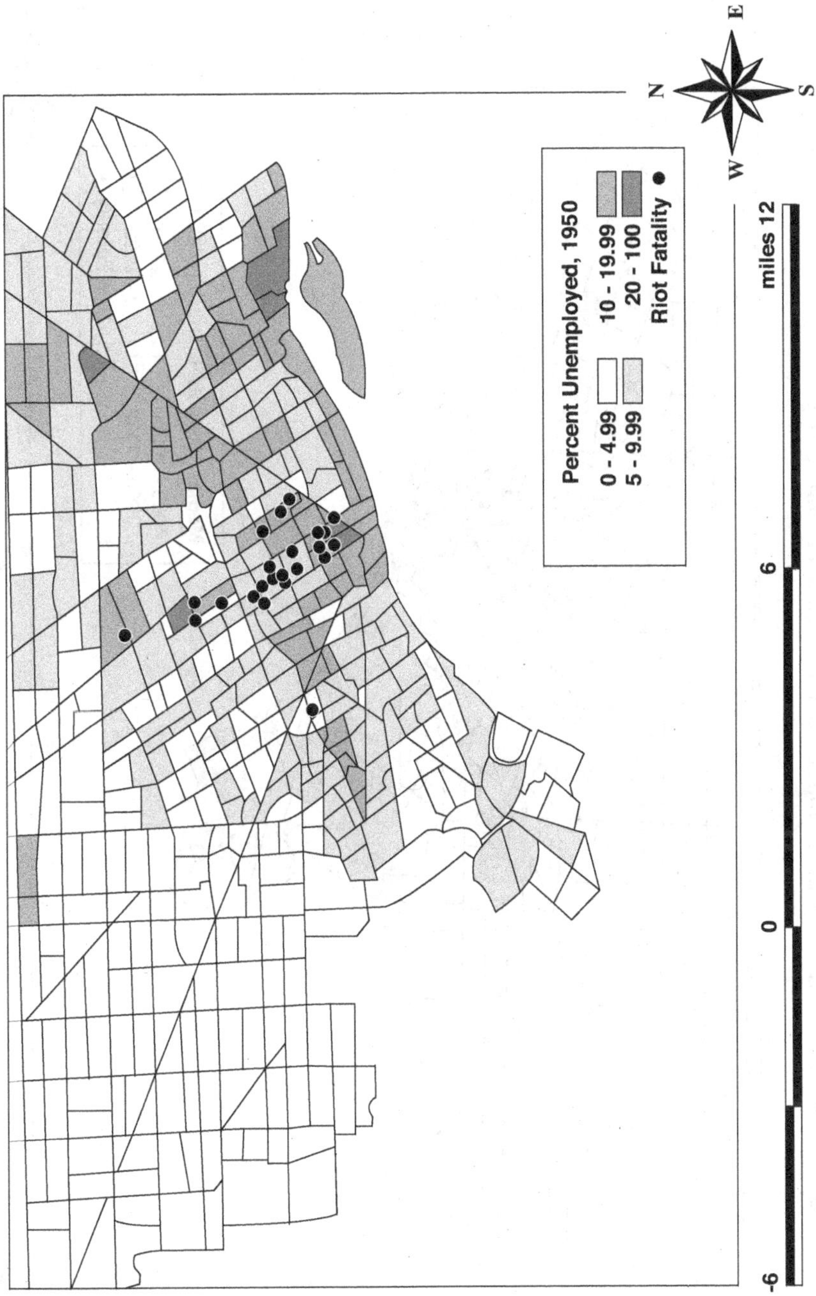

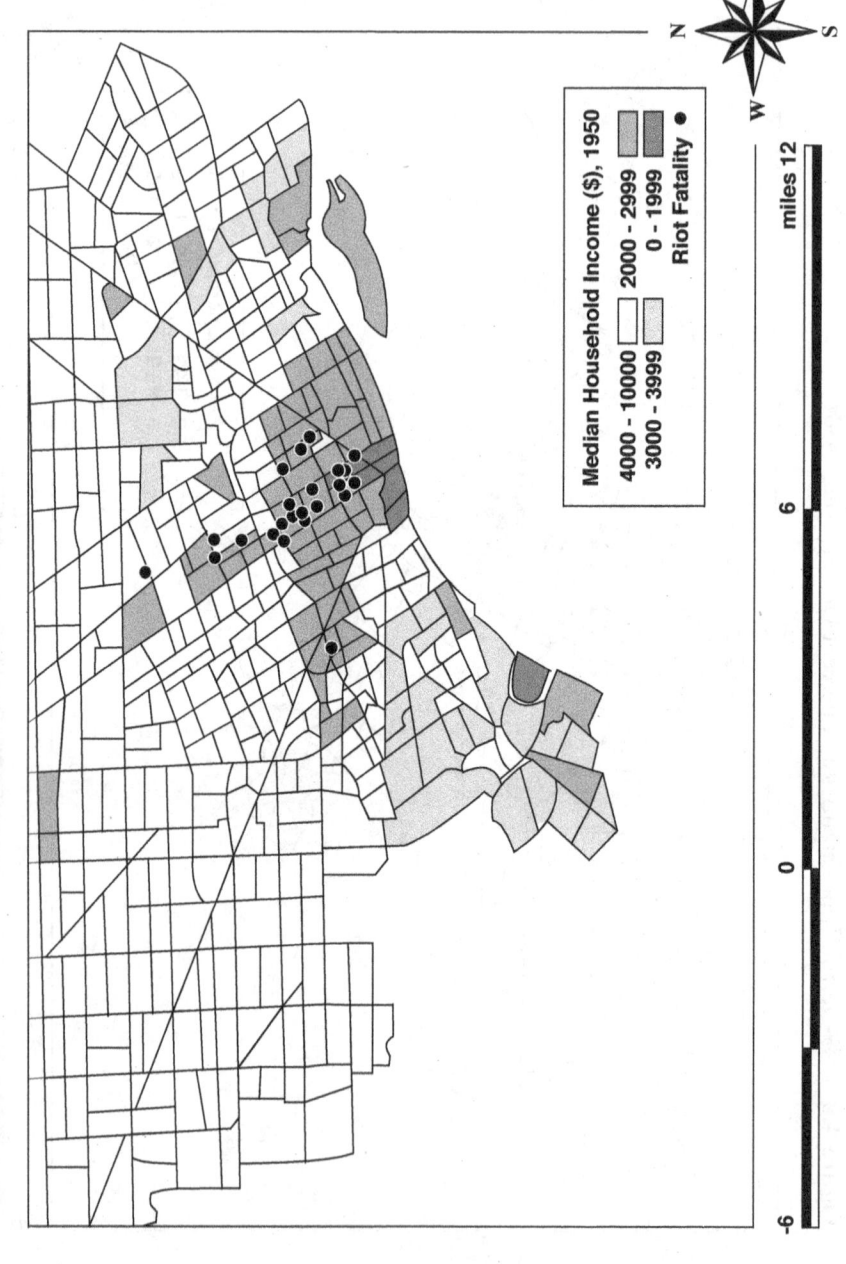

Figure 4.9 1943 Detroit Riot Fatalities and Median Household Income, 1950

population increased by 20 percent or more over the course of the decade. This is strong visual evidence that rapid population change was associated with the location of violence in the 1943 riot.

At least one economic factor also appears to have been associated with violence that occurred during the 1943 Detroit riot. Figure 4.9 implies a relationship between median household income levels and riot violence. Riot fatalities clearly clustered in tracts where median household income was below $3,000 per annum. As with Chicago, however, there is no clear pattern between rates of male unemployment and the location of riot deaths (Figure 4.8). GIS analysis for Detroit suggests that a combination of ethnic succession and poverty (but not unemployment) was associated with collective violence that occurred during the summer of 1943. Had income measures been available for 1919 Chicago, it is quite possible that I would have obtained a similar finding for both cities.

Statistical Tests of Ecological Hypotheses

Up to this point I have cautiously stated that the results of my GIS analysis only represent visual associations. These relationships are merely implied and must be tested with formal statistical techniques. To do so, I employ two kinds of statistical analysis, difference of means tests and Poisson regression. These tests will help ascertain whether the associations among population change, economic characteristics, and riot violence visually displayed in the GIS maps are statistically significant as well.

Difference of Means Test (T-Test)

The difference of means test is designed to ascertain whether there is a statistically significant difference in the mean values of a particular variable among two groups. By dividing census tracts into two groups—those where riot fatalities occurred and those where riot fatalities did not occur —I test for significant differences among these groups on a series of demographic variables. Table 4.1 presents the results of these tests for Chicago and Detroit.

For the city of Chicago there were twenty-four tracts that experienced riot fatalities and 476 that did not during the events of July 1919. Compared to tracts where riot fatalities did not occur, tracts containing riot-related deaths had a significantly higher rate of change in percent black over the period 1910–1920. On average, a riot death tract had a black population increase of 14.4 percent, while nondeath tracts had only a 1.8 percent gain in black population. This finding, which is significant at the .01 level for a two-tailed test, further supports an ethnic succession explanation for riot violence in Chicago. Tracts where deaths occurred had on average a higher rate of black in-migration and concomitantly higher rate of white out-migration. By 1920, tracts where deaths took place had a significantly higher percentage of black residents than those where no deaths occurred,

Table 4.1 Demographic Measures for Census Tracts with and without Riot Fatalities by City (Chicago and Detroit)

City	N	Percent Change		Mean Percent (End of Ten-Year Period)			
		Black	Foreign Born	Black	Foreign Born	Males Unemployed	Median Household Income
Chicago 1910–1920							
Tracts with Fatalities	24	15.8***	-------	24.1***	23.3**	14.6	-------
Tracts without Fatalities	476	2.3	-------	3.4	30.6	17.4	-------
Detroit 1940–1950		Black	Foreign Born	Black	Foreign Born	Males Unemployed	Median Household Income
Tracts with Fatalities	21	28.8***	-8.9***	85.8***	3.2	3.7	$2,346***
Tracts without Fatalities	440	5.4	-4.0	10.9	14.9	2.1	$3,630

*=p<.05 **=p<.01 ***=p<.001

Sources: NHGIS data for census tract and enumeration districts of Chicago, 1910. Ernest Burgess. *Census Data for the City of Chicago, 1920*. University of Chicago Press, Chicago: 1932. U.S. Census of Population and Housing for the Detroit SMSA (1940, 1950 paper volumes).

26.9 percent versus 3.7 percent. This too is a statistically significant finding, although tracts where deaths occurred also had a higher black percentage to begin with. Testing the economic deprivation hypothesis, I found no significant differences in male unemployment among death and nondeath tracts. This confirms the results obtained using GIS, which suggested that unemployment was not a significant predictor of the location of riot fatalities. Neither GIS nor difference of means analysis support an economic deprivation account for riot violence in Chicago. Yet, because income data were not available for Chicago in 1910 or 1920, I cannot conclusively rule out an economic deprivation explanation. Nonetheless, both GIS and difference of means analysis provide support for the ethnic succession thesis.

For Detroit, I obtained similar results. In Detroit there were sixteen tracts where a riot related fatality took place and 197 tracts where no deaths occurred during the events of June 1943. As with Chicago, Detroit tracts containing riot deaths on average had a higher rate of black in-migration than did tracts where no riot deaths took place. Tracts with riot-related deaths experienced an average increase of 28.8 percent in black population while tracts without fatalities experienced a 5.4 percent increase in black population on average. This difference is statistically significant at the .001 level for a two-tailed test. Likewise, tracts where deaths occurred in Detroit experienced a higher rate of out-migration by foreign-born residents, 8.9 percent versus 4.0 percent, respectively. This finding is significant at the .001 level, two tailed. By the end of the period, tracts where riot fatalities occurred had a much greater average black population size than nondeath tracts, 85.8 percent versus 10.9 percent. This figure may be somewhat skewed by the larger black population of these tracts at the beginning of the period. The difference of means tests confirm the intensification of black population in the riot zone as well as the flight of the remaining white population, particularly white immigrants, from those areas of downtown Detroit where blacks were moving in most rapidly. Finally, economic deprivation must be given some consideration as a factor leading to the onset of riot hostilities. The difference of means tests reveal statistically significant differences in median household income and male unemployment rates between those tracts with and without riot fatalities. Tracts where riot deaths occurred had, on average, significantly higher rates of unemployment (contrary to the random pattern suggested by GIS analysis) and lower median household incomes (confirmed by GIS analysis). These findings further suggest that economic deprivation, as well as population change indicative of ethnic succession, was associated with the location of deaths that occurred in the 1943 Detroit riot.

Poisson Regression Analysis

Thus far my conclusions have been based on visual association and a simple inferential statistical test. To confirm these results, more powerful statistical tests that can control for several factors simultaneously are needed. In this section, I describe the results obtained by Poisson regression analysis, a form of regression modeling most suitable for count data. Using Poisson regression models I estimate the number of riot-related deaths that occurred with a census tract as a function of racial/ethnic composition and economic characteristics, thus testing whether particular demographic factors are most predictive of riot severity. The results of this analysis are displayed in tables 4.2a–4.2b.

TESTING FOR NONLINEAR EFFECTS OF BLACK POPULATION SIZE According to Blalock's "power threat" and "competition" formulations we should expect to find nonlinear effects of percent black on the number of riot-related fatalities in a given census tract. If power threat is operative, the relationship will be positive and ever increasing, exemplified by a positive coefficient for percent black and a positive coefficient for percent black squared. If competition is the operative case, we should find a positive nonlinear relationship with a slope that decreases at the highest levels of percent black, exemplified by a positive coefficient for percent black and a negative coefficient for its squared term.

For Chicago the coefficient for percent black regressed on the number of riot deaths is positive and statistically significant, controlling for economic indicators (male unemployment and housing density). See table 4.2a, model 1. The squared term was negative but not statistically significant. Therefore the relationship between percent black and riot violence in Chicago appears to be linear. Increases in percent black lead to an increased probability of riot violence in a tract. Thus for Chicago, neither Blalock's power threat nor competition formulations are supported.

For Detroit, I found a curvilinear relationship between percent black and the number of deaths in a tract. The coefficient for percent black is positive and significant (table 4.2b, model 1). The coefficient for percent black squared is negative but also significant. The effect of black population size on riot violence increases steadily but diminishes at the highest levels of percent black. This inverted U-shape curve is indicative of Blalock's competition formulation. Increasing levels of black population increase the likelihood of riot violence in a tract, but once a neighborhood has become mostly black, the probability of riot-related violence decreases. Riot-related violence was most likely to take place in neighborhoods of Detroit where neither whites nor blacks constituted a clear majority of residents. In contrast to Spilerman's hypothesis, the number of riot-related deaths in Detroit peaked where black and white populations were closest to parity. Highly segregated (almost exclusively white or black) tracts were less

Table 4.2a Poisson Regression Estimates of the Number of Riot Fatalities in Chicago Census Tracts as a Function of Change in Racial/Ethnic Composition and Economic Characteristics, 1910–1920

Independent Variables Dependent Variable: Number of Riot Fatalities

Model	(1)	(2)	(3)	(4)	(5)	(6)
Percent Black (1920)	6.04*** (3.01)	-----	-----	-----	3.93*** (.540)	3.33*** (.570)
Percent Black Squared (1920)	-.030 (.030)	-----	-----	-----	-----	-----
Percent Black (1910)	-----	3.22*** (1.04)	-----	-----	-----	-----
Change in Percent Black (1910–1920)	-----	3.54*** (.810)	4.31*** (.680)	4.14*** (.720)	-----	-----
Change in Percent Black (1910–1920) * Percent Males Unemployed (1920)	-----	-----	.090 (.090)	-----	-----	-----
Change in Percent Black (1910–1920) * Ratio of Persons/Dwellings	-----	-----	-----	.250 (.600)	-----	-----
Percent Black (1920) * Percent Males Unemployed (1920)	-----	-----	-----	-----	1.60* (.080)	-----
Percent Black (1920) * Ratio of Persons/Dwellings (1920)	-----	-----	-----	-----	-----	-.220 (.360)
Percent Males Unemployed (1920)	-4.44 (3.77)	-4.80 (3.69)	-9.57* (4.26)	-7.26* (3.54)	-9.96* (4.40)	-4.90 (3.80)
Ratio of Persons/Dwellings (1920)	9.46*** (2.20)	9.39*** (2.19)	7.16*** (2.36)	7.73*** (2.34)	7.44*** (2.40)	9.38*** (2.21)
Constant	-3.349*** (.8039)	-3.203*** (.7787)	-2.16*** (.833)	-2.57*** (.733)	-2.25*** (.855)	-3.18*** (.793)
Log Likelihood	-103.629	-104.306	-107.399	-107.788	-102.438	-104.148
D.F.	494	494	494	494	494	494

*p<.05 **p<.01 ***p<.001 One-tailed Test.   Standard errors are in parenthesis.

Sources: Ernest W. Burgess. *Census Data for the City of Chicago, 1920.* University of Chicago Press, Chicago: 1932.
1910 Chicago Census Data provided by the NHGIS Project, University of Minnesota.

Table 4.2b Poisson Regression Estimates of the Number of Riot Fatalities in Detroit SMSA Census Tracts as a Function of Change in Racial/Ethnic Composition and Economic Characteristics, 1940–1950

Independent Variables	Dependent Variable: Number of Riot Fatalities						
	(1)	(2)	(3)	(4)	(5)	(6)	(7)
Percent Black (1950)	12.126*** (4.124)	------	------	------	------	4.854*** (.8362)	5.022*** (.9158)
Percent Black Squared (1950)	-5.875* (2.969)	------	------	------	------	------	------
Percent Black (1940)		4.690*** (.8154)					
Change in Percent Black (1940-1950)	------	1.618* (.8602)	------	2.792*** (.8837)	.7890 (1.686)	------	------
Change in Percent Foreign Born (1940-1950)			-3.079* (1.594)				
Percent Foreign Born (1940)			-23.525*** (4.039)				
Change in Percent Black (1940-1950) * Percent Males Unemployed (1950)	--------	------	------	119.784*** (41.021)	------	------	------
Change in Percent Black (1940-1950)* log Median Household Income (1950)	--------	------	------	------	-10.472*** (4.617)	------	------
Percent Black (1950) * Percent Males Unemployed (1950)	--------	------	------	------	------	.4106 (31.089)	-----
Percent Black (1950)* log Median Household Income (1950)	--------	------	------	------	------	-----	.5862 (1.776)
Percent Males Unemployed (1950)	10.755 (10.265)	10.701 (10.515)	14.591 (10.273)	-43.530*** (14.661)	-10.643 (11.827)	15.256 (22.029)	15.110 (10.030)
Median Household Income log (1950)	-1.546** (.6624)	-2.161** (.7947)	-2.301** (.6529)	-6.159*** (.8664)	-4.754*** (.6508)	-1.408** (.6591)	-1.792 (1.316)
Constant	5.287 (5.684)	11.516* (6.519)	17.243*** (5.207)	47.327*** (7.127)	35.362*** (5.340)	5.741 (5.643)	8.785 (10.585)
Log Likelihood	-58.692	-59.461	-67.639	-83.617	-85.041	-61.187	-61.135
D.F.	456	456	456	456	456	456	456

* $p < .05$ ** $p < .01$ *** $p < .001$ One-tailed test. Standard errors are in parenthesis.

Source: U.S. Census of Population and Housing, Census Tract Data for the Detroit SMSA (1940, 1950 paper volumes).

likely than more integrated tracts to experience the most severe manifestations of riot violence.

TESTING FOR EFFECTS OF CHANGING RACIAL COMPOSITION

Whereas Blalock's postulates focus on the relative size of minority and nonminority populations at a given point in time, ethnic succession theorists argue that *change* in the relative size of migrant and nonmigrant groups over time is most predictive of ethnic collective action and interethnic violence. Model 2 of Table 4.2a presents the results of such analysis for Chicago, examining the relationship between black in-migration (as measured by change in percent black) and the number of deaths in a tract while controlling for economic indicators (unemployment, ratio of persons/dwellings) and percent black in 1910.

Controlling for black population size at the beginning of the period (percent black 1910) and economic indicators (unemployment, housing density), there was a positive and significant effect of the rate of change in percent black on the number of riot fatalities in Chicago census tracts (Table 4.2a, model 2). The greater the rate of change in black population for a tract, the more likely that tract had been touched by riot-related violence. This lends support to an ethnic succession explanation for riot violence in Chicago. Not only did the size of the black population help in determine where riot violence was most intense in Chicago (as shown in Model 1), but the rate of change in the relative size of the black population was also predictive of the intensity of violence in Chicago neighborhoods during the events of July 1919.

The results for the Poisson regression analysis of fatal violence on changing racial/ethnic composition of Detroit census tracts are presented in Table 4.2b (models 2 and 3). Controlling for the relative size of the black population (percent black 1950) along with economic indicators (male unemployment, log median household income), change in percent black is a significant predictor of the number of deaths in Detroit census tracts (Table 4.3, model 2, p< .05 single-tailed test). As with Chicago, the size of the black population is not the only measure associated with the location of violence in Detroit. Furthermore, when controlling for percent foreign born at the beginning of the period, the rate of change in percent foreign born has a significant impact on the number of riot-related fatalities in a tract (Table 4.2a, model 3). Yet, unlike the positive effect of percent black on the number of riot deaths, the coefficient for change in percent foreign born is negative. Where the percentage of immigrant residents was decreasing the potential for riot violence was higher. Taken together, these models suggest that riot-related violence in Detroit was most likely to occur in neighborhoods where black migrants were moving in and immigrants (mostly white) were moving out. Such findings lend support to an ethnic succession interpretation for riot violence that took place in Detroit.

To summarize these findings, in both cases, Chicago (1919) and Detroit (1943), Poisson regression analysis supports Spilerman's claim that black population size is associated with the presence and intensity of riot violence. Yet, for both cities there is also evidence that the number of riot-related deaths in a tract was related to changes in the racial and ethnic composition during the years preceding each riot event. Although it is difficult to sort out the effects of changing racial and ethnic composition from black population size, this analysis suggests that both factors are important predictors of where riot-related violence is most likely to occur. In both cities ethnic succession played a role in the genesis of riot violence.

TESTING FOR ETHNIC COMPETITION: INTERACTION EFFECTS

Susan Olzak, one of the founders of ethnic competition theory (Olzak and Nagel 1986; Olzak 1992), posits that riot violence is related to the relative size of majority and minority ethnic groups. Yet unlike Blalock and Spilerman she looks beyond static measures of minority population size to examine the effects of demographic change on the composition of labor markets. She hypothesizes that waves of migration/immigration combine with slack labor markets to induce competition for jobs and wages. To test this notion, I utilized interaction terms to examine the multiplicative effects of change in percent black and economic indicators (the percent of males unemployed and median household income, respectively) along with housing density (ration of persons to housing units).

In Chicago, neither the interaction terms for change in percent black and male unemployment nor the interaction of change in percent black and housing density had significant effects on the number of riot fatalities in a tract (Table 4.2a, models 3 and 4). Income statistics were not available for that city. By contrast, in Detroit the interaction of change in percent black and male unemployment was significant and positive. In Detroit neighborhoods, changes in relative black population size combined with higher levels of unemployment to enhance the effect of black population size on riot violence. This supports Olzak's variant of ethnic competition. Furthermore, for Detroit census tracts, the interaction effect for change in percent black and median household income was significant and negative. Higher levels of income diminished the effect of increasing black population size on the number of riot fatalities in Detroit census tracts. This finding also supports Olzak's ethnic competition claim.

Several urban historians such as Spear (1967), Philpott (1978), and McGreavey (1996) emphasize how shortages of housing in Chicago and Detroit led to struggles among white ethnics and black migrants for living space. In model 4 for Chicago and in a separate analysis for Detroit, I looked at the interaction of housing demand (as measured by the ratio of persons to dwellings) and black in-migration. In neither city did I find a significant interaction of black migration and housing demand/density on the probability of riot violence. In both cases, however, strong correlations among the interaction term and change in percent black made it difficult to untangle the effects of change in percent black from the interaction of change in percent black and demand for housing. As the historical accounts suggest, the increase in black population and housing demand went hand in hand. While the Poisson regression analysis fails to provide support for a housing competition explanation of riot violence in Chicago and Detroit, I cannot conclusively rule out such claims.

TESTING THE ECONOMIC DEPRIVATION HYPOTHESIS

Poisson regression analysis yields mixed results for the economic deprivation thesis in Chicago (Table 4.2a). In three of the six regression models, the percent of males who were unemployed was a significant predictor of riot violence. Yet, the direction of this relationship runs contrary to the economic deprivation hypothesis. We would expect that higher rates of unemployment would be associated with a greater presence of riot fatalities in a tract, but this finding suggest the contrary. Controlling for ethnic composition and housing density, higher unemployment rates actually decreased the likelihood of riot-related deaths in Chicago census tracts.

Despite the mixed results for the main effects of male unemployment on riot violence in Chicago, there is a significant interaction effect of percent black and male unemployment on the number of deaths in Chicago census tracts (Table 4.2, model 5). Where percent black is held constant, as in model 5, the effect of male unemployment on the number of deaths in a tract is negative. Yet, when the interaction of percent black and unemployment is taken into account, the effect of unemployment becomes positive. In tracts where the black population percent was greatest, the impact of unemployment on the intensity of riot violence was most pronounced. Thus, while absolute economic deprivation appears to be unrelated to riot severity when controlling for other population measures, high levels of black segregation and male unemployment work together to increased the likelihood of riot-related violence in Chicago census tracts during the summer of 1919.

In Detroit, Poisson regression analysis yields similarly mixed results for an absolute deprivation explanation of riot violence. In only one of the six Poisson regression models did percent males unemployed attain statistical significance as a predictor of riot intensity (Table 4.2b). By contrast, in five of the six regression models there was a significant association between median household income and the number of deaths in a tract. This relationship was negative across all models, suggesting that tracts with higher levels of median household income were less likely to sustain multiple deaths than tracts with lower levels of median household income.

Thus while male unemployment levels seem unrelated to riot violence in Detroit neighborhoods, differences in income levels did play a significant role in predicting where the most intense violence occurred. This finding is consistent with an economic deprivation perspective, suggesting that riot violence in Detroit during the summer of 1943 was fueled, at least in part, by income inequality.

The interaction of percent black and economic deprivation indicators (unemployment, income), however, did not appear to add any predictive power above and beyond that of the base economic deprivation measures. Neither the interaction of unemployment nor median household income with percent black significantly altered the main effects of unemployment and income on the number of deaths in a tract. Therefore, regardless of levels of black population, poverty itself remained a significant predictor of riot severity for Detroit census tracts in 1943.

CONTROLLING FOR SPATIAL AUTOCORRELATION

As discussed in the previous chapter, the potential presence of spatial autocorrelation raises questions about the reliability of regression estimators in models that employ data from closely spaced geographic units. Because spatial autocorrelation implies serial dependence among observations, it must be controlled for in order to perform hypothesis testing. To do so, I have reestimated the base Poisson regression models as linear regression models that control for spatial autocorrelation. Table 4.3 presents the results of these models for both cities.

Controlling for spatial autocorrelation, the proportion of black residents remained a significant predictor of the presence of riot fatalities in Chicago and Detroit census tracts. Controlling for proportion black at the beginning of the decade as well as spatial autocorrelation, the effect of change in relative black population size on riot violence also remained statistically significant in both cities. In Chicago, the ratio of persons to dwellings (a measure of housing density) also remained statistically significant controlling for spatial autocorrelation, but male unemployment was not a statistically significant predictor of the number of riot-related deaths in Chicago. Likewise, in Detroit, when controlling for spatial autocorrelation, percent males unemployed did not remain statistically significant as a predictor of number of deaths in a tract. Furthermore, in Detroit, median household income also failed to attain statistical significant when controlling for spatial autocorrelation. Thus, when controlling for spatial autocorrelation, economic deprivation appears to have had little impact on the number of riot-related fatalities in Chicago and Detroit neighborhoods. We should be careful, however, when interpreting these results, since the spatial regression models assume a linear relationship between the independent and dependent variables, which is generally not true for count data, e.g., the number of deaths in a tract. Nonetheless, in Poisson

Table 4.3 Linear Regression Estimates of the Number of Riot Fatalities in Chicago and Detroit Census Tracts as a Function of Change in Racial/Ethnic Composition and Economic Characteristics (Controlling for Spatial Autocorrelation)

Independent Variables	Dependent Variable: Number of Riot Fatalities			
	Chicago 1910–1920		Detroit 1940–1950	
	(1)	(2)	(3)	(4)
Racial/Ethnic Composition				
Change in Percent Black (Ten-Year Period)	-------	.385** (.175)	-------	.383* (.223)
Percent Black (End of Ten-Year Period)	.410*** (.130)	-------	.846*** (.134)	--------
Percent Black (Beginning of Ten-Year Period)	-------	.658** (.231)	-------	1.12**** (.167)
Economic Indicators				
Percent Males Unemployed	-.160 (.230)	-.002 (.002)	.046 (.714)	.121 (.698)
Median Household Income log	--------	--------	.000 (.000)	.000 (.000)
Ratio of Persons/Dwellings	.033*** (.006)	.0325*** (.005)	--------	-------
Constant	-.202** (.077)	-.185** (.070)	-.039 (.143)	-.0238 (.1404)
Residual Standard Error	.278	.309	.493	.495
D.F.	494	493	355	356

* p < .05   ** p < .01   *** p< .001   One-tailed test.   Standard errors are in parenthesis.

Sources: Chicago Census Tract Data, NHGIS Project, University of Minnesota.
U.S. Census of Population and Housing, Census Tract Data for the Detroit SMSA (1940, 1950 paper volumes).

regression models and in linear regression models that control for spatial autocorrelation, relative black population size (percent black) and changes in percent black are associated with riot violence in Chicago (1919) and Detroit (1943). The data both clearly support an ethnic succession hypothesis for riot violence in Chicago and Detroit and confirm Spilerman's claim regarding the effects of minority population size on the severity of urban unrest.

CONCLUSION

Having examined the available historical and statistical evidence pertaining to these two cases of urban unrest in Chicago and Detroit during the first half of the twentieth century, I found empirical support for both ethnic competition and ethnic succession perspectives on ethnic collective violence. Waves of black migration from the South to the North altered the composition of labor markets and neighborhoods in these two cities, fostering competitive relations among black migrants and white immigrants for control of jobs, space, and housing. As my analysis indicates, the intensity of riot violence in Chicago and Detroit was associated with these changes in the racial/ethnic composition of labor markets and neighborhoods that resulted from black in-migration and white flight.

Despite considerable job growth spurred by wartime increases in industrial production, the sheer number of migrants entering Chicago and Detroit continued to place pressure on the local labor markets, exacerbating emergent tensions between white and black workers. The "split labor market" in which white and black workers were divided in the tasks they performed and the wages they received (with whites receiving higher wages for less dirty or dangerous work) helped foster a perception among whites that black workers would undercut their wages and privileges (Bonacich 1972, 1976). The influx of black migrants from the South and their use as strikebreakers magnified whites' fears and spurred violence against black migrants during the summers of 1919 and 1943. Yet, economic competition alone cannot precisely explain why violence broke out when and where it did. In Chicago and Detroit, the effects of rapid black in-migration went beyond battles for jobs and wages.

For ethnic whites the mass migration of black folk to the North implied not only a threat to their precarious economic status but also a danger to the cultural fabric of their communities. Having recently established ethnic enclaves, carving out their own "ecological niches" amidst the chaotic order of the industrial city, Irish, Italian, Polish, and Easten European Jewishimmigrants were determined to defend the racial and ethnic "purity" of their communities against the onslaught of an unfamiliar black race. In Chicago and Detroit they drew imaginary "lines in the sand" (concrete). In those formerly white areas where black migrants succeeded in moving, differences in dress, speech, music, and religious practices were highlighted. New institutions sprouted in both emerging and expanding black neighborhoods. Black Baptist congregations began to inhabit formerly white Catholic churches. Stores catering to the tastes of Southern and Central European immigrants began sell products geared specifically for black consumers. Racial transition thus came to be associated in the minds of white ethnics with economic and cultural displacement, generating defensive sentiments that led to aggression against the recent wave of black newcomers.

Historical accounts, GIS maps, and statistical analyses all reflect a fundamental point regarding the origins of riot violence in Chicago and Detroit during the wartime years: the neighborhoods most likely to have experienced riot-related violence were those whose racial/ethnic composition had changed rapidly as a result of black migration. During the respective eras in which these riot events took place, these former white immigrant enclaves were transformed into highly segregated black communities. During the two World Wars, despite black migrants' concerted efforts to establish a place for themselves in the "promised land" of the urban North (Lemann 1992), white immigrants refused them "a piece of the pie" (Lieberson 1980). Attempts by black migrants to move into white working-class neighborhoods resulted in backlash violence at the hands of these white ethnics. Such was the nature of urban unrest in the first half of the twentieth century

CHAPTER FIVE

White Flight and Black Power:
Newark and Detroit (1967)

In contrast to "race riots" in the first half of the twentieth century, the urban unrest that erupted in America's cities during the mid- to late 1960s appears to constitute a different class of phenomena. The riots that took place earlier in the century pitted groups of white and black civilians against one another over access to recreational and residential space. Participants sought to inflict bodily harm on one another as a means of defending their turf. Few riot-related deaths in Chicago (1919) or Detroit (1943) were attributed to police action. By contrast, episodes of the urban unrest that took place during the 1960s were marked primarily by conflict between black residents and predominantly white police/military forces (Hahn and Feagin 1970:183). The vast majority of riot-related deaths in these cases were attributed to the police or National Guard (Bergesen 1980).

Furthermore, the main targets of rioters during the 1960s were business establishments operated by white merchants in black neighborhoods, not civilians of different racial/ethnic backgrounds. Thus, as Janowitz (1969) notes, the form that urban unrest took during the 1960s differs notably from riots that occurred earlier in the century. Violence during the 1960s was inflicted by rioters primarily on property rather than people, with the exception of police officers and security guards whose job it was to protect property. Given this orientation toward property violence, the 1960s era events may best be characterized as "commodity riots," distinguished from the "communal" riots of previous decades. Yet, despite these differences of form, we must be sensitive to similarities in the underlying structural conditions that gave rise to these events. To address this matter, I turn to the cases of Newark and Detroit in the summer of 1967.

The summer of 1967 represents the apex of the 1960s cycle of urban unrest, with 164 "civil disorders" breaking out in 128 cities (National

Advisory Committee on Civil Disorder 1968:113). Of these disturbances, Newark (July 12–17) and Detroit (July 23–28) were the most severe in terms of property damage and loss of life. In Newark, over 10 million dollars' worth of property was damaged and twenty-three people were killed (all but two were African American). In Detroit, 22 million dollars of property was damaged and forty-three people were killed (National Committee on Civil Disorders 1968:107). Such figures would not be matched again until the Los Angeles riot of 1992.

Both disturbances were set off by police activities. In Newark, an African-American cab driver named John Smith drove around a parked police car. He was subsequently stopped and arrested, during which time he was severely beaten. As he was dragged into the 4th Precinct headquarters, a crowd began to assemble from a public housing project across the street. When police allowed a small group of civil rights leaders to visit the prisoner, they demanded that Smith be taken to a hospital. Emerging from the building, these civil rights leaders begged the crowd to stay calm but were shouted down. Soon a volley of bricks and bottles was launched at the precinct house and police stormed out to confront the assembly. As the crowd dispersed they began to break into stores on the nearby commercial thoroughfare, Springfield Avenue. The riot had begun. Within forty-eight hours, National Guard troops entered the city, and with their arrival the level of violence intensified.

In Detroit, police vice squad officers executed a raid on an illegal after-hours drinking club known as a "blind pig" located at 12th Street and Clairmount Avenue. They were expecting to round up a few patrons, but instead found eighty-two people inside holding a party for two returning Vietnam veterans. The officers attempted to arrest everyone who was on the scene. While the police awaited a "clean up crew" to transport the arrestees, a crowd gathered around the establishment in protest (Locke 1969:27; National Advisory Committee on Civil Disorders 1968:85). After the last police car left, a small group of men who were "confused and upset because they were kicked out of the only place they had to go" lifted up the bars of an adjacent clothing store and broke the windows (personal interview, Roosevelt Hurt, June 17, 2001). Further acts of vandalism followed. As police and military troops sought to regain control of the city, violence escalated.

The incidents that touched off these events were not isolated occurrences. Rather, they reflected an ongoing pattern of harassment at the hands of predominantly white police forces. In Detroit, during the 1960s, a unit known as the "Tac Squad," also referred to as the "Big Four" because of their worked in teams of four to a cruiser, patrolled the streets, searching for bars to raid and prostitutes to arrest. The unit frequently stopped youths who were driving or walking through the 12th Street neighborhood, asking them who they were and where they were going

(Fine 1989:98). During these encounters, officers were known to speak in racially charged terms, addressing the youths as "boy" or "nigger." Likewise, in Newark, police stops of black motorists and pedestrians were routine. A community activist whose organization worked with police officers to help foster mutual understanding recalls being stopped almost every night on his way home from work (personal interview, Tom Carmichael, June 21, 2002). Most of the time, black residents were asked to produce identification and eventually allowed to proceed on their way. However, an inability to produce "proper" identification could lead to arrest or worse. In a few notable cases, police stops led to the injury or death of those who were detained.

In Newark, the case of Lester Long stands out. On June 12, 1965, while cruising around the city in their 1955 Chevrolet, Long and his companions drove past an unmarked police car that was traveling in the opposite direction. They were immediately tailed, stopped at a nearby corner, and asked to produce identification. The officers on duty doubted the authenticity of Long's papers. As a result, they released his companions but placed him in the back of the patrol car. While the police were checking into his prior arrest record, Long jumped out of the patrol car and fled along the adjacent boulevard toward a crowd of patrons that had just left a local nightclub. Before he could reach the sidewalk, he was shot in the back of the head by one of the patrolmen. Despite the fact that deadly force was not warranted under the circumstances, and despite inconsistencies in the officers' testimonies, neither of the patrolmen involved in the shooting was prosecuted.

That same summer, Bernard Rich, a twenty-six-year-old African-American male, was arrested during a "routine Friday night check" and died while in police custody. Allegedly, he "went berserk," banging his head on the walls and setting himself on fire. The official coroner's report lists his death as "asphyxiation" due to the fire, but on his death certificate the cause of death remained blank for five months (Porambo 1971). Two weeks later, the police shot a twenty-seven-year-old black motorist during a high-speed pursuit. Then, on Christmas Eve, while investigating an alleged mugging outside a Ukrainian social club, police detained a group of teenagers. In the process of searching the youths who were pushed up against a brick wall, one of the officer's guns discharged, fatally wounding Walter Mathis, age seventeen. No officers were indicted for this shooting; On the other hand, Mathis's brother Walter and three companions were arrested on suspicion of larceny (Porambo 1971:39–59; Wright 1968:4–5).

As suggested by these examples, few cases of police abuse in Newark ever made it to a jury. Police-related shootings and beatings for the most part were not prosecuted, and efforts by the black community to generate a civilian police review board were stymied by city hall (National Advisory Committee on Civil Disorders 1968:58).

> The police have always been defensive about the brutality charge. Since 1960, they have had a complaint system of their own. Of sixty complaints made in six years, the police investigators have substantiated the charge of brutality two times. In addition, although rejecting CORE'S demand in 1965 for a civilian review board, the Mayor decided to refer future complaints of brutality to the FBI and county prosecutor. From September 1965 until August 1967, 7 cases were reported but no action was taken on any. The case of cab-driver Smith was the first referred to the FBI in more than a year. (Hayden 1968:15)

Police in Newark were not only brutal but notoriously corrupt, running gambling rackets, operating car theft rings, and shaking down local merchants for protection money. It was widely believed that the Mafia had substantial contacts within the police force, affording them an informal veto on police appointments (Porambo 1971:64–65). In December 1965, an Essex County grand jury investigation revealed that there were overlapping payroll records of Newark police department employees and a mob-related contractor (Wright 1968:5). This combination of police misuse of force, rampant corruption, and the intransigence of the justice system when dealing with police misconduct cases deeply damaged black people's faith in the police. In a postriot press release, the Committee of Concern, a local civil rights organization, stated,

> A large segment of the Negro people are convinced that the single continuously lawless element operating in the community is the police force itself, and its callous disregard for human rights. Many independent observers believe this position has merit. (Governors Select Commission on Civil Disorders, 1968:32)

In Detroit, black civilians fared little better than their Newark counterparts with respect to encounters with the police. As in Newark, many black Detroiters believed that the police were themselves a criminal element who acted in concert with Mafia bosses to reap profits from vice activity in the ghetto. Police Commissioner George Edwards confirmed this view in his testimony before the National Advisory Commission on Civil Disorders, testifying that the police had "strong tie-ins" with reputed mobsters (Fine 1989:101). But the main issue in the minds of Detroit's black residents was police harassment and police brutality, which they identified in a *Detroit Free Press* survey as the number one problem they faced in the period leading up to the riot (*Detroit Free Press* 1968; Fine 1989; Thomas 1997).

Police sometimes used excessive force against their prisoners in the station house or against individuals in the ghetto, where white policemen believed themselves both hated and in the presence of danger. The likelihood that misuse of force might occur was increased by the fact that most police contacts with civilians were not subject to close surveillance and the police could claim they had acted in self-defense or because the suspect had resisted arrest. The head of the Detroit NAACP remarked in 1965 that at one time in Detroit "every Negro arrested somehow fell down and suffered a cracked skull" (Fine 1989:100).

Other high profile cases of police brutality in Detroit included the 1962 police shooting of a black prostitute named Shirley Scott who, like Lester Long of Newark, was shot in the back while fleeing from the back of a patrol car; the severe beating of another prostitute, Barbara Jackson, in 1964; and the beating of Howard King, a black teenager, for "allegedly disturbing the peace" (Fine 1989:117).

A number of citizens in both cities suggested that the police might not have been so brutal had they been more racially representative of the communities they served. "The most frequent recommendation of Negro community people for improving police-community relations was to increase the number of Negro policemen" (Governor's Select Commission on Civil Disorders 1968:35). The fact of the matter is that African Americans were woefully underrepresented on both police forces. Although the number of black police officers had nearly doubled in Detroit between July 1966 and May 1967 from 134 to 227, blacks still constituted only 5 percent of the overall police force. Furthermore, as of April 1966, only one out of every eight black officers held a rank higher than that of patrolman (Fine 1989:109). In Newark, black officers accounted for 145 of 1,322 total officers or 10.9 percent; though this figure was somewhat better than Detroit's, still, only nine black officers held a rank above that of patrolman (Report for Action 1968: 24). Given these numbers, black residents of Detroit and Newark saw the police not as part of the community but as an occupation force. According to the president of the Detroit NAACP in 1965, "The Negroes in Detroit feel they are part of an occupied country. The Negroes have no rights which the police have to respect" (*Detroit Free Press*, January 10, 1965). In a similar vein, activist Tom Hayden made the following pronouncement:

> Dominated by Italians who run Newark politics, tainted by alleged underworld connections, including a token of about 150 blacks among its 1400 members (all of them in subordinated positions) the police department seems to many Negroes to be an armed agency defending the privileges of the city's shrinking white community. (Hayden,1968:15)

Residents' negative attitudes toward the police were matched by policemen's negative attitudes toward the black community. Lower-level white officers in Detroit saw themselves as defenders of the white majority against the rising black minority. They saw blacks as a "privileged" minority who were "ready to use violence" to attain a "greater advantage vis-à-vis the white community" (Fine 1989:97). Such views provided ready justification for police violence against black civilians. According to journalist Ron Porambo, Newark police officers felt that "a little brutality would keep 'them' in their place" (Porambo 1971:64). This proclivity for violence against blacks spilled over to police actions during the riots themselves, which may explain why 69 percent of Detroit riot fatalities and 80 percent of Newark riot fatalities were attributed to police and armed forces. Given the high percentages of police shootings, Bergesen (1980) labeled the events that took place in Newark and Detroit "police riots."

The mutual suspicion and hostility that characterized the relationship between black citizens and the police in Newark and Detroit were matched by feelings of political powerlessness and acrimony toward political officials. By the late 1960s, both Newark and Detroit had sizable black communities. In Newark, African Americans constituted a numerical majority. In Detroit, the black population share was rapidly approaching the 50 percent mark. Yet despite these numbers, in neither city did black people hold the reigns of political power.

This disparity of political power was underscored in Newark when Mayor Hugh Addonizio, who had professed sensitivity to black concerns during his election campaign, failed to appoint blacks to leadership positions in his administration. Assemblyman George Richardson, who served briefly in Addonizio's administration, testified that "Negroes supported Mr. Addonizio for mayor with the idea that he would appoint black people to responsible positions, where they could get the experience needed to take over the city when a Negro mayor was elected." Richardson continued, "Negroes found out immediately after the election that the supposed partnership did not really exist" (Governor's Select Commission on Civil Disorders 1968:7).

Most telling was the manner with which the mayor handled a school board vacancy by appointing an Irish high school graduate, Councilman James T. Callaghan, over Wilbur Parker, the first African-American certified public accountant in New Jersey history. Based on their respective credentials, it was obvious which candidate was the most qualified, but political favors carried more weight than formal qualifications. Members of the black community, particularly those who had a stake in the education system, were incensed. Fred Means, president of an organization named Negro Educators of Newark, even alluded to the possible of riot if the decision were not reversed. He bluntly stated, "The Negro community is in turmoil over this injustice. If immediate steps are not taken, Newark might become another Watts" (Governor's Select Commission on Civil Disorders 1968:15).

Further contention resulted over the administration of federal antipoverty funds. As part of President Lyndon Johnson's War on Poverty, the federal government sought to channel funds to community groups in poor neighborhoods as a means of empowering poor people to address their indigenous problems. Under the Community Action Program (CAP), groups like Newark's United Community Corporation (UCC) could apply for federal funds to launch jobs programs, day care centers, and other programs people in the community felt were needed at the time. Mayor Addonizio feared that the UCC would become an alternative power base, which would then challenge his leadership. To a certain degree, Addonizio was right. The UCC took on functions akin to those of a government in waiting, resolving problems that the city government was unable or unwilling to handle, such as confronting slumlords about building conditions.

> Largely excluded from positions of traditional political power, Negroes, tutored by a handful of militant social activists who had moved into the city in the early 1960s, made use of the anti-poverty program, in which poor people were guaranteed representation, as a political springboard. This led to friction between the United Community Corporation, the agency that administered the anti-poverty program, and the city administration. (National Advisory Commission on Civil Disorders 1968:59)

Addonizio petitioned the federal government for changes in the Community Action Program that would make funding of community groups subject to mayoral approval. Eventually, not withstanding the Mayor's efforts, Congress declined to renew funding for CAP. Black residents who had been politically empowered by CAP, though deeply disappointed, were unwilling to fade into the shadows. They channeled their anger against Addonizio and the federal government into a campaign to halt construction of a proposed medical school complex. Militant leaders such as Amiri Baraka, then known as LeRoi Jones, spoke of revolution. The black community had become politically organized and self-aware. The genie was out of the bottle.

In Detroit, the situation was somewhat different. The new mayor was young, charming, and idelogically liberal. His desire to help the black community was more sincere than his Newark counterpart's. In his first term in office, Mayor Jerome Cavanagh revived the Committee on Community Relations and instructed it to enforce fair employment practices among firms holding municipal contracts. Making good on campaign promises, he appointed several African Americans to positions in his cabinet including Alfred Pelham as city comptroller and appointed a white liberal, George Edwards, as commissioner of police. One NAACP official described Edwards's appointment to the post as akin to Lyndon Johnson's appointment of Thurgood Marshall to the U.S. Supreme Court (Fine 1989:19). Compared to its counterpart in Newark, Detroit's black community was well represented, with two black congressmen, three municipal judges, and twelve members of the state legislature (Fine 1989:32). With a liberal mayor responsive to black people's concerns, it seemed that Detroit was a "model city" for race relations. Nicholas Hood, a black city councilman, summarized this spirit prior to the riots, stating that "Detroit is far ahead of any major city in America because we have a city administration that will not only listen to the concerns brought to it but will set out to work on these concerns" (Fine 1989:33).

Yet, despite these prominent appointments, black political leadership, and Mayor Cavanagh's good working relationship with mainstream civil rights groups, a significant segment of the black community in Detroit felt disenfranchised, frustrated by what they perceived to be the relatively slow pace of racial change and persistent racial inequality. Although black Detroiters had higher incomes, lower unemployment rates, and higher levels of education than their peers in other cities, these measures paled in comparison with the gaps in income, employment, and education in Detroit between whites and blacks. According to one long-time community activist, blacks in Detroit did not compare themselves to blacks in other cities. Rather, they compared themselves to whites in Detroit. Such comparisons helped give rise to militancy in the black community (personal interview, Ron Hewitt, June 29, 2001). Local militant leaders like the Reverend Albert Cleague spoke of self-determination and separatism, arguing that whites were incapable and or unwilling to share power. At a black power rally in Detroit in early July 1967, H. Rap Brown foreshadowed the course of future events, stating that if "Motown" didn't come around, "we are going to burn you down." The irony of this statement is that in Detroit Mayor Cavanagh, unlike Newark Mayor Addonizio, was making a real effort to turn the city around, to make the city government more responsive to black people. Yet, despite his best efforts, the reforms instituted by Cavanagh failed to address many of the fundamental problems faced by black residents in Detroit such as shortages of affordable housing, loss of industrial jobs, and the increased concentration of poor blacks in poor neighborhoods. Given these structural conditions, no amount of incremental reforms could stanch the rise of black militancy

Police brutality and a sense of political powerlessness were far from the only major problems experienced by Detroit and Newark residents in the period leading up to the riots. Both cities were beset by a myriad of social trouble with the potential for fomenting collective violence. Of these, the quality and availability of housing was a major source of contention among black residents and government officials. In a public opinion survey by the Governor's Select Commission on Civil Disorder in New Jersey, known as the Hughes Commission, 54 percent of black respondents indicated that "housing problems had a 'great deal to do with the riot.'" This was a larger margin than those who said that unemployment (53 percent), lack of equal job opportunities (52 percent), broken promises by city officials (52 percent), and unresponsiveness of city officials to Negro wishes (46 percent) had a "great deal to do with the riot." Notably, only 46 percent of black respondents indicated that police brutality was a key factor in causing the riot. When asked to consider Newark's most serious problem, 37 percent of black respondents mentioned housing, second only to high living costs (44 percent). These responses were indicative of the dire need for affordable housing in Newark at that time (Governor's Select Commission on Civil Disorders 1968:55).

Much of the existing housing in Newark during the mid- to late 1960s was uninhabitable by modern safety and health standards. The city's own application for the Model Cities program in 1966 "described over 40,000 of the city's 136,000 housing units as substandard or dilapidated" (Governor's Select Commission on Civil Disorders 1968:55). Slumlords collected rent but often failed to perform regular maintenance, let alone improvements, to their properties (Sternlieb 1969). Sometimes landlords simply set fire to their property in hope of receiving an insurance windfall. Between 1961 and 1967, Newark averaged 3,620 structural fires per year (Winters 1979:5). Due to their limited housing options, blacks in Newark paid more money for lesser-quality domiciles:

> There can be no question that Newark's non-whites pay more than whites for substandard housing. In a special report of the U.S. Census of Housing HC(S1)-94, the variation in the prices paid by whites vs. non-whites is highlighted. If we analyze the data for substandard housing alone, the median rent was $61.00 per month; for non-whites it was $72.00 per month. Thirty percent of the white renters of substandard housing paid less than $55.00 per month, as contrasted with only 12.4% of non-whites. On the other hand, only 10.5% of whites paid $80.00 or more, while 22.2% of the non-whites paid that amount. (Sternlieb and Barry 1967:9)

The alternative to private housing for many low-income Newark residents was not much better. Public housing, which consisted of high-density high-rise projects, was neither conducive to residents' well-being nor the people who served them. Yet by 1967, "a vast constellation of low-income public housing projects was already standing in the Central Ward." Eleven percent of all Newarkers lived in such projects, one of the highest concentrations of public housing in the nation (Winters 1979:8).

> Some 18,000 people are now crowded into an area with a radius of about a mile and a half. There is little grass or open space around the project grounds. There are no lavatory facilities on first floors or near playgrounds. It is virtually impossible in densely populated vertical silos for parents to supervise their youngsters, for maintenance workers to keep up with their chores, or for policemen to do their job adequately. (Governor's Select Commission on Civil Disorders 1968:56)

Public housing in Newark merely helped concentrate poverty and despair in one centralized location. This further isolated the black poor from the community at large. One former public housing resident, whose family left the projects just before the 1967 riot, states,

> I remember being in the projects and during the daytime there would be just as many people walking around during the week as on a Saturday, so that should give you some indication of what is what like. In the summertime there were lots of folks just sitting on the benches or just hanging around the corner.... There was so much depression and lack of hope; the people just had no hope. (personal interview, Gerard Drinkard, October 5, 2001)

Affordable housing, or the lack thereof, was also a fundamental concern for black Detroiters. When polled by the *Detroit Free Press* regarding the problems that contributed most to the rioting in the previous year, respondents listed "poor housing" as one of the most important issues, second only to police brutality (*Detroit Free Press* 1968; Thomas 1997:130–131). Detroit had a long history of housing discrimination stretching back to the turn of the century when black migrants first arrived in the city and middle-class African Americans sought to integrate predominantly white neighborhoods. During the 1940s and 1950s, white Detroiters sought to block the entry of blacks into their neighborhoods by legal and extralegal means, in one instance building a six-foot-high, one-foot-wide concrete wall to separate themselves from potential black neighbors. During those years, white residents engaged in several bitter campaigns to prevent the integration of public housing located in predominantly white areas (Farley, Danzinger, and Holzer 2000:154–161). By the 1960s, with the exception of some movement of blacks into formerly white neighborhoods, little had changed. In fact segregation had become more pronounced. "Despite the spatial expansion of black residences in the 1950s, 'invisible walls' continued to separate whites and blacks. Blacks, indeed were actually more segregated in their housing in 1960 than they had been 30 years earlier" (Fine 1989:10).

The quality and cost of housing differed substantially for blacks and whites in Detroit:

> Whereas 69.6 percent of Detroit's whites in 1960 lived in housing built before 1939, 91 percent of nonwhites lived in such dwellings. The homes non-whites lived in were less valuable and less soundly built than white-owned homes. The median value of owner-occupied non-white homes in 1960 was $10,200, that of owner occupied white homes, $12,600; and 27.9% of non-white homes, as compared to 9.8% of white homes, were dilapidated or deteriorating. Unlike Detroit whites, 64.7 percent of whom owned their homes, 61.1% of non-whites lived in rental units. Although non-whites lived in inferior dwellings as compared to whites, they nevertheless paid approximately the same rent as their white counterparts: $76 was the median rent per month for non-whites, $77 for whites. Since they had lower incomes than whites, rent absorbed 29.2 percent of the income of non-white renters, as compared to 19.7 percent of the income of white renters. (Fine 1989:11)

For black residents who could not afford private housing, public housing in Detroit was not much better than public housing in Newark. Like Newark's public housing, Detroit's projects were mostly high density and hypersegregated, "reinforcing isolation by race and income and reducing informal supervision over children and youth." Yet applicants for public housing in Detroit continued to outpace the number of available units (Thomas 1997:26–27). This pattern occurred by design as "slums" were cleared and residents relocated to the already crowded projects of the center city (Sugrue 1996:87).

In both cities the shortage of housing was further exacerbated by "urban renewal" projects. In Detroit, entire neighborhoods were bulldozed to make way for freeways that linked city and suburbs. Not surprisingly, the neighborhoods that met their fate in such manner were predominantly black. To build Interstate 75, Paradise Valley or Black Bottom, the neighborhood that black migrants and white ethnics had struggled over during the 1940s, was buried beneath several layers of concrete. As the oldest established black enclave in Detroit, Black Bottom was not merely a point on the map, but the heart of Detroit's black community, commercially and culturally. The loss for many black residents of Detroit was devastating, and the anger burned for years thereafter. In the meantime, former residents had to find shelter. Moving westward, they poured into the second established black enclave in Detroit, the 12th Street neighborhood, a seemingly stable middle-class area. As a result of the influx of less affluent residents from the east side, this neighborhood soon experienced overcrowding and decay. It would become the epicenter of the 1967 riot.

In Newark, "urban renewal," or "Negro removal" as it was referred to by local residents, would play an equally important role in fomenting rebellion. Plans were already in place to build superhighways that would bisect the black community (Winters 1979:4–5; www.nycroads.com/roads/NJ-75). Then, in the early months of 1967, the city proposed the "clearance" of 150 acres of "slum" land to build a medical school/hospital complex. Of course, this would involve the demolition of numerous homes in the predominantly black Central Ward. Given the shortage of housing in other areas, the effects of such displacement were potentially devastating. A Rutgers University study stated that "if the total of units 'in poor condition' was calculated, only 4,133 vacant units were actually available." This report further noted that "a substantial part of the housing outside the core area (3,223 or these 4,133 units) was too high priced for the people who would need relocation" (Chernick, Indik, and Sternlieb cited in Governor's Select Commission on Civil Disorders 1968:62). Tom Hayden summarized the resident's fears:

> The city's vast programs for urban renewal, highways, downtown development, and most recently, a 150 acre Medical School in the heart of the ghetto seemed

almost deliberately designed to squeeze out this rapidly growing Negro community that represents a majority of the population. (Hayden 1968:6)

Upon hearing of the proposal, members of the local community quickly mobilized and began to hold protest rallies. Some of the same people who attended these rallies were present at the 4th Precinct house where the riot started that summer. The city's plan to build the medical school, while demolishing black occupied homes, would help set the stage for future confrontation (Winters 1979:48).

Against a backdrop of police brutality and housing crisis, a profound change was underway in the economic structure of cities like Newark and Detroit. By the late 1960s, both cities were caught in the throes of industrial decline, of which black workers bore the brunt. The flight of manufacturing jobs that had begun in the 1950s accelerated during the 1960s. In Newark, the famed breweries that drew water from the polluted Passaic River shut down, as did the tanneries that fouled the water to begin with. The big conglomerates, Westinghouse and General Electric, who manufactured large appliances in Newark soon followed. In their wake, thousands of jobs were lost.

Aggravating the growing deficit of resources even further was the postwar abandonment by industry, leaving fewer employment opportunities nearby for the lower skilled and unskilled who remained in or came into the city. Stripped of much of its leadership and other resources and faced with problems from before and after the war, the city came to be like a house ransacked (Wright 1968:57).

As a result of previous discrimination and poor education, black workers, who were concentrated in heavy industry, felt the impact of these changes more than white workers who had moved upward into managerial and professional jobs.

> When inadequate education is coupled with lack of work experience and training, and overt or built in discrimination the picture becomes even bleaker for the non-white. Although the Newark labor market has a total unemployment rate hovering around 4.3%, the Negroes in the city suffer an unemployment rate of 11.5%, twice as high as among whites (5.9%). (Governor's Select Commission on Civil Disorders 1968:66)

But it was black youth, just entering the labor market, who seemed to have suffered the most in the long run. The 1968 Hughes Commission reported the following grim statistics:

> Among 16–19 year old Negro men, more than a third—37.8% are jobless. Considering that more than 40% of Newark's Negroes are under the age of 15, an even more serious crisis lies ahead." (Governor's Select Commission on Civil Disorders 1968:66)

Detroit, internationally recognized as a center of automobile production, seemed to fare a little better economically than Newark. But beginning in the 1950s, the big car manufacturers, Ford, Chrysler, and GM, began to automate their assembly lines and outsource parts production to subcontractors located in other municipalities and foreign countries (Sugrue 1996:128). Detroit, like Newark, was deindustrializing and black workers "felt the brunt" of this change:

> Data from the 1960 census make clear the disparate effect of automation and labor market constriction on African American workers. Across the city 15.9 percent of blacks, but only 5.8 percent of whites were out of work. In the motor vehicle industry, the black-white gap was even greater. 19.7 percent of black auto workers were unemployed, compared to only 5.8% of whites. Discrimination and de-industrialization proved to be a lethal combination.... By the early 1960s, observers noted that a seemingly permanent class of underemployed and jobless blacks had emerged, a group that came to be known as the "long-term unemployed." (Sugrue 1996:144)

As was the case in Newark, it was the black youth of Detroit who were most impacted by the tidal wave of economic restructuring; it was these unemployed, alienated youth who would serve as foot soldiers in the urban uprising that followed.

> The combination of discrimination and deindustrialization weighed most heavily on the job opportunities of young African-American men. Young workers, especially those who had no post-secondary education, found that entry-level operative jobs that had been open to their fathers or older siblings in the 1940s and early 1950s were gone. The most dramatic evidence of the impact of industrial change on young black workers was the enormous gap between black and white youth who had no attachment to the labor market.... By the end of the 1950s, more and more black job seekers, reported by the Urban League, were demoralized, "developing patterns of boredom and hopelessness with the present state of affairs." The anger and despair that prevailed among the young, at a time of national promise and prosperity, would explode on Detroit's streets in the 1960s. (Sugrue 1996:147)

ETHNIC SUCCESSION

Accompanying this economic transformation was an equally significant demographic shift. As early as the 1950s, when industrial enterprises shut down their urban manufacturing plants and relocated jobs to the suburbs, white residents followed. This trend would intensify in Newark, Detroit, and other American cities during the 1960s as throngs of white homeowners packed up and moved to the greener pastures of suburbia. The federal government played a key role in promoting this urban exodus, subsidizing the construction of housing by offering low-interest loans to veterans and other "qualified" applicants, generally nonwhites. Federal highway funds built the interstate system that would carry white workers from the suburbs to downtown offices and back. Blacks, facing discrimination at the hands of realtors and/or lacking the resources necessary to move, were increasingly abandoned in the central cities. A "chocolate city, vanilla suburb" pattern had begun to take hold.

In Newark, as a result of postwar suburban migration, the white population plummeted to approximately 158,000 in 1967 from 363,000 in 1950 and 266,000 in 1960. Correspondingly, the black population of Newark rose from 70,000 in 1950 to 125,000 in 1960 and an estimated 220,000 in 1967. By 1967, a majority of Newark residents (55 percent) were African American. According to educator Nathan Wright's *Ready to Riot* (1968), "No typical American city has as yet experienced such a precipitous change from a white to a black majority" (16).

Demographic changes at the city level were reflected in particular neighborhoods, namely the Central Ward, formerly home to a sizable concentration of immigrant and second-generation Jews. Abandoning their homes and synagogues, these Jews, along with some Catholic Poles and Italians, fled for the suburbs of nearby South Orange, West Orange, and Livingston. There they rebuilt the institutions they had left behind. (Helmreich 1998). Between 1960 and 1967, two-thirds of the white population of the Central Ward moved out (Winters, 1979:87). By the time of the riot, the Central Ward was a predominantly black neighborhood, yet served by mostly Jewish-owned businesses—a recipe for ethnic tension.

Population change in Detroit led to a similar outcome. Like Newark, Detroit was swept by a wave of white flight. During the 1950s the white population of Detroit declined by 23 percent. Correspondingly, the percentage of nonwhites rose from 16.1 percent to 29.1 percent. In absolute numbers, the black population of Detroit increased from 303,000 to 487,000 during that decade (Fine 1989:4). By 1967, the black population of Detroit stood at an estimated 40 percent of the total population (National Advisory Committee on Civil Disorders 1968:89–90). As in Newark, some neighborhoods were more affected by white flight than others. This was particularly true for the 12th Street neighborhood, where rioting broke out in the summer of 1967. According to historian Thomas Sugrue:

> The consequences of flight were clear in the racial composition of the Twelfth Street area. Whereas virtually no blacks lived there in 1940 (the area was 98.7% white), the area was over one-third (37.2%) non-white in 1950. By 1960, the proportion of blacks to whites had nearly reversed: only 3.8 percent of the area's residents were white. Given that the first blacks did not move to the area until 1947 and 1948, the area underwent a complete racial transition in little more than a decade. (1996:244)

This rapid turnover in population in the neighborhoods of Detroit and Newark brought with it the attendant ills of social disorganization, crime, and further discrimination. With respect to Newark, though the point is applicable to Detroit as well, Wright stated:

> All societies strive more for order than for orderly but needed changes. Thus it would seem immediately fallacious to deny that gross discrimination did not exist in a city that has moved from an 85 percent white urban oriented majority in 1940 to a nearly 60 percent black, strongly rural oriented black majority in 1965. Newark has been—and is—the scene of massive urban change. Such change brings disorganization. (1968:8)

In the words of historian Sidney Fine, the impact of demographic change on Detroit's 12th Street neighborhood was devastatingly clear:

> The transition from white to black on Detroit's near northwest side occurred at a remarkably rapid rate.... In a familiar pattern of neighborhood succession, as blacks moved in after World War II, the Jews moved out. The first black migrants to the area were middle class persons seeking to escape the confines of Paradise Valley. They enjoyed about "five good years" in their new homes until underworld and seedier elements from Hastings Street and Paradise Valley, the poor and indigent from the inner city, and winos and derelicts from skid row flowed into the area. Some of the commercial establishments on Twelfth Street gave way to pool halls, liquor stores, sleazy bars, pawn shops, and second hand businesses. Already suffering from a housing shortage and lack of open space, Twelfth Street became more "densely packed" as apartments were subdivided and six to eight families began to live where two had resided before. The 21,376 persons per square mile in the area in 1960 were almost double the city's average. "The blight—human misery—was setting in," a black man who lived in the area at the time recalled. "You could feel it in the air, smell it coming rancid out of the bars, watch it...on the faces of kids not 20 years old yet." (Fine 1989:4)

TESTING THE ETHNIC SUCCESSION HYPOTHESIS

Geographic Information Systems Analysis

Some twenty-four years earlier in Detroit and forty-eight years prior in Chicago, one could observe these same essential conditions: crowding, poverty, vice, and crime, all corresponding to the mass migration of rural blacks into the former immigrant ghettos of the urban North. In the previous chapter, I proposed that the violence that marked the Chicago riot of 1919 and the 1943 Detroit riot was a product of demographic flux, rooted in social disorganization that accompanied racial change. I will now address whether the violence that swept Newark and Detroit neighborhoods during the summer of 1967 can be explained according to this same hypothesis.

Using a combination of census data and information on the location of riot-related fatalities culled from official riot commission reports, I address whether there is an association between riot violence and the rate of demographic change in neighborhoods The first step involved gathering demographic data at the census tract level for the entire city or MSA. Such data included indicators of racial/ethnic composition (percent black, percent white, change in percent black, change in percent white) and indicators of economic well-being (percent males unemployed, median household income). In the maps and statistical models that follow, I used the census tract as my main unit of analysis.

The second step involved compiling a database of riot-related fatalities for each riot, including the name, age, race, gender, and circumstances of death, as well as the day, time, and street address where each fatality occurred. Using the address mapping or "geocoding" feature of ArcView GIS software, I located each fatality on a map of census tracts for the city. I then used ArcView to overlay the position of the riot fatalities with the demographic data. This allowed me to produce a series of thematic maps that examine the location of riot fatalities with respect to the changing racial/ethnic composition and economic characteristics of census tracts. These maps are presented in Figures 5.1–5.10.

Figures 5.1–5.3 display the relationships among the location of Newark riot fatalities and the changing racial/ethnic composition of Newark census tracts during the era preceding the riot (1950–1960). Figure 5.1 shows the location of riot fatalities with respect to the distribution of black population (percent black) in 1950. Figure 5.2 looks at the black population distribution in 1960. Figure 5.3 examines the change in black population composition between 1950 and 1960.

Figures 5.1 and 5.2 reveal a significant expansion and concentration of black population in Newark's Central Ward during the 1950s. In 1950, only eight census tracts had a black population greater than 50 percent of the tract's total population and fourteen had a black population between 25 to 50 percent of the tract's total. By contrast, in 1960, thirty census tracts had a black population of 50 percent or more and ten tracts had a black population of 25–50 percent. Figure 5.3 reveals that the preponderance of riot fatalities took place in census tracts where the black population increased by more than 20 percent during the decade. This lends support to an ethnic succession explanation of riot violence. The areas that experienced the most demographic change had a greater likelihood of being touched by riot related homicides than tracts that did not experience such a magnitude of change

Figures 5.4–5.5 look at the relationship between riot-related fatalities and economic indicators (percent males unemployed and median household income). Figure 5.4 reveals a general correspondence between high rates of male unemployment and the riot violence. The preponderance of

Figure 5.1 1967 Newark Riot Fatalities and Percent Black, 1950

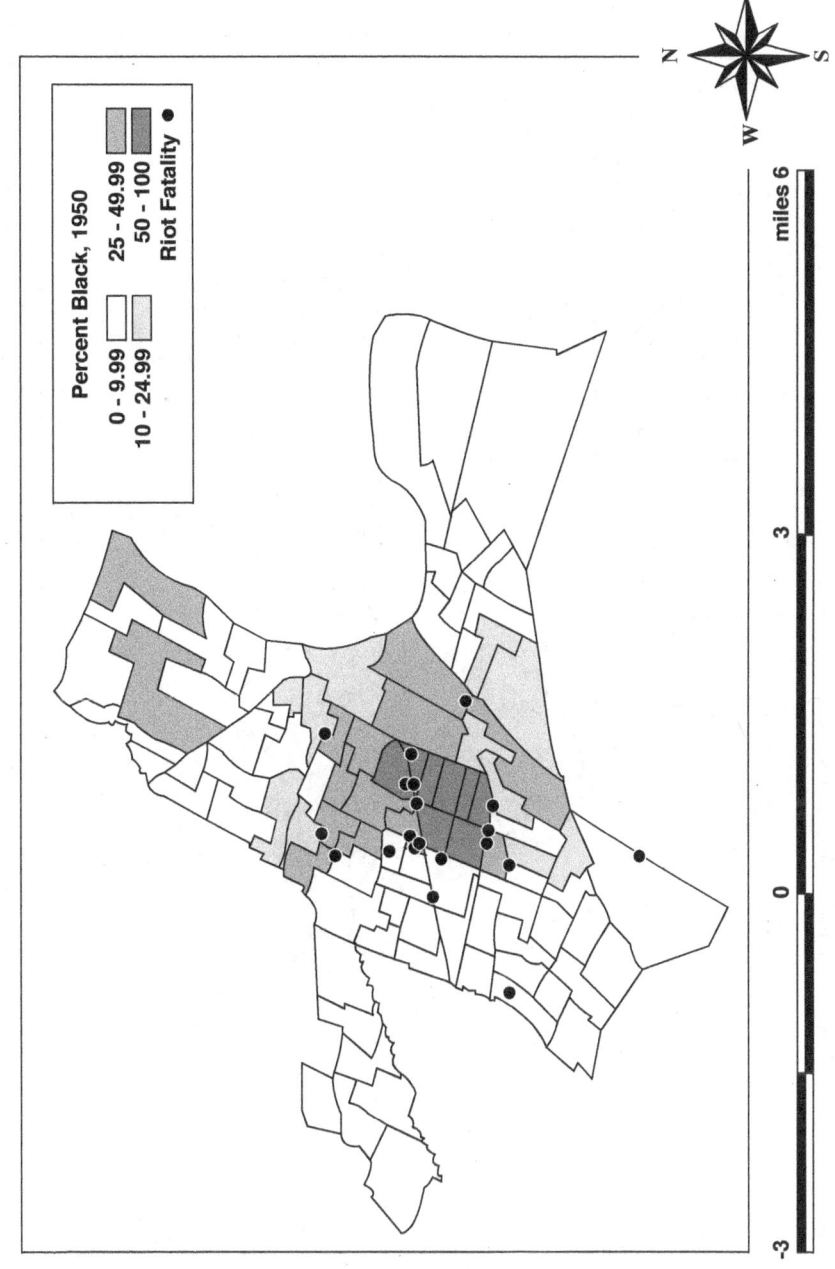

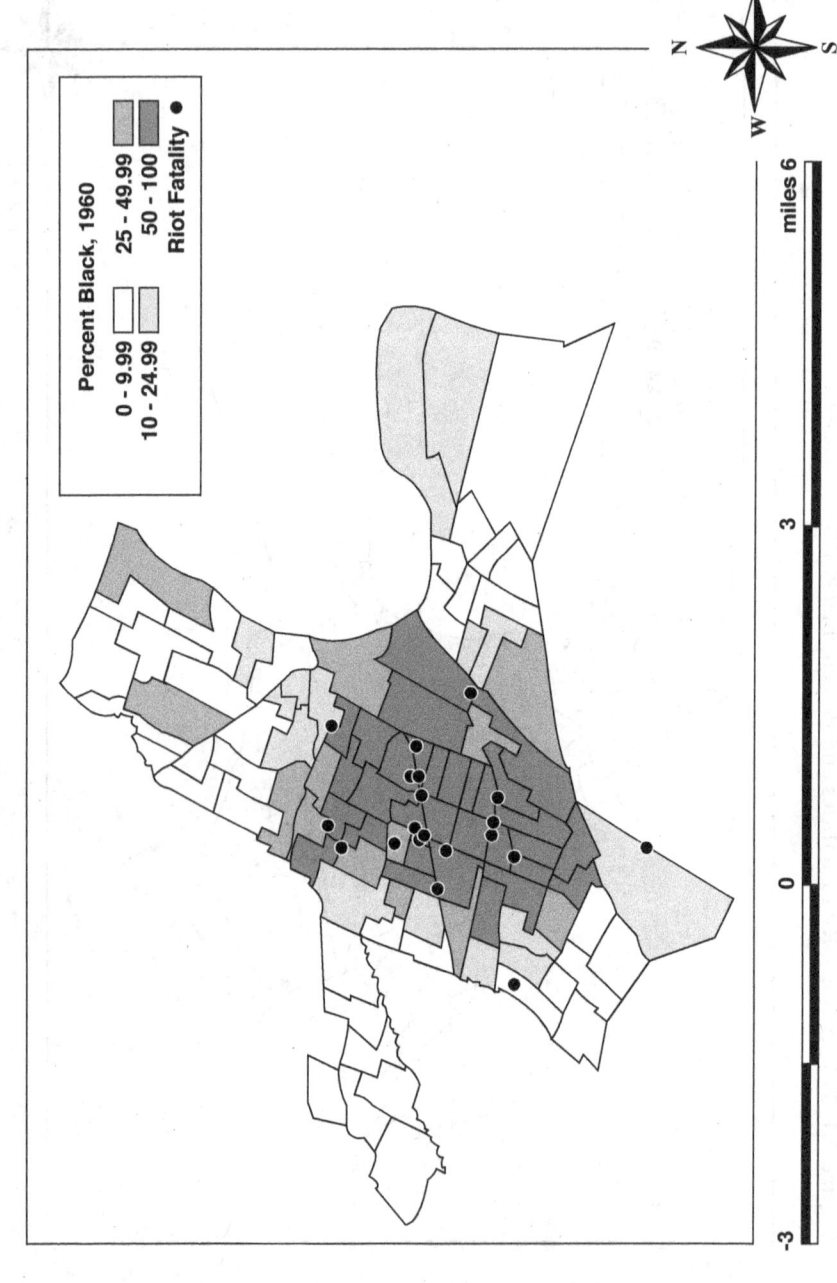

Figure 5.2 1967 Newark Riot Fatalities and Percent Black, 1960

Figure 5.3 1967 Newark Riot Fatalities and Change in Percent Black, 1950–1960

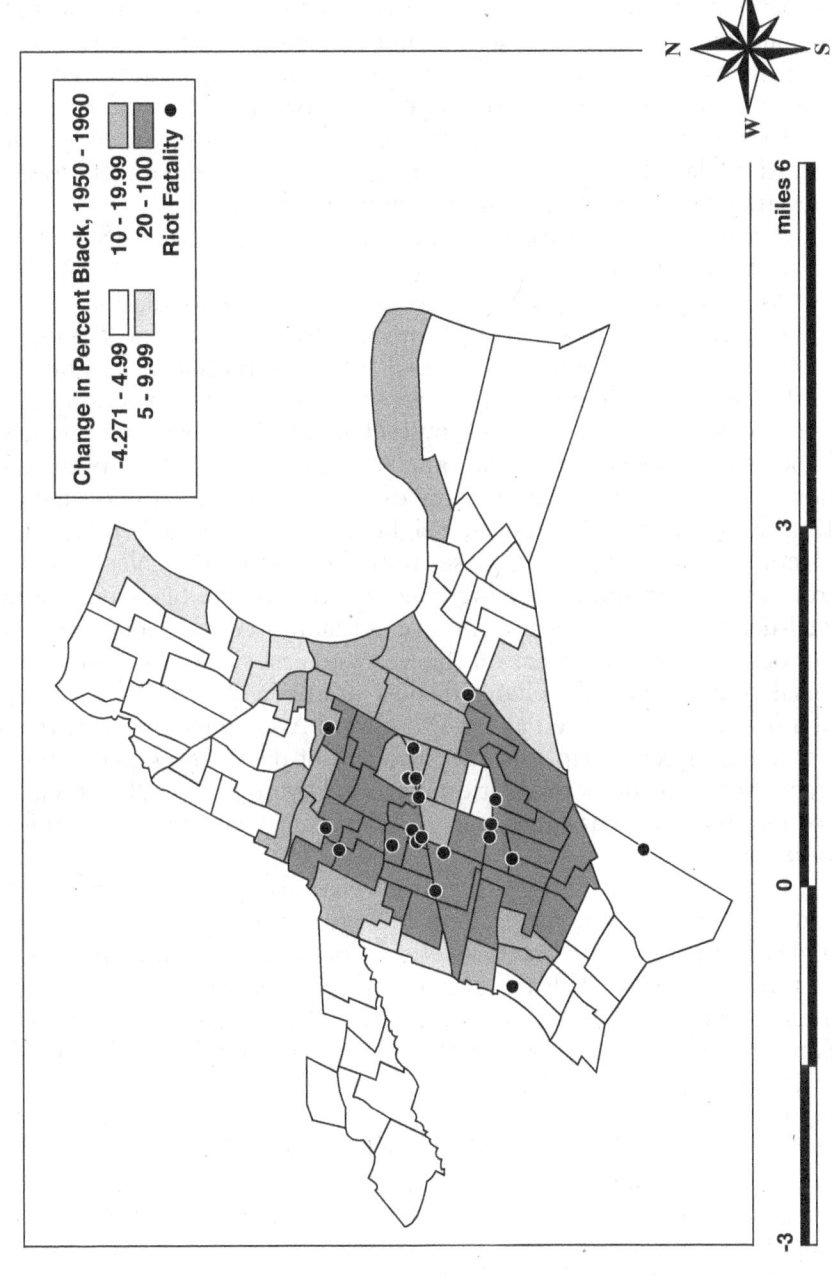

deaths occurred in tracts where male unemployment was between 10 and 20 percent, with the exception of a cluster of fatalities along Springfield Avenue, which was a commercial, not residential, area. Figure 5.5 shows that riot fatalities were also generally associated with tracts that had the lowest levels of average household income. Based on this GIS map analysis, I tentatively conclude that both ethnic succession and economic deprivation played a role in contributing to the presence of riot violence in Newark neighborhoods during the summer of 1967.

Figures 5.6–5.10 present the results of a comparable GIS analysis for Detroit riot fatalities by census tract.

As illustrated by Figure 5.6, in 1950 the black population of Detroit was concentrated in the center of the city, the area known as Paradise Valley/Black Bottom. Between 1950 and 1960, several homes and businesses in that area were demolished to make way for the construction of Interstate 75. As shown in Figure 5.7, by 1960 much of the black population had relocated to enclaves on the east and west sides of Detroit. The concentration to the northwest, where many of the riot fatalities are located, is the 12th Street neighborhood—the neighborhood where the 1967 riot began. Overall, from 1950 to 1960, we see both dispersion of the black population from the center and increasing concentration of the black population in well-defined clusters. Figure 5.8 reveals that most of the riot-related fatalities occurred in these areas on the west and east side of Detroit where the racial composition had changed most dramatically. With the exception of a few deaths clustered along Woodward Avenue (center north), which was a commercial strip, the vast majority of deaths took place in census tracts where the black population increased by more than 20 percent. This correspondence lends support to an ethnic succession explanation for riot violence.

Figures 5.9 and 5.10 examine the relationship between riot fatalities and economic well-being in Detroit. Figure 5.9 shows that the majority of deaths took place in tracts where the percentage of unemployed males was between 10 to 19.9; tracts marked by the most severe rates of male unemployment (20 percent or greater) were largely untouched by violence. Similarly, Figure 5.10 shows that a majority of riot-related fatalities in Detroit took place in neighborhoods where the median household income was between $3,635 and $5,585 per year, while relatively few fatalities occurred in tracts marked by the lowest levels of household income (less than $3,635 per year). This suggests that riot-related violence in Detroit was not centered in the most economically deprived neighborhoods. Rather, riot-related fatalities were clustered in tracts that were a step or two above those with the most severe levels of poverty and unemployment. Such a finding confirms the result of a survey of rioters in Newark and Detroit conducted by Nathan Caplan and Jeffrey Paige (1968), which revealed that riot participants in Newark and Detroit were somewhat better educated and more

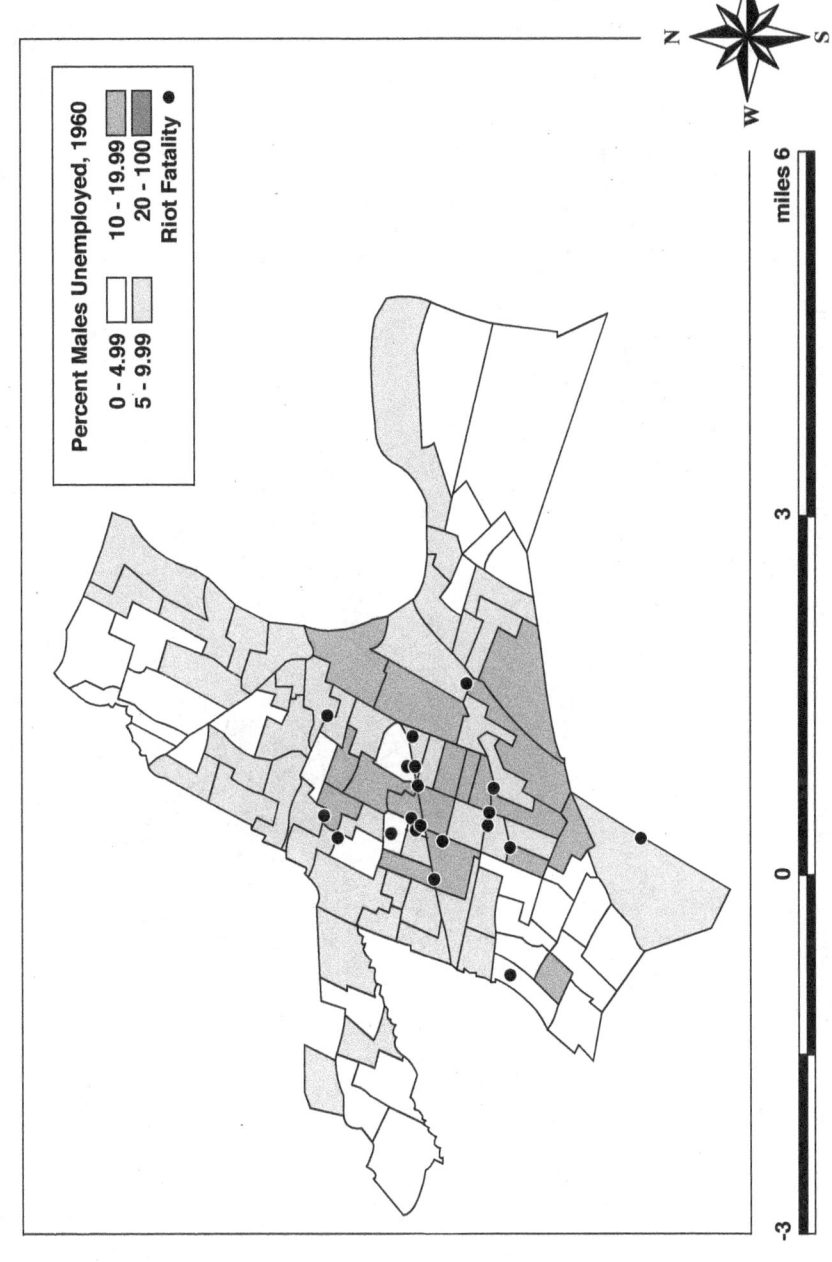

Figure 5.4 1967 Newark Riot Fatalities and Percent Males Unemployed, 1960

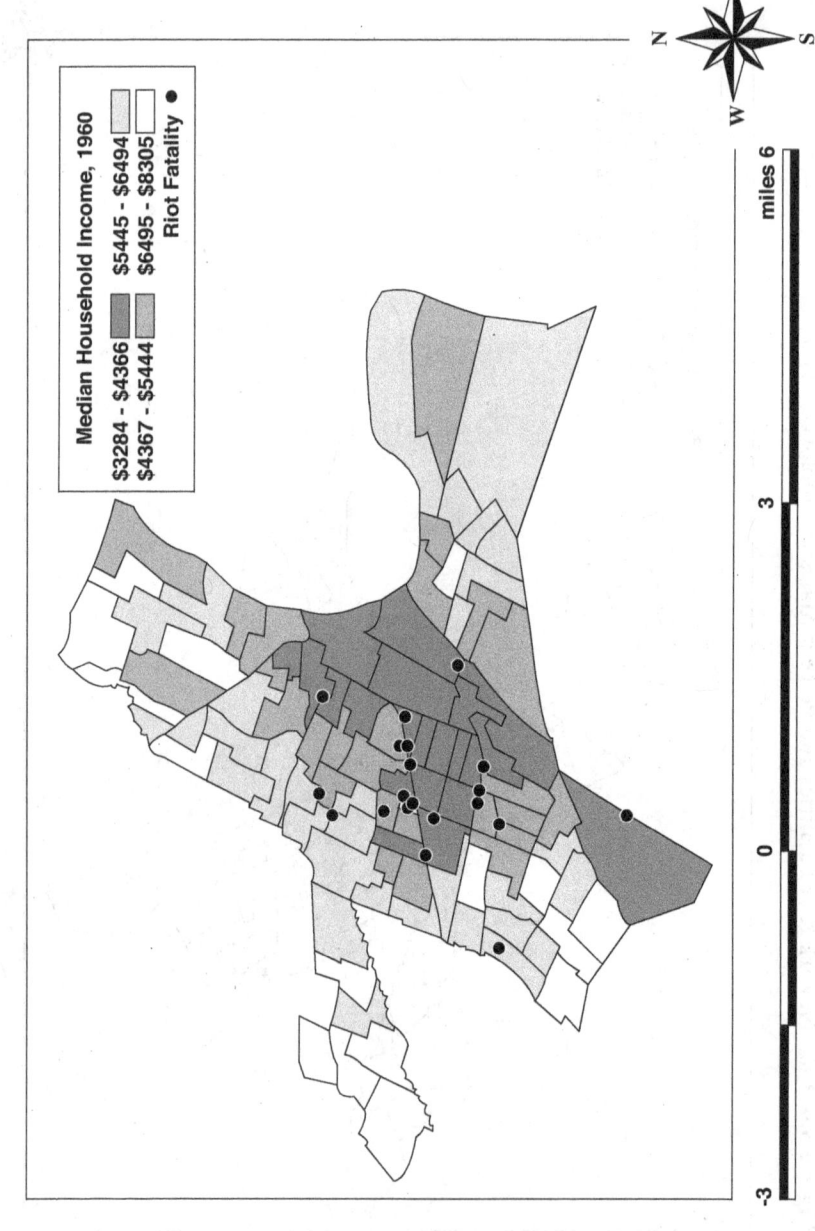

Figure 5.5 1967 Newark Riot Fatalities and Median Household Income, 1960

White Flight and Black Power 97

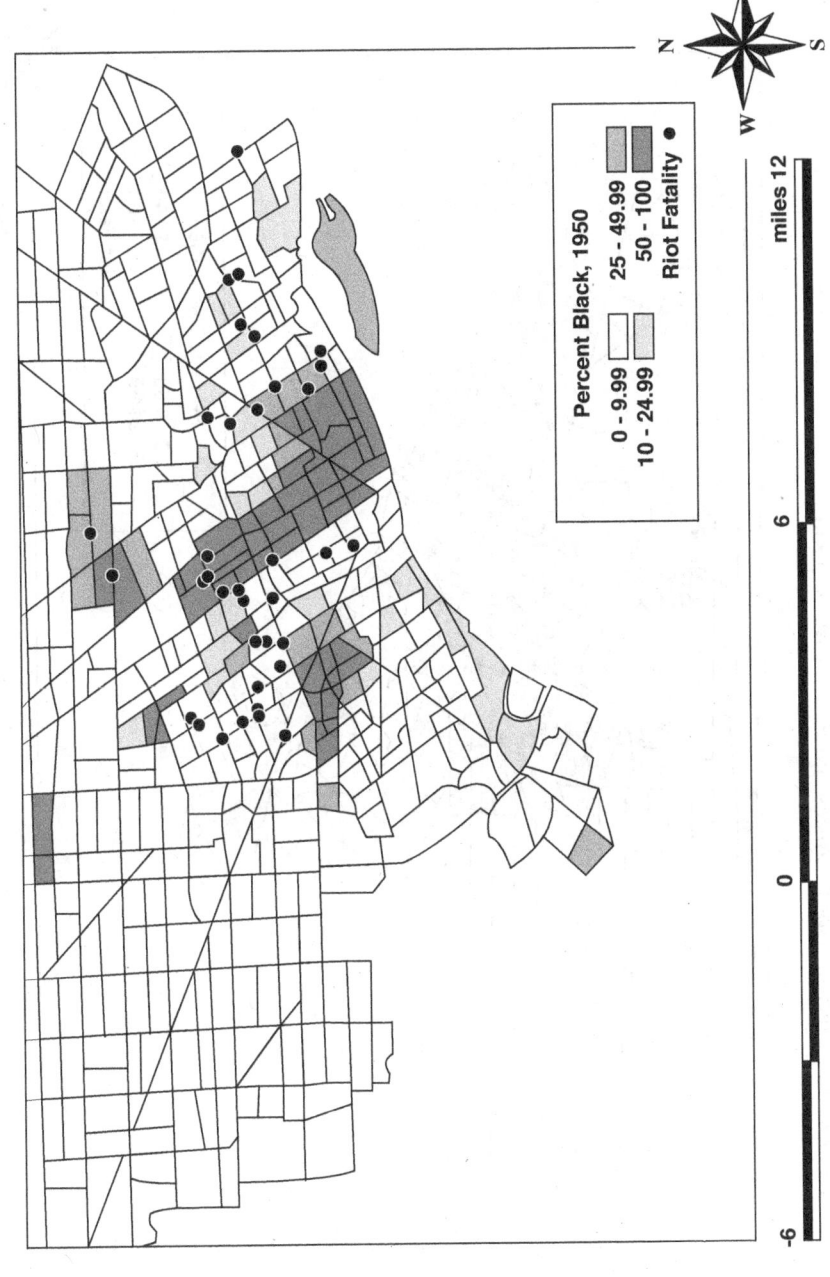

Figure 5.6 1967 Detroit Riot Fatalities and Percent Black, 1950

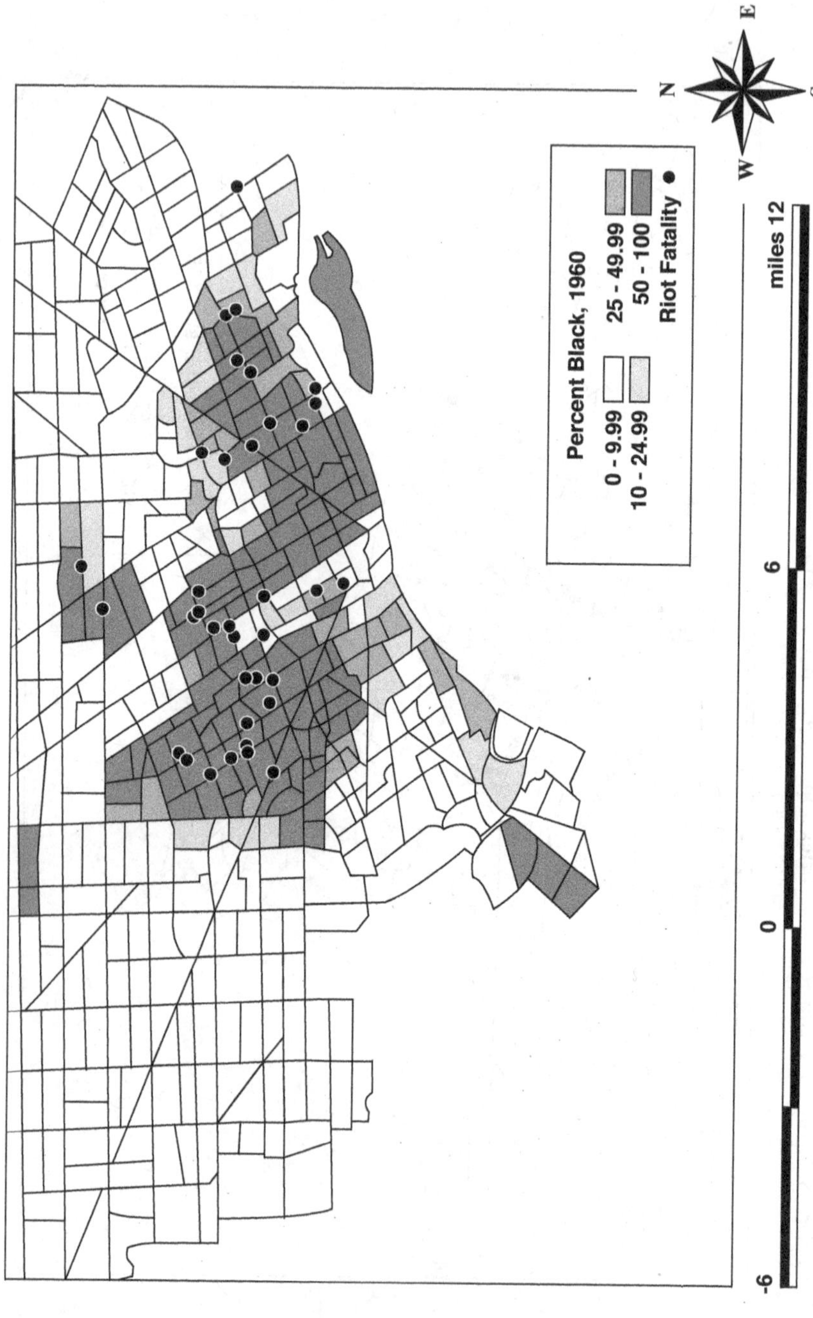

98 FIGHTING IN THE STREETS

Figure 5.7 1967 Detroit Riot Fatalities and Percent Black, 1960

Figure 5.8 1967 Detroit Riot Fatalities and Percent Chance in Percent Black, 1950-1960

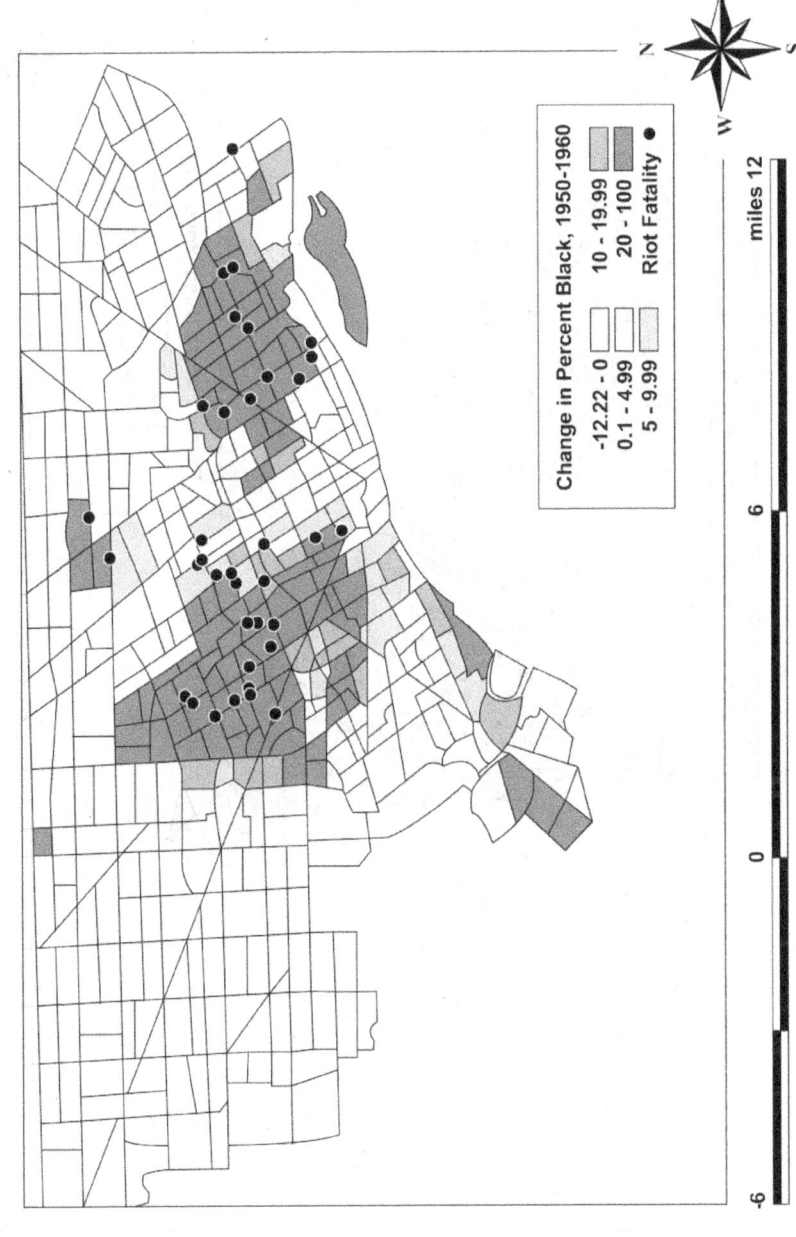

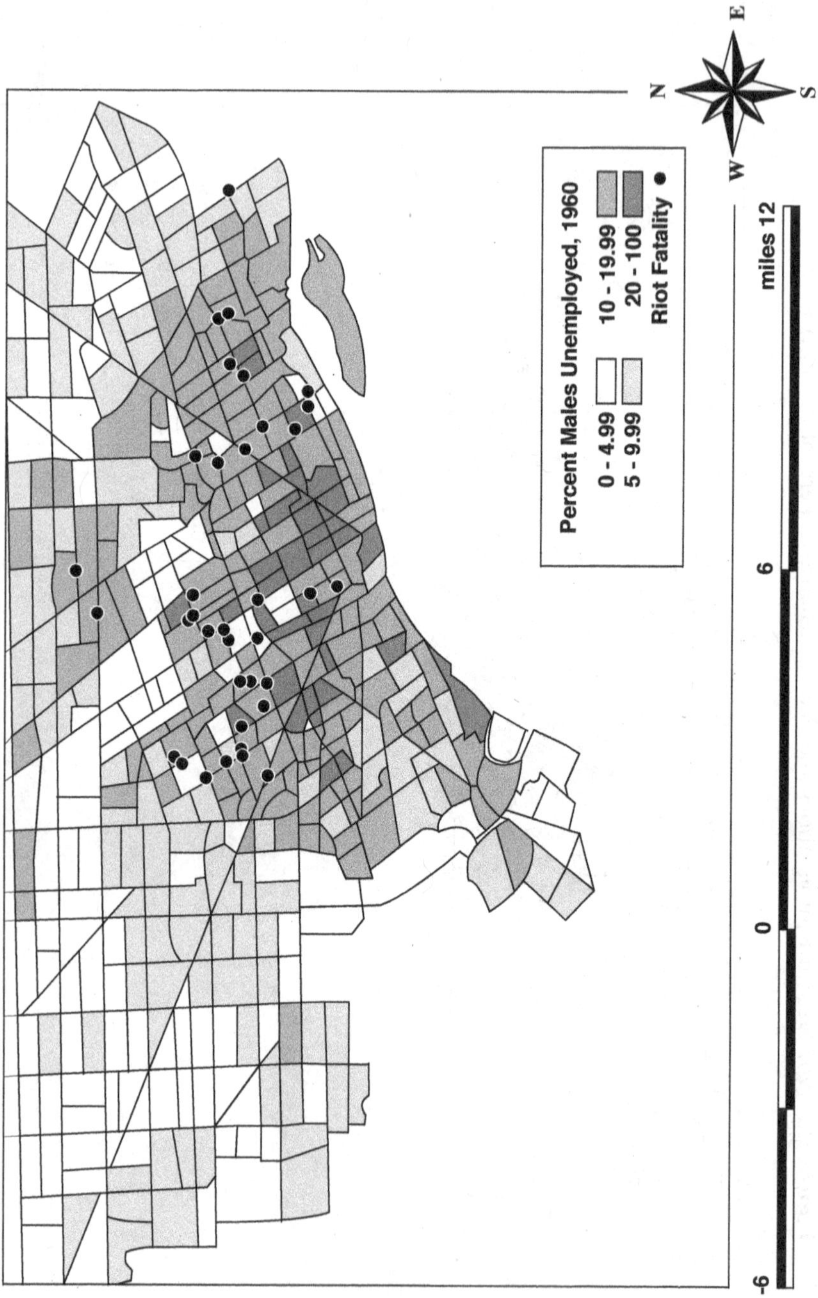

Figure 5.9 1967 Detroit Riot Fatalities and Percent Males Unemployed, 1960

White Flight and Black Power 101

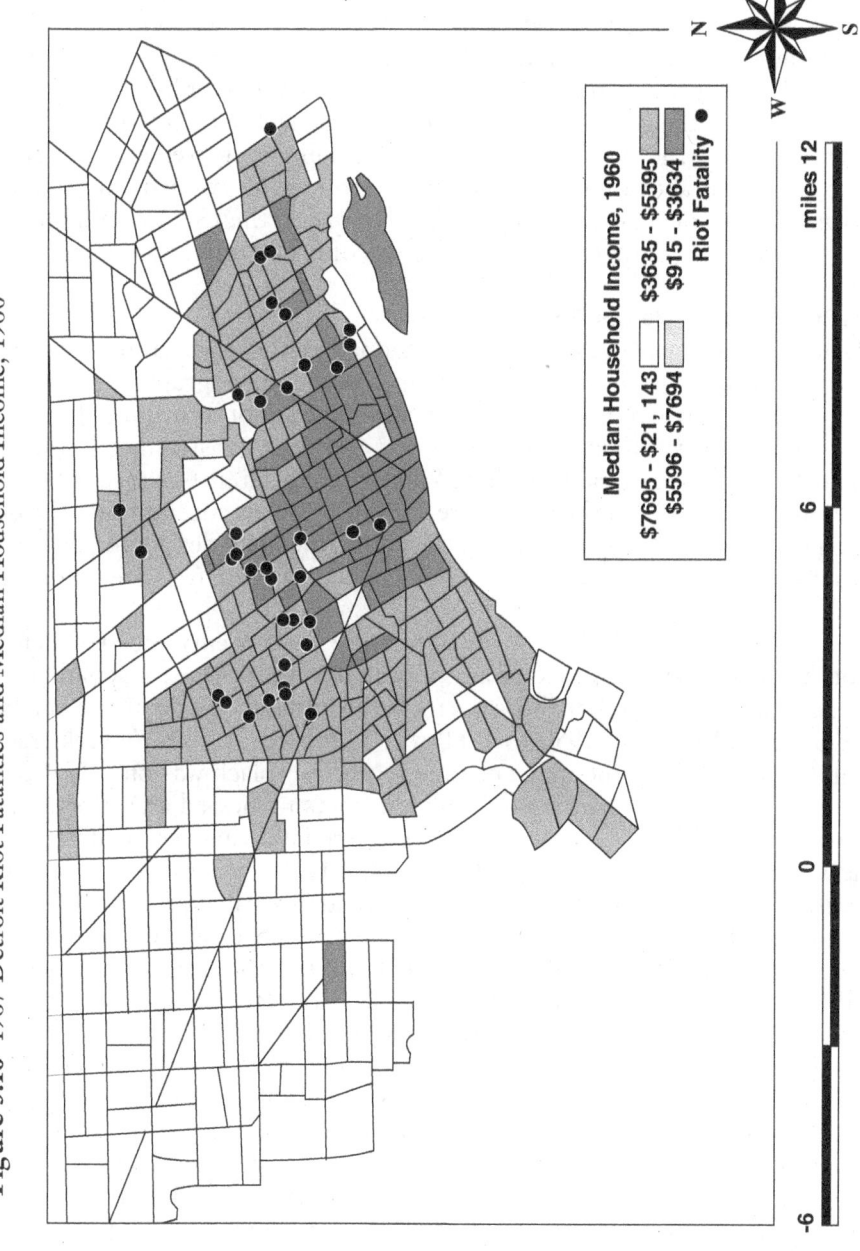

Figure 5.10 1967 Detroit Riot Fatalities and Median Household Income, 1960

likely to have been employed than people in the riot neighborhoods who did not participate in the riots. This finding also resonates with the work of numerous scholars of revolution and rebellion who claim that the poorest of the poor rarely revolt (Davies 1971; Gurr 1970). These "relative deprivation" theorists, including Caplan and Paige, argue that people are most likely to riot when their aspirations are frustrated or blocked or when they see that others have what they do not. The fact of the matter is that in Detroit during the 1960s, some blacks were doing quite well economically. But as argued above, black people in Detroit didn't compare themselves with black people in others cities. They compared their situation with that of whites. This comparison fueled the fire of urban unrest in Detroit.

Difference of Means Test (T-Test)

Although GIS map analysis allows us to make visual associations between the presence of riot fatalities and the underlying demographic features of neighborhood where they occur, map analysis cannot inform us about the strength of these associations or whether they are statistically significant. A fairly simple statistical technique known as a difference of means test allows us to address whether there are significant differences among the demographic characteristics of tracts that contained riot deaths versus tracts where riot deaths did not occur. The results of this analysis are contained in Table 5.1.

As shown in Table 5.1, for Newark there were twenty-four tracts that contained a riot-related fatality as opposed to seventy-three tracts that did not contain a fatality. For those tracts with riot fatalities the mean change in percent black from 1950 to 1960 was 32.6 percent. For Newark tracts without riot deaths, the mean change in percent black was only 12.4 percent. Whereas both death and nondeath tracts witnessed a proportionate increase in black population, the tracts where fatal violence occurred witnessed a much greater increase. Because the 1960s census treats black and white persons as mutually exclusive and exhaustive categories, the increase in percent black for these census tracts was matched by a corresponding decrease in percent white from 1950 to 1960. In short, tracts with riot fatalities, on average, had greater rates of relative black population increase and white population loss than tracts without fatalities.

Based on 1960s census figures, on average tracts with riot fatalities in Newark had a significantly proportion of black residents and a significantly lower proportion of white residents. As suggested by Spilerman (1970, 1971), riot fatalities in Newark tended to cluster in areas with sizable black population. Finally, tracts where riot-related fatalities occurred in Newark had significantly higher rates of unemployment (8.6 percent vs. 6.5 percent) and significant lower household income ($5,697 vs. $4,657) than tracts where riot-related fatalities did not take place. These findings confirm the results of the GIS map analysis for Newark. Tracts with riot

Table 5.1 Demographic Measures for Census Tracts with and without Riot Fatalities by City, Newark and Detroit

City	N	Percent Change		Mean Percent (End of Ten-Year Period)			Median Household Income
		Black	Foreign Born	Black	Foreign Born	Males Unemployed	
Newark 1950–1960							
Tracts with Fatalities	24	32.6***	10.2***	62.2***	7.4***	8.6***	$4,657***
Tracts without Fatalities	476	12.4	2.4	22.7	14.5	6.5	$5,697
Detroit 1950–1960		Black	Foreign Born	Black	Foreign Born	Males Unemployed	Median Household Income
Tracts with Fatalities	21	44.6***	-11.9	62.9***	12.8***	14.6**	$4,752***
Tracts without Fatalities	440	13.0	-7.7	25.9	7.1	10.6	$6,121

*=p<.05 **=p<.01 ***=p<.001

Sources:
U.S. Census of Population and Housing, Census Tract Data for the Newark SMSA (1950, 1960 paper volumes).
U.S. Census of Population and Housing, Census Tract Data for the Detroit SMSA (1950, 1960 paper volumes).

deaths were characterized by greater rates of demographic change and greater economic distress than tracts without riot-related deaths

Difference of means tests for Detroit yielded similar results as for Newark. In Detroit, which covers a larger geographical area than Newark, there were 33 tracts that contained a riot fatality and 386 census tracts with no fatalities. Detroit census tracts marked by riot fatalities had, on average, a 44.6 percent increase in percent black, compared to a 13 percent average increase in relative black population size for tracts without riot deaths. The black population proportion was increasing in most Detroit neighborhoods, but the neighborhoods where riot deaths took place had a significantly greater rate of black population increase. By 1960, tracts marked by riot-related fatalities had a significantly larger average black population proportion (62.9 percent vs. 25.9 percent) and a significantly smaller average white population proportion (37 percent vs. 74.1 percent) than tracts without fatalities, once again confirming Spilerman's hypothesis regarding the relationship between riot violence and black population size (Spilerman 1970, 1971).

In terms of economic indicators, Detroit tracts with deaths had a significantly larger average male unemployment rate (14.6 percent vs. 10.6 percent) and a significantly lower median household income ($4,752 vs. $6,212) than tracts without fatalities. As a package, these difference of means tests for Detroit confirm the visual associations uncovered in the GIS maps displayed in Figures 5.6–5.10. This preliminary statistical analysis provides further support for ethnic succession and economic deprivation as key factors in generating urban unrest.

Difference of means analysis, like GIS, is limited in scope. The main drawback of such tests is that they can only be performed on one variable at a time and thus cannot control for the effects of other independent variables at the same time. To simultaneously examine the effects of demographic, economic, and housing factors on the number of riot deaths in a tract, I employ Poisson regression models that are best suited to event counts. The Poisson regression models displayed in Table 5.2a and 5.2b estimate the number of deaths likely to occur in Newark and Detroit census tracts based on their racial/ethnic composition and economic characteristics.

Testing for Nonlinear Effects of Black Population Size
According to Blalock's "power threat" and "competition" formulations we should expect to find nonlinear effects of percent black on the number of riot-related fatalities in a given census tract. If power threat is operative, the relationship will be positive and ever increasing, exemplified by a positive coefficient for percent black and a positive coefficient for percent black squared. If competition is the operative case, we should find a positive nonlinear relationship with a slope that decreases at the highest levels of

Table 5.2a Poisson Regression Estimates of the Number of Riot Fatalities in Newark Census Tracts as a Function of Change in Racial/Ethnic Composition and Economic Characteristics, 1950–1960

Independent Variables	Dependent Variable: Number of Riot Fatalities					
	(1)	(2)	(3)	(4)	(5)	(6)
Percent Black (1960)	5.52* (2.84)	------	------	------	3.64*** (.770)	3.98*** (.890)
Percent Black Squared (1960)	.020 (.020)	------	------	------	------	------
Percent Black, 1950	------	3.22*** (.840)	------	------	------	------
Change in Percent Black (1950-1960)	------	4.20*** (.940)	2.61*** (1.03)	2.63** (1.03)	------	------
Change in Percent Black (1950–1960)* Percent Males Unemployed	------	------	.040 (.240)	------	------	------
Change in Percent Black (1950–1960) * Median Household Income	------	------	------	.0000 (.0000)	------	------
Percent Black (1960) * Percent Males Unemployed (1960)	------	------	------	------	-.030 (.210)	------
Percent Black (1960) * Median Household Income (1960)	------	------	------	------	------	.000 (.000)
Percent Males Unemployed (1960)	-4.92 (5.48)	-5.93 (5.69)	-1.94 (7.00)	-2.48 (5.74)	-3.25 (10.12)	-4.16 (.054)
Median Household Income (1960)	-.030 (.020)	-.040 (.030)	-.090*** (.020)	-.090*** (.020)	-.020 (.020)	-.040 (.030)
Constant	-1.433 (1.659)	-.4163 (1.730)	3.023 (1.437)	3.111 (1.282)	-1.285 (1.775)	-.5383 (1.769)
Log Likelihood	-45.447	-44.676	-52.311	-52.314	-45.692	-45.3325
D.F.	86	84	84	84	84	84

* $p < .05$ ** $p < .01$ *** $p < .001$ One-tailed test. Standard errors are in parenthesis.

Source: U.S. Census of Population and Housing, Census Tract Data for the Newark SMSA (1950, 1960 paper volumes).

Table 5.2b Poisson Regression Estimates of the Number of Riot Fatalities in Detroit Census Tracts as a Function of Change in Racial/Ethnic Composition and Economic Characteristics, 1950–1960

Independent Variables	Dependent Variable: Number of Riot Fatalities					
	(1)	(2)	(3)	(4)	(5)	(6)
Percent Black (1960)	7.88*** (1.94)	------	------	------	2.31 (.53)	3.00 (.640)
Percent Black Squared (1960)	-.060*** (.020)	------	------	------	------	------
Percent Black, 1950	------	.850 (.630)	------	------	------	------
Change in Percent Black (1950–1960)	------	2.79*** (.570)	2.40*** (.490)	2.18** (.710)	------	------
Change in Percent Black (1950–1960)* Percent Males Unemployed	------	------	.050 (.070)	------	------	------
Change in Percent Black (1950–1960) * Median Household Income	------	------	------	.0000 (.0000)	------	------
Percent Black (1960) * Percent Males Unemployed (1960)	------	------	------	------	-.210** (.070)	------
Percent Black (1960) * Median Household Income (1960)	------	------	------	------	------	.000001** (.000000)
Percent Males Unemployed (1960)	-4.30 (3.26)	-4.32 (3.19)	-.440 (4.28)	-3.21 (3.06)	10.66 (6.17)	-.2.64 (3.17)
Median Household Income (1960)	-.040*** (.020)	-.060*** (.020)	-.060*** (.020)	-.070*** (.020)	-.030* (.020)	-.090*** (.020)
Constant	-1.564 (1.12)	.1695 (.974)	.946 (1.04)	.5528 (.956)	-2.61 (1.33)	1.16 (.960)
Log Likelihood	-123.991	-124.147	-124.738	-124.9390	-125.707	-124.29
D.F.	405	405	405	405	405	405

* $p < .05$ ** $p < .01$ *** $p < .001$ One-tailed test. Standard errors are in parenthesis.

Source: U.S. Census of Population and Housing, Census Tract Data for the Detroit SMSA (1950, 1960 paper volumes).

percent black, exemplified by a positive coefficient for percent black and a negative coefficient for its squared term.

For Newark the coefficient for percent black regressed on the number of riot deaths is positive and statistically significant, controlling for economic indicators (male unemployment and housing density). (See Table 5.2a, model 1). The squared term was positive but not statistically significant. Therefore the relationship between percent black and riot violence in Newark appears to be linear. Increases in percent black lead to an increased probability of riot violence in a tract. Thus for Newark (1967), neither Blalock's power threat nor competition formulations are supported.

For Detroit (1967), I found a curvilinear relationship between percent black and the number of deaths in a tract. The coefficient for percent black is positive and significant (Table 5.2b, model 1). The coefficient for percent black squared is negative but also significant. The effect of black population size on riot violence increases steadily but diminishes at the highest levels of percent black. This inverted U-shape curve is indicative of Blalock's competition formulation. Increasing levels of black population increase the likelihood of riot violence in a tract, but once a neighborhood has become mostly black, the probability of riot-related violence decreases. Riot-related violence was most likely to take place in neighborhoods of Detroit where neither whites nor blacks constituted a clear majority of residents. In contrast to Spilerman's hypothesis, the number of riot-related deaths in Detroit peaked where black and white populations were closest to parity.

Testing for Effects of Changing Racial Composition

Whereas Blalock's postulates focus on the relative size of minority and nonminority populations at a given point in time, ethnic succession theorists argue that *change* in the relative size of migrant and nonmigrant groups over time is most predictive of ethnic collective action and interethnic violence. Model 2 of Table 5.2a presents the results of such analysis for Newark, examining the relationship between black in-migration (as measured by change in percent black) and the number of deaths in a tract while controlling for economic indicators (unemployment, ratio of persons/dwellings) and percent black at the beginning of the decade.

For Newark, when controlling for the effects of economic indicators (percent males unemployed, median household income) as well as black population size at the beginning of the period (percent black 1950), change in percent black from 1950 to 1960 had a significant effect on the number of deaths in a census tract (Table 5.2a, model 2, p<.05). As change in percent black increased, the likelihood of multiple riot fatalities in a tract also increased. Similar results were obtained for Detroit (Table 4.2b). In Detroit, controlling for the effects of economic indicators (percent males unemployed, median household income) and percent black in 1950, the change in percent black between 1950 and 1960 also had a significant effect on the number of deaths in a census tract (model 2). As change in percent black increased, the likelihood of multiple riot fatalities in Detroit census tracts also increased. In Detroit, the effect of change in percent black on riot intensity was so strong that the independent effect of black population size at the beginning of the period (percent black 1950) failed to attain statistical significance. These results provide strong support for an ethnic succession interpretation of violence in both Newark and Detroit.

Testing the Economic Deprivation Hypothesis

Poisson regression analysis yields mixed results for the economic deprivation thesis in Newark and Detroit. For Newark (Table 5.2a, models 1 and 2), when controlling for change in percent black, black population size, and median household income, the percent of males who were unemployed had no statistically significant impact on the number of riot-related deaths in a tract. The same result was obtained for Detroit, controlling for black population change, black population size, and median household income (Table 5.2b, models 1 and 2). In Newark, when controlling for changes in percent black, black population size, and male unemployment rates, median household income failed to have a statistically significant effect on the number of deaths in a tract. In none of the six regression models presented for Newark in Table 5.2a did the effect of median household income attain statistical significance. By contrast, for Detroit, median household income did appear to have some impact on riot severity. Controlling for changes in percent black, black population size at the beginning of the period, and male unemployment rates, the effect of median household income on the number of riot-related deaths in Detroit census tracts was positive and significant. Yet, when controlling for percent black at the end of the period, this effect did not remain significant. Thus, neither male unemployment nor median household income had consistently significant effects on riot violence in Newark and Detroit when controlling for ethnic composition.

This result makes sense in light of the historical evidence. During the late 1960s, manufacturing industries in Newark and Detroit were performing well. In Newark, companies like General Electric and Westinghouse continued to employ thousands of men. For the most part, the 1960s was a prosperous decade. Yet, not all shared in this prosperity. Poverty and unemployment were concentrated among people of color, thereby making it difficult to disentangle the effects of racial composition and economic deprivation.

To examine the joint effects of racial/ethnic segregation and economic deprivation in Newark and Detroit, I computed interaction terms for percent black and male unemployment as well as percent black and median household income (models 6 and 7 of Tables 5.2a and 5.2b). In Newark, neither of these interaction terms had statistically significant effects on the number of riot deaths in a census tract. Percent males unemployed and median household income neither enhanced nor diminished the main effect of percent black on riot violence. By contrast, in Detroit, both interaction terms were statistically significant, yet ran in a direction counter to the expectations of economic deprivation theorists. Higher rates of male unemployment diminished the effect of percent black on riot fatalities and higher levels of median household income enhanced the effect of percent black on riot-related violence in a tract. Yet, in these models, the main effects for percent males unemployed and median household income were not significant and, therefore, the effects of the interaction terms were not interpretable. In short, the interaction of male unemployment and median household income with percent black (used here as measure of segregation) did not add predictive power above and beyond the main effect of percent black on the number of riot-related deaths in Detroit census tracts.

Testing the Ethnic Competition Hypothesis
As mentioned previous, Olzak and other ethnic competition theorists look at the impact of population change on labor markets as indicative of competition relations between ethnic racial groups. Higher rates of unemployment and low incomes should theoretically interact with increasing minority population to generate a higher likelihood of riot violence. To test this hypothesis I created interaction terms that examine the joint effects of black population change and economic characteristics (percent males unemployed, median household income) for both Newark and Detroit. The results of these analyses are presented in Table 5.2a, models 4 and 5 (Newark) and Table 5.2b, models 4 and 5 (Detroit).

As was the case with the interaction of black population size and economic indicators, there were no significant interactive effects of change in percent black and male unemployment or median household income on the number of riot-related fatalities in Newark census tracts. Nor were there significant interaction effect for changes in percent black and male unemployment or median household income for Detroit. Higher levels of male unemployment or lower levels of household income neither enhanced nor diminished the main effects of black population change on riot fatalities in these two cities. Therefore, Olzak's competition hypothesis is not supported by the Poisson regression analysis for these two cities.

Controlling for Spatial Autocorrelation
As discussed in the previous chapter, the potential presence of spatial autocorrelation raises questions about the reliability of regression estimators in models that employ data from closely spaced geographic units. Because spatial autocorrelation implies serial dependence among observations, it must be controlled for in order to perform hypothesis testing. To do so,

Table 5.3 Linear Regression Estimates of the Number of Riot Fatalities in Newark and Detroit Census Tracts as a Function of Change in Racial/Ethnic Composition and Economic Characteristics (Controlling for Spatial Autocorrelation)

Independent Variables	Dependent Variable: Number of Riot Fatalities			
	Newark 1950–1960		Detroit 1950–1960	
	(1)	(2)	(3)	(4)
Racial/Ethnic Composition				
Change in Percent Black (Ten-Year Period)	-------	1.46*** (.420)	-------	.330** (.120)
Percent Black (End of Ten-Year Period)	1.74*** (.340)	-------	.200* (.100)	--------
Percent Black (Beginning of Ten-Year Period)	-------	1.94*** (.420)	-------	.070 (.120)
Economic Indicators				
Percent Males Unemployed	-2.90 (2.80)	-2.93 (2.81)	.000 (.005)	.11 (.580)
Median Household Income log	.000 (.000)	.000 (.000)	.000 (.000)	.000 (.000)
Constant	.312 (.645)	.337 (.642)	.164 (.135)	.148 (.135)
Residual Standard Error	.639	.639	.403	.404
D.F.	91	90	405	404

* $p < .05$ ** $p < .01$ *** $p < .001$ One-tailed test   Standard errors are in parenthesis.

Sources: U.S. Census of Population and Housing, Census Tract Data for the Newark SMSA (1950, 1960 paper volumes). U.S. Census of Population and Housing, Census Tract Data for the Detroit SMSA (1950, 1960 paper volumes).

I have reestimated the basic Poisson regression models as linear regression models that control for spatial autocorrelation. Table 5.3 presents the results of these models for both cities.

In Newark, when controlling for spatial autocorrelation, percent black at the end of the period (1950–1960) continued to have a positive and significant effect on the number of riot fatalities within a tract (model 1). Likewise, change in percent black from 1950 to 1960 continued to have a significant effect on the number of riot deaths in Newark census tracts when spatial autocorrelation is taken into account (model 2). By contrast, when controlling for spatial autocorrelation and ethnic composition measures, neither male unemployment rates nor median household income remained significant predictors of riot-related violence in Newark (Table 5.3, models 1 and 2).

Similar results were obtained for Detroit, where the relative size of the black population (percent black 1960) remained statistically significant when controlling for spatial autocorrelation and economic indicators (model 3). As shown in model 4, for Detroit, the change in percent black continued to have a significant impact on the number of riot deaths in a tract when controlling for spatial autocorrelation and economic indicators. As with Newark, the impact of economic indicators is reduced when controlling for spatial autocorrelation. Neither the effect of male unemployment nor median household income remained significant predictors of riot violence in Detroit.

Such findings challenge the applicability of an economic deprivation explanation for the Newark and Detroit riots of 1967. By contrast, these findings support the ethnic succession hypothesis and also confirm Spilerman's findings regarding black population size on the severity of riot violence during the 1960s.

SUMMARIZING THE RESULTS

While Poisson regression models for Newark and Detroit yield varying results for the effects of housing and economic factors on the presence of riot-related fatalities, for both cities a tract's black population size was a significant predictor of riot violence. I conclude that neighborhoods most susceptible to violence were those with the largest black populations as a percent of the total. In this respect, Spilerman's claim (1970, 1971) is confirmed. Riot intensity is a function of black population size. But for Newark and Detroit, the location of riot violence was also determined by the changing racial composition of census tracts. While the relationship between change in percent black and the presence of riot fatalities was stronger in Detroit than Newark, riot violence in both cities could also be attributed to ethnic succession. Together, racial change and segregation (as measured by the concentration of black population) in census tracts serve as predictors of riot violence, independent of the economic and housing characteristics of these areas.

Poisson regression analysis indicates that ethnic succession was significantly related to riot violence in both cities, thus confirming the results of both the GIS map analyses and the difference of means tests presented earlier. The convergence of results from three separate forms of geographical and statistical analysis offers strong proof that measures of demographic change are essential for predicting *where* riot violence was most likely to occur during the summer of 1967 in Newark and Detroit. To address *why* riot violence took place, however, we must reexamine the historical context of the communities where the riots occurred. By doing so, we may further specify how ethnic succession fostered urban unrest.

CONCLUSION

By the mid-1960s, cities like Newark and Detroit were in the midst of a second phase of demographic transition. The first phase had taken place when black migrants arrived from the rural South in the years between 1910 and 1950, encountering strong resistance from first- and second-generation white ethnics who sought to maintain their the racially and culturally exclusive enclaves. This phase culminated with the expansion of ghetto boundaries but reinforced the persistence of racial segregation and political marginalization. By the 1950s, many blacks found themselves living in high-rise public housing projects that concentrated poverty and isolated them from mainstream society (Hirsch 1988).

The second phase of demographic transition occurred when whites, who only a few decades earlier sought to repel the "invasion" of black residents into their communities and workplaces, abandoned the cities for greener suburban pastures. New residential black majorities rose in their place and inner-city neighborhoods that had previously been home to white immigrants, like Newark's Central Ward and Detroit's 12th Street, became predominantly black.

Nonetheless, by the mid- to late 1960s the succession was still not complete. Despite having relocated residentially from the central cities, whites still held prominent positions in politics and commerce and constituted the vast majority of ranking officers on the municipal police forces. Although blacks had the numbers, they lacked the formal control of political and economic power, which remained in white hands. Cities with new black residential majorities continued to be governed predominantly by white politicians and police, while industrial jobs disappeared and unemployment among black youth rose dramatically. Given the rising expectations unleashed by the successes of the Civil Rights Movement, black residents of Newark and Detroit could not help but notice the disparities of power and persistence of economic inequality within their cities.

Sugrue provides a succinct comparison of the conditions that gave rise to rioting in Detroit during the 1940s and two decades later in the summer of 1967:

> The riot of 1943 came at a time of increasing black and white competition for jobs and housing; by 1967 discrimination and deindustrialization had ensured that blacks had lost the competition. White resistance and white flight left a bitter legacy that galvanized black protest in the 1960s. Detroit's attempts to take advantage of the largesse of the Great Society offered too little, too late for Detroit's poor, but raised expectations nonetheless. Growing resentment, fueled by increasing militancy in the black community, especially among youth, who had suffered the brunt of economic displacement, fueled the fires of 1967. (1996:260)

Although it did not experience a major riot during the first half of the twentieth century, Newark had essentially gone through the same cycle as Detroit. Black migration met with white resistance, only to give way to white flight a few decades later. As industrial enterprises shut down, blacks found themselves trapped in cities with declining opportunities and little hope for the future. In Newark and Detroit, ethnic succession was marked by demographic change but little political or economic progress. The sense of status inconsistency produced by this incomplete succession is central to understanding why the riots occurred. The places where people rioted were the neighborhoods that had undergone the greatest transition in the shortest period of time—neighborhoods where white-owned businesses now catered to predominantly black residents. These were neighborhoods where white police encountered black youth whom they too often regarded with disdain and treated with contempt. They were "slums" where many white politicians feared to tread except when accompanied by a bulldozer. As Nathan Wright (1968) put it, these were places where people were "ready to riot."

For the black people of Newark and Detroit, the riots were a mixed blessing. The riots brought African Americans together, channeling their anger and spawning new political movements that would soon bear fruit (personal interviews, Ron Hewitt, June 19, 2001; Tom Carmichael, June 21, 2002). Within a few years, both cities elected their first black mayors. Small businesses changed ownership from white to black. Black residents moved into homes abandoned by whites. Blacks entered the rolls of the police and fire departments in substantial numbers. Yet, after the riots, larger business establishments like Bamberger's (Newark) and Hudson's (Detroit) that had catered mainly to the white middle class also fled from the now predominantly black cities. In turn, the tax base continued to erode, leaving the new black political regimes and, by extension, the cities, nearly bankrupt. For African Americans in Newark and Detroit, the succession, while finally complete, was achieved at great cost.

CHAPTER SIX

New Immigrants and Black Resentment:
Miami (1980) and Los Angeles (1992)

From 1970 to 1980, American cities were relatively quiet. With the notable exception of the Boston busing crisis of 1974–1975, there had been no major episodes of urban racial unrest since the late 1960s. In cities like Newark, Detroit, and Los Angeles, voters elected black mayors and city councilpersons. Politically, blacks had acquired a piece of the pie. It seemed that the riots of the 1960s had run their course. Yet, on May 17, 1980, rioting resurfaced in Miami, resulting in eighteen fatalities, numerous injuries, and an estimated 80 million dollars' worth of property damage. Twelve years later, on April 29, 1992, Los Angeles erupted, with a total of fifty-one people killed and over 1 billion dollars' worth of property destroyed.

At first glance, these episodes of urban unrest bear an uncanny resemblance to the civil disorders of the 1960s. The Miami riot of 1980 and the 1992 Los Angeles riot, like the "uprisings" of the 1960s in Newark and Watts, were sparked by the beating of black motorists by police. In Miami, Arthur McDuffie, a thirty-three-year-old insurance agent, was killed by police officers after allegedly running a red light on his motorcycle. Police officers beat him to death with batons and flashlights and then attempted to cover up the incident as a motorcycle accident. The subsequent trial was held outside of Miami in predominantly white Tampa. Despite eyewitness testimonies of other officers who had been on the scene and forensic experts who testified on behalf of the prosecution, all three of the defendants were found not guilty. Twelve years later, despite videotape evidence that indicated otherwise, an all-white jury in Simi Valley acquitted four Los Angeles Police Department officers of assaulting Rodney King, a thirty-four-year-old African-American motorist. Shortly after the verdict was announced, Los Angelenos took to the streets to protest the jury's decision.

Despite these similarities in the initial incidents that sparked unrest, the 1992 Los Angeles and 1980 Miami riots differed from their 1960s predecessors. Although many of the victims of the later riots were African Americans, a significant number of those killed, injured, and arrested were neither black nor majority white. In Miami, 12 percent of the victims were Hispanic. In Los Angeles, 30 percent of the fatalities were Hispanic and 4 percent were Asian (and 51 percent of those arrested were Hispanic). This diversity of victims has led some scholars, such as Edward Chang (1993), to label these events as the first "multicultural riots."

Furthermore, unlike the 1960s riots, the majority of deaths that resulted from the riots in Miami and Los Angeles were attributed to civilians, not police. Of the eighteen people who were killed during the 1980 Miami riot, only four (22 percent) were shot by police. In Los Angeles, of the fifty-one total deaths, only eight (15.6 percent) were attributed to police. By contrast, in Watts (1965), twenty-two of the twenty-five deaths (78 percent) were linked to police/military action; in Newark (1967), seventeen of the twenty-six fatalities (65 percent) were attributed to police/military forces; and in Detroit (1967), twenty-nine of forty-two killings (69 percent) were committed by police or armed forces.

This ethnic diversity of victims and participants, as well as the relatively small percentage of deaths attributed to police and military forces, clearly distinguish the riots in Miami and Los Angeles from their 1960s predecessors and challenges the characterizations of the Miami and Los Angeles riots as black rebellions against white police brutality. Although it is clear that some people took to the streets of Miami to protest the Arthur McDuffie verdict and of Los Angeles to protest the Rodney King verdict, the motives of other participants in these events are less evident. Why would Latinos raid Korean-owned stores if they were protesting the Rodney King verdict? Why would African Americans target Latino and white motorists if the object of their wrath was the police?

The precipitating incidents and the motives of the participants in these cases do not always match. This suggests that we should be careful not to conflate the sparks with the fuel that enabled rioting to erupt. Had it not been for the McDuffie or King verdicts, it is questionable whether rioting would have occurred in either Miami or Los Angeles. Without the resentment that had been building among the various racial/ethnic groups over several years, it is also unlikely that full-scale riots would have developed in either city. To understand the origins of violence in Miami and Los Angeles during the latter half of the twentieth century, we must address the long-term structural conditions that preceded these events. We must also move beyond the traditional black/white paradigm of the American "race relations model" to examine the rapidly shifting demographic terrain of urban America in the 1980s and 1990s.

THE CHANGING DEMOGRAPHY OF MIAMI AND LOS ANGELES

During the period between 1980 and 1990, 8.6 million immigrants entered the United States. In sheer numbers this was the largest wave of immigration to hit the United States since 1900–1910. In addition to New York City, the main entry points for these immigrants were the sunbelt cities of the South and the West Coast. Throughout the 1970s and 1980s, Miami and Los Angeles served as primary destinations for international migration. By 1980, these cities were already ranked first and second nationally in proportion of foreign-born residents. Between 1970 and 1990, over half a million immigrants moved to Miami, increasing the proportion of foreign-born residents from 23.7 percent to 45.1 percent (U.S. Census of Population and Housing, STF 3a). In Los Angeles, over the same time period, the number of foreign-born residents increased by 2.8 million. Their share of the population correspondingly rose from 10.9 percent to 27 percent. A few decades earlier Miami and Los Angeles were comprised of mostly non-Hispanic white majorities, established but segregated black minorities, as well as a few pockets of Asians and Hispanics. From 1970 to 1990, however, Miami's non-Hispanic white population decreased by 193,000, falling from 61.4 percent to 30.3 percent of the city's total population. In Los Angeles, during the same time period, the white population declined by 190,244, a decrease from 71 percent to 47.5 percent of the population.

This decline in non-Hispanic white population corresponded with a substantial increase in Hispanic population. In Miami, three waves of Cuban immigration and a smaller Central American influx during the 1960–1980 period increased the size of the Hispanic population from 299,000 to 953,000. By 1990, Hispanics accounted for 49.2 percent of Miami's total population. In Los Angeles, led by increased immigration from Mexico, the Hispanic population also grew dramatically, from 1,399,000 in 1970 to 4,697,509 in 1990. By 1990, Hispanics accounted for approximately one-third of Los Angeles's population, up from 14 percent in 1970.

In neither Miami nor Los Angeles did black population growth keep pace with the phenomenal increase in Hispanic population. From 1970 to 1990, the black population of Miami increased by approximately 170,000, but blacks' share of Miami's population increased only slightly, from 15 percent to 19.5 percent, over this period. Likewise, in Los Angeles, the black population numerically increased from 781,000 in 1970 to 1.1 million in 1990. Yet, relative to the overall population of the city in 1990, the black population stood at 7.9 percent, an increase of a mere one-tenth of 1 percent from two decades earlier. In both cities, by the time the riots began, Hispanics had surpassed African Americans to become the largest "minority" group. In Los Angeles, a substantial influx of Asians added to the increasingly diverse ethnic mix. The Asian population increased from approximately 250,000 in 1970 to 1.3 million in 1990

These demographic changes served as a harbinger of blacks' declining political and economic influence. The dramatic influx of immigrants, stagnation in black population share, and continued white flight took place over a relatively short period of time and had profound effects on relations among members of the different racial/ethnic groups in these cities, particularly among African Americans who increasingly defined Latino and Asians immigrants as rivals for economic and political power (Ladner et al. 1981, Porter and Dunn 1982, Miles 1992, Piatt 1997, Suro 1998).

LABOR FORCE COMPETITION

Of those who lived in Miami and Los Angeles during the height of Latino in-migration, African Americans expressed particular concern regarding the economic impact of new arrivals. African Americans in Miami, who had traditionally occupied the lowest-wage, least-skilled jobs in the hotel and garment industries, worried that they were at risk of being "displaced" by the new immigrant labor (Governor's Dade County Citizens Commission 1980; Ladner et al. 1981; U.S. Commission on Civil Rights 1982; Porter and Dunn 1984; Dunn and Stepick 1992).

African Americans in Los Angeles, who were once employed predominantly in the industrial sector but were then laid off when manufacturing was shifted overseas, expressed similar sentiments. Given the few blue-collar jobs that remained, black workers in Los Angeles now viewed recent immigrants as a further threat to their shattered employment prospects (Miles 1992; Piatt 1997; Suro 1998).

The degree of displacement of blacks by Hispanics in the workplace in Miami, Los Angeles, and other "postindustrial cities" is a topic of much debate among contemporary scholars (Steinberg 1995; Waldinger and Bozorgmehr 1996). Portes and Stepick (1993) argue that that Hispanics did not displace blacks from jobs in Miami. Rather, the new Hispanic immigrants filled positions mostly vacated by whites. In the garment industry, for example, blacks neither gained nor lost jobs. As the proportion of whites in this industry declined from 94 percent in 1960 to 10.4 percent in 1980, the proportion of Hispanic garment workers jumped to 39.6 percent. By contrast, the proportion of black garment workers increased slightly, from 5.6 percent in 1960 to 7 percent in 1980. Furthermore, during this period, many Latinos established their own business enterprises, thus "transforming Miami's economy" (Portes and Stepick 1993:40) but not displacing blacks per se.

There was no one-to-one substitution of Blacks by Cubans in the labor market, nor was there direct exploitation of one minority by the other. There was, however, a new urban economy in which the immigrants raced past other groups, leaving the native minority behind. Hence, after decades of striving for a measure of equality with whites, Miami blacks found that the game had drastically changed. Anglos were leaving and other whites who spoke a foreign language were occupying their positions. As a result, most blacks were in a similar position as before (Portes and Stepick 1993:43).

While Portes and Stepick's findings challenge the notion of displacement, Porter and Dunn (1984) provide evidence to the contrary. Drawing data from a Dade County Planning Department document that compares black employment rates in 1968 and 1978, these authors argue that considerable job displacement did indeed occur. This displacement, they argue, coincided with Cuban in-migration:

> Blacks who held jobs as clerical workers dropped from 13.3 percent of the black population to 11.1 percent. Machine operators went from 10.3 percent of the black population to 2.2; service workers, from 23.1 to 18.8; household workers, from 11.2 to 6.5. At the same time that blacks holding white-collar and semi-skilled jobs declined, those doing general labor, at the bottom of the economic heap, rose dramatically. It went from 12.4 percent of the population to 25 percent. (1984:195)

Porter and Dunn offer further evidence of economic displacement, citing a survey by Jan B. Luytjes of Florida International University. This survey showed a decline in black ownership and rise in Hispanic ownership of Dade County gas stations.

> In 1960, some 25 percent of all the gas stations in Dade County were owned by blacks. In 1979, the figure had dropped to 9 percent, while the number of Hispanic owned gas stations rose from 12 percent to 48 percent in the same period" (195–196).

According to Porter and Dunn, the effect of Cuban migration on black workers was "like seeing economic progress suddenly thrown into reverse gear" (195).

For political scientist Sheila Croucher, author of *Imagining Miami* (1997), the displacement of black workers by Latino immigrants was more perceptual than real. She emphatically states that there is little empirical evidence to support the job displacement thesis in Miami. Combining postmodernist and Marxist theory, Croucher argues that Anglo political and economic elites generated a hegemonic discourse that emphasized black-Latino tensions rather than elite domination. Croucher contends that the rhetoric of black-Latino animosity is meant to deflect criticisms of the predominantly Anglo power structure for its decades-old exclusion of black and other minorities. This "discourse of displacement," Croucher argues, was utilized by Anglo elites to prevent the formation of multiethnic alliances that might have challenged their power.

This thesis is problematic. While Miami's Anglo economic elite is largely responsible for having created and perpetuated the ghettoization of Miami's black community in the not-so-distant past, Hispanics are now part of that elite and thus bear some responsibility as well for the plight of Miami's black population. Grenier and Stepick (1992) document the rise of Latinos in Miami's shipping, insurance, and import/export industries, culminating with the selection of a Latino as head of the Miami Chamber of Commerce. Citing a report by Botifol (1985), they state, "by the mid-1980s 40 percent of Miami's banks were owned by Latinos" (Grenier and Stepick 1992:10). According to Portes and Stepick, "by 1979 Cubans owned approximately 50% of all major construction firms, which together accounted for more than 90% of commercial and residential construction in the southwest zone of the county" (1993:132). Furthermore, a large portion of businesses in the black ghetto were owned and operated by Cubans, placing them in the role of "middleman minority" (Bonacich 1973), a buffer between the white power structure and the black community.

Addressing the issue of economic competition among blacks and Cubans, a clear pattern of preference for Hispanics emerged in the distribution of small business loans.

> SBA data for Dade County indicate that during fiscal years 1968 through 1980, the agency made a total of 780 direct loans—37 to blacks, 469 to Hispanics, and 267 to non-minorities. Of 1,148 guaranteed loans, 58 went to blacks, 525 to Hispanics, and 557 to non-minorities. (U.S. Commission on Civil Rights 1982:111)

A similar pattern of preferential treatment existed with respect to contracts for public transit projects, with Hispanic-owned firms receiving 61.6 percent of minority set-asides compared to 17.5 percent for black-owned companies (U.S. Commission on Civil Rights 1982:119). Although the available data do not provide definitive proof of direct economic competition or displacement of black workers by Latinos, the preferences that Cuban businessmen received and the financial power they accrued may help explain the resentment that many African-American residents expressed toward Hispanic immigrants.

At the same time as the third wave of Cubans was arriving in Miami, another group of immigrants entered the scene—the Haitians. Unlike the majority of Cuban immigrants, Haitians were for the most part classified as "black." Yet native-born blacks in Miami did not readily embrace their Caribbean counterparts. Many American-born blacks perceived the Haitians as foreigners rather than "brothers." Because most Haitians lacked the fiscal capital and skills of the previous Cuban refugees, native-born blacks feared that Haitians might compete with them for unskilled, low-wage jobs (Grenier and Stepick 1992:62; Portes and Stepick 1993:55). As native blacks had feared, such competition did eventually develop.

> True, prominent blacks had defended the newcomers against government deportation, but they had done so in the interest of racial equality-because they were black, not because they were immigrants. Once settled, however, the newcomers proceeded to compete directly with Black Americans for manual labor jobs, accepting almost any wages and work conditions. For Liberty City, Overtown and other Black areas reeling under the impact of double marginalization, the appearance on the labor scene of yet another competitor was not welcome. (Portes and Stepick 1993:55)

For their part, Haitians did not see themselves as being part of the same cultural category as American blacks. Rather they saw themselves as immigrant entrepreneurs and sought to build an enclave similar to the Cuban's Little Havana (Portes and Stepick 1993:55–56). Haitians succeeded in their entrepreneurial ventures and carved out a sociocultural niche for themselves, fostering further resentments by native blacks. Bypassed economically by the Cubans, native-born black Miamians felt squeezed economically by the Haitians as well. Despite the apparent commonality of racial ancestry, the division between native-born and foreign-born blacks was salient in Miami.

In Los Angeles, there has been a similar debate regarding the displacement of black workers by Latinos. Unlike their mostly Cuban counterparts in Miami, Hispanics in Los Angeles, who are of predominantly of Mexican origin, have yet to be incorporated into the economic and political elite. While some Mexicans and Central Americans have made progress toward attaining economic and political power, most of the recent immigrants from these countries lack the human resources and financial capital that would enable them to integrate into the primary sector of America's postindustrial economy. Suro (1998) suggests that Hispanic immigrants are at risk of becoming an immigrant "underclass." The most recent Hispanic arrivals to Los Angeles primarily tend gardens, wash dishes, clean offices, or toil in garment factories—low-wage, unskilled jobs in which African Americans are sparsely represented.

One must be careful not to attribute the absence of blacks in these occupations to their presumed lack of motivation, e.g., the popular notion that blacks are not interested in performing low-wage labor. The paucity of black workers in jobs held primarily by Hispanics does not imply that blacks are uninterested in such work. On the contrary, several studies report that black workers in Los Angeles have experienced competition with Hispanic immigrants for unskilled positions and have lost in this struggle (Waldinger and Bozomehr 1996; Waldinger 1997; Grant, Oliver, and James 1996; Ong and Valenzuela 1996).

One well-documented example of job displacement in Los Angeles involves the janitorial services industry. Citing a General Accounting Organization report, Grant, Oliver, and James (1996), Miles (1992), Piatt

(1997), and Suro (1998) all note the precipitant decline of black employment in an industry that blacks had once dominated.

> Consider the example of janitors, the single largest black occupational niche from 1970 on. In 1970, one in three janitors was black and one in fourteen was foreign born. The next two decades saw the number of janitors double, yet the number of black janitors fell by more than three thousand while the number of immigrant Latino janitors rose by more than thirty-nine thousand. A transformation of this type is difficult to explain. It is unlikely that African Americans simply did not want or were unavailable to fill the growing number of janitorial positions; more likely however is the possibility that janitorial jobs became increasingly difficult for blacks to get. (Grant, Oliver, and James 1996:390)

Waldinger (1997) found that employers in Los Angeles were more willing to hire Latino workers than blacks. This was in in part because they could exploit Latinos' extended kinship ties for recruitment purposes. This hiring practice serves employers' interests in two important ways. First, they don't have to pay to advertise the jobs in question, and second, in their opinion, kinship ties lead to a cohesive workplace environment free of cultural conflicts. The end result is that blacks have lost positions in the garment industry, construction work, and restaurant employment—occupations that Hispanics now dominate. Ong and Valenzuela (1996) suggest that employers hire workers of tenuous immigration status in the belief that they can be more readily exploited than native-born blacks. Again, blacks lose.

Ong and Valenzuela (1996) further argue that to fully see the effects of immigration on black employment in Los Angeles we must distinguish among workers' levels of education and occupational skill across metropolitan areas. If one looks at particular industries nationwide, it appears that immigration has not hurt the employment opportunities of native-born black workers. Indeed, it seems that immigration has helped increase salaries for blacks. Yet, on closer examination, this benefit tends only to accrue to black workers who occupy skilled positions in the labor market. Among unskilled blacks, immigration has negative net consequences for their employment status. This was particularly true for blacks in Los Angeles:

> A comparison of raw rates indicates that joblessness, is more prevalent in Los Angeles than in other metropolitan areas among both young and less-educated blacks.... Amazingly, most of the difference is associated with level of recently arrived less-educated Latinos. (Ong and Valenzuela 1996:174)

The displacement of black workers in the janitorial and hospitality industries, combined with recruitment along ethnic kinship lines, effectively excluded African Americans from a variety of occupations in Los

Angeles. Given evidence that suggests that employers prefer to hire Latinos, this dynamic has fueled resentment among blacks. In a few notable cases, before and after the 1992 riot, blacks vented their frustrations upon Latino workers whom they saw as impeding their economic progress. Piatt (1997) cites two such examples. One standoff occurred at the Martin Luther King Medical Center in Watts, where black and Hispanic county employees clashed over hiring and promotion issues. At another incident at a construction site, Latino laborers claimed they were attacked by blacks protesting the paucity of jobs for African-American workers. Such conflicts may have spilled over into the neighborhoods of South Central Los Angeles and Compton, where blacks and Latinos both reside.

In addition to the conflicts among Latinos and blacks, another fault line was developing within the Latino community. Recent arrivals from Central America and those who had immigrated earlier, typically from Mexico, fought over access to jobs and housing as well. As Latino immigrants continued to stream into Los Angeles, their relative lack of skills led them to compete for low-wage jobs occupied by those who had arrived just a few years before them. Despite being commonly classified by the Census Bureau as Hispanic, regional and other cultural differences among these groups, along with differences in when they arrived in the United States, reinforced the notion that many fellow Latinos were not "brothers" but competitors (Suro 1998). Like native-born blacks in Miami who resented the increased presence of Haitians, more established Latinos in Los Angeles felt that the recent Hispanic immigrants posed a threat to their jobs and their way of life.

Adding fuel to the fire was the increased presence of Korean shopkeepers in South Central Los Angeles. Occupying a middleman role, similar to that of Cuban entrepreneurs in Miami's black ghetto, Koreans owned and operated mini-marts and swap meets on the streets of South Central. This role brought them into direct contact with blacks and Latinos of limited economic means. In this milieu, cultural misunderstandings augmented economic inequalities (Abelman and Lie 1995; Joyce 2003). Since most Korean storeowners did not live in South Central, they were frequently perceived as outsiders who siphoned money away from poor communities. Because their mini-marts traded in alcoholic beverages, Koreans acquired a notorious reputation as liquor merchants and ultimately began to be targeted by community leaders bent on "cleaning up the neighborhood" (Abelman and Lie, 1995). More crucially, African-American residents who lacked access to capital necessary to own and operate small businesses resented the relative success of these new immigrants (Wong 1994). Latinos also developed an intense antipathy toward Korean merchants (Oliver, Johnson, and Farrell, 1993). In 1992, an African-American teen, Leticia Harlins, was shot and killed by a Korean storeowner while allegedly stealing a bottle of orange juice. When the storeowner received a suspended sentence for "voluntary manslaughter," acrimony among these groups was further intensified (Joyce 2003:145). Whether the destruction of Korean-owned stores was a political act of vengeance or a result of opportunism is uncertain, but the sense of resentment that both blacks and Latinos expressed toward Korean merchants was clear. Nonetheless, this mutual antagonism directed by blacks and Latinos against Korean merchants did not alleviate the hostility that blacks and Latinos expressed toward each other in the neighborhoods of South Central and Compton, where these groups competed for both jobs and space.

CONTESTED SPACE

While much public and private debate focused on the "real" versus "perceived" role of immigrants in displacing African-American workers, a noticeable change was occurring in Los Angeles's traditionally black neighborhoods. South Central Los Angeles, Watts, and Compton had developed since the 1940s as officially recognized black communities. Hemmed in historically by segregated housing markets, these areas became, in essence, black enclaves. Industrial enterprises such as Uniroyal Tire Company employed thousands of African-American workers from the surrounding area, anchoring the black community with the prospect of steady employment. When these factories began to close their doors in 1970s, the black community suffered greatly. While segregation persisted, unemployment rose dramatically. Soon thereafter, blacks began moving to adjacent suburban areas that promised a better standard of living and better access to jobs. In their wake, an "urban underclass" comprised of those who could not find work nor afford to move was left behind. As a result of this process, which was taking place in inner-city neighborhoods across the nation, blacks in South Central and Compton experienced economic and social dislocation (see Wilson 1987).

During the 1980s, the pace of middle-class black flight quickened as upwardly mobile blacks moved out of the inner city and in some cases out of Los Angeles County. Morrison and Lowry (1994) report that black out-migration from Los Angeles County "offset" the natural increase of the county's black population, leading to stagnation in black population growth for the Los Angeles region. Within the county, they report, blacks also moved to the west and southeast, away from South Central, Watts, and Compton to places such as Inglewood, Hawthorne, Downey, Paramount, and Long Beach. They note that "these residential shifts reflect upward social mobility, for the most part, as those blacks who prospered moved to better housing and better neighborhoods" (1994:29).

At the same time as middle-class blacks were moving out of the inner-city neighborhoods of South Central, Watts, and Compton, there was an influx of Hispanic residents. During the 1980s, South Central Los Angeles was becoming increasingly Hispanic. At the beginning of the decade,

African Americans accounted for approximately 74 percent of South Central's population (U.S. Census of Population and Housing STF3a, 1980). By 1990, their share of the population had fallen to 55 percent, while the Latino population had risen to 45 percent (U.S. Bureau of the Census Report CB92-145). As Oliver, Johnson, and Farrell (1993) note, "today nearly one-half of the South Central Los Angeles population is Latino" (121) According to Morrison and Lowry, "by 1990, Hispanics had become the dominant ethnic group in the northeastern half of South Central Los Angeles" (29). By Joe Domanick's estimation, "more than half of Compton and two-thirds of Watts are now Latino" (1996:77).

Such rapid demographic transition had profound effects on the relations among blacks and Latinos in these areas. As early as 1984, sociologists Melvin Oliver and James Johnson conducted survey research that documented rising levels of hostility between blacks and Latinos in Los Angeles and warned of the potential for interethnic conflict. Nine years prior to the riots, they wrote:

> Researchers should be sensitive and concerned with the potential for social conflict that exists between the have-nots who are increasingly forced to live together in our nation's ghettos.... The impact of the "new immigration" is that the new groups, for the most part are ethnically and culturally different from the traditional inhabitants of these areas and therefore each are perfect targets for the other's displaced hostility. (Oliver and Johnson quoted by Tierney 1994:158)

Oliver and Johnson's prediction rang true during the late 1980s and early 1990s as blacks and Latinos wrestled for control of institutions in demographically changing communities. Public schools became the scene of pitched battles among these groups as blacks resolved to defend their turf against Latinos. In Compton High School, for example, blacks went from dominant majority to sizable minority. Whereas the student body had been almost entirely black in the 1980s, by 1992, African Americans accounted for only 40 percent of all students, while Latinos attained a majority of 60 percent. According to a teacher describing his first year at Compton High School,

> It was like stepping into another world. There were three race riots, one of which lasted almost six hours.... In another riot in 1994, one Latino student was beaten so badly that when his father arrived and saw the bloodied boy, he punched the first black student he saw. (Domanick 1996:78)

Such conflict, according to Davis, was mirrored in schools throughout Southern California, e.g., in the cities of South Bay and the San Fernando Valley, where "black versus Latino tensions have erupted in wild melees involving hundreds of kids" (1993a:39–40). According to Domanick's

(1996) account, even an elementary school was a site of conflict between mostly black teachers and the parents of mostly Latino students, ultimately requiring the intervention of a federal mediator. For Davis, however, school-based conflicts pale in comparison with hostilities that occurred among blacks and Latinos in the local prisons:

> Since the 1990s, the jails have been rocked by almost monthly rioting between Blacks and Latinos. A thousand inmates have been seriously injured and the jail system has become a factory of hate, manufacturing animosities that are invariably sent back to the neighborhoods. (1993a:42)

Davis also offers documentation that black-Latino conflict also took place in residential settings, a testament to the intense competition for control of housing:

> In public housing projects meanwhile, sinister omens of ethnic cleansing have recently appeared. The arson deaths of a Latino family in Watts' predominantly black Jordan Downs Housing Project were reciprocated by the fire-bombing of Black families in Ramona Gardens, an eastside housing complex ruled by the so-called "Mexican Mafia."... Black families in the tiny Latino governed city of Hawaiian Gardens have recently complained about "living under a reign of terror...of death threats and arson." (1993:42)

Taken together, these accounts imply an association between ethnic succession and battles for institutional control culminating in interethnic violence in Los Angeles. Steven Frie, a political science professor at the University of California-San Diego, makes this thesis clear:

> It was no accident that the flash points for the '92 rebellion and riot were in those neighborhoods that have undergone the greatest ethnic transition-around Florence and Normandie, and then up in Pico Union. The breakdown of community institutions is what happens when you have this kind of very quick and sharp ethnic transition. (Quoted in Domanick 1996:76)

Given the pace of this demographic transition and their corresponding loss of social control of community institutions, it is not surprising that blacks in South Central took to the streets during the 1992 riot, nor is it surprising that several of the first riot victims were Latinos (*U.S. News and World Report* 1993).

On the surface, competition for space appears to be less of a contentious issue in Miami than in Los Angeles. In Miami, blacks are more highly segregated and remain more geographically isolated from both the Anglo and Latino populations than blacks in Los Angeles. As a Southern city, Miami developed with specific areas reserved for occupancy by blacks and restricted blacks from living elsewhere. One of these areas, named Overtown, had historically served as the spatial and cultural center for Miami's black community. During the early 1960s, however, a substantial portion of the neighborhood was targeted for "urban renewal," involving the destruction of housing and the building of freeways (Mohl 1996). Consequently, much of the black population was displaced from the neighborhood. Around the same time, the first wave of Cuban immigrants arrived and settled in the area just south of Overtown, where they quickly established an enclave, often referred to as Little Havana. As later waves of Cubans arrived, they sought inexpensive housing near the expanding enclave, consequently undermining the ability of blacks to find new housing close to their old neighborhood (Mohl 1996:275). As a result of urban planning policies, blacks found themselves concentrated in new housing developments in the area known as Liberty City. Not unlike South Side Chicago with its corridor of deteriorating public housing projects, Liberty City has been left to whither in relative isolation from downtown Miami and the increasingly white suburbs. The name Liberty City thus came to represent a cruel joke, referring not to the freedom of middle-class suburban living but to a black ghetto characterized by severe concentrations of poverty.

Blacks who wished to leave Liberty City during the 1960s and 1970s found discrimination and low incomes to be obstacles to residential mobility. New waves of Cuban and Haitian immigrants began arriving in the mid- to late 1970s, further exacerbating an already tight housing market. Oliver Kerr, a Dade County planning official, summarized the problem:

> Essentially what you are seeing is no vacancies at all, no reasonable chance of movement. All that you have is turnover in units.... [The recent influx of Haitian and Cuban refugees] has had a major impact. The market prior to the influx was already extremely tight. As I say, half of one percent. No other metropolitan area in the country has such a rate.... That's added to the severity of the situation, particularly for low income [families] because these refugees, of course, have absorbed every available room, every shack, every available space in the county. (U.S. Commission on Civil Rights 1982:23)

In Miami, we have not seen the same kinds of residential succession that have been noted in Los Angeles. But this is largely a vestige of racial discrimination in housing in Miami. Blacks simply cannot move outside of their established enclaves, and even the new Hispanic immigrants express little desire to live in these predominantly black and poor neighborhoods. Instead of blacks moving out of Liberty City, the population density of this area has actually increased, due largely to an increased demand for low-cost housing among blacks. According to Glenn Shuman, then acting director of Legal Services of Greater Miami,

> The areas that may...[have been] occupied by low income people are now being occupied by people who have a little bit of money, so they can afford those

houses, thereby increasing the density of the Liberty City area.... The influx of refugees...has only compounded the problem. (U.S. Commission on Civil Rights 1982:69)

Despite the relative stability of black neighborhoods in Miami, blacks express feelings of resentment toward Latino and Haitian immigrants who have established enclaves of their own on the fringe of an increasingly dense black ghetto. Preliminary evidence to suggest that ethnic competition for jobs and housing has been a key factor in generating riot violence in both Miami and Los Angeles, albeit in a different manner. Whereas black communities in South Central Los Angeles experienced an increasing influx of Latinos and out-migration of wealthier African Americans, blacks in Miami remained stuck in their highly segregated enclaves—their residential mobility blocked by a combination of racist real estate practices and an influx of immigrants into adjoining areas.

TESTING ECOLOGICAL HYPOTHESES FOR RIOT VIOLENCE

Geographic Information Systems Analysis

Figures 6.1–6.5 display relationships among the changing demographic characteristics of Miami census tracts from 1970 to 1980 and the location of fatalities that occurred during the 1980 riot. Figure 6.1 shows the location of riot fatalities with respect to the distribution of black and Hispanic population in 1970 Miami. The lighter shaded areas represent tracts where Latinos account for more than 50 percent of the population, and the more heavily shaded areas represent tracts where African Americans account for more than 50 percent of the population. Figure 6.2 updates the demographic data for black and Hispanic populations in 1980, again displaying the geographic coordinates of riot fatalities.

As shown in Figures 6.1 and 6.2, from 1970 to 1980 Miami witnessed a geographical expansion of both black and Latino populations as non-Hispanic whites fled from central Miami. Yet, these expanding black and Hispanic populations do not appear to overlap with one another. Hispanics were not moving into African-American neighborhoods, nor were blacks moving into Latino neighborhoods. Furthermore, as Figure 6.3 shows, riot deaths in Miami do not appear to be associated with the pace of black population change.

As Figure 6.3 shows, riot deaths did not cluster in areas where black population had increased rapidly (20 percent or more) during the decade. Nor did riot deaths cluster in tracts where Hispanic population had increased by 20 percent or more. These maps thus challenge the applicability of the residential ethnic succession explanation to riot violence in Miami.

New Immigrants and Black Resentment 129

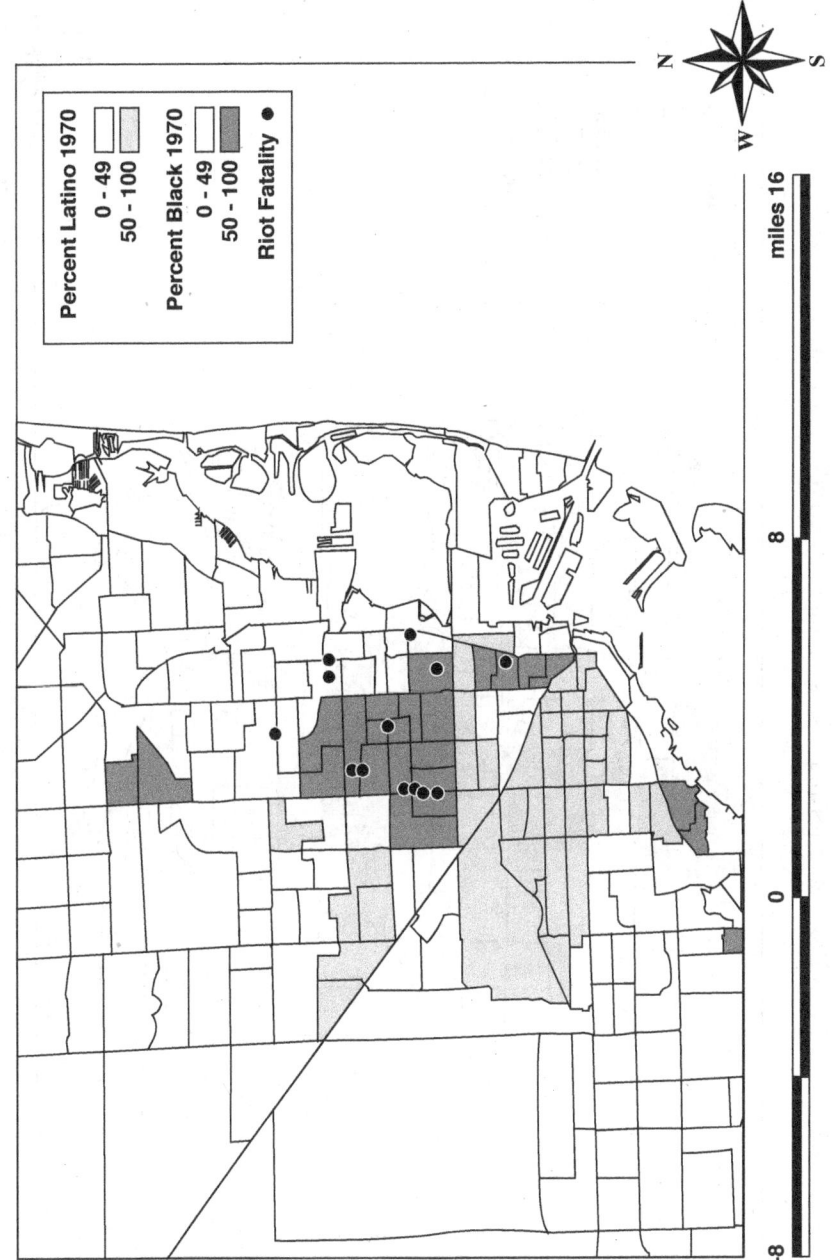

Figure 6.1 1980 Miami Riot Fatalities and Ethnic Composition, 1970

130 FIGHTING IN THE STREETS

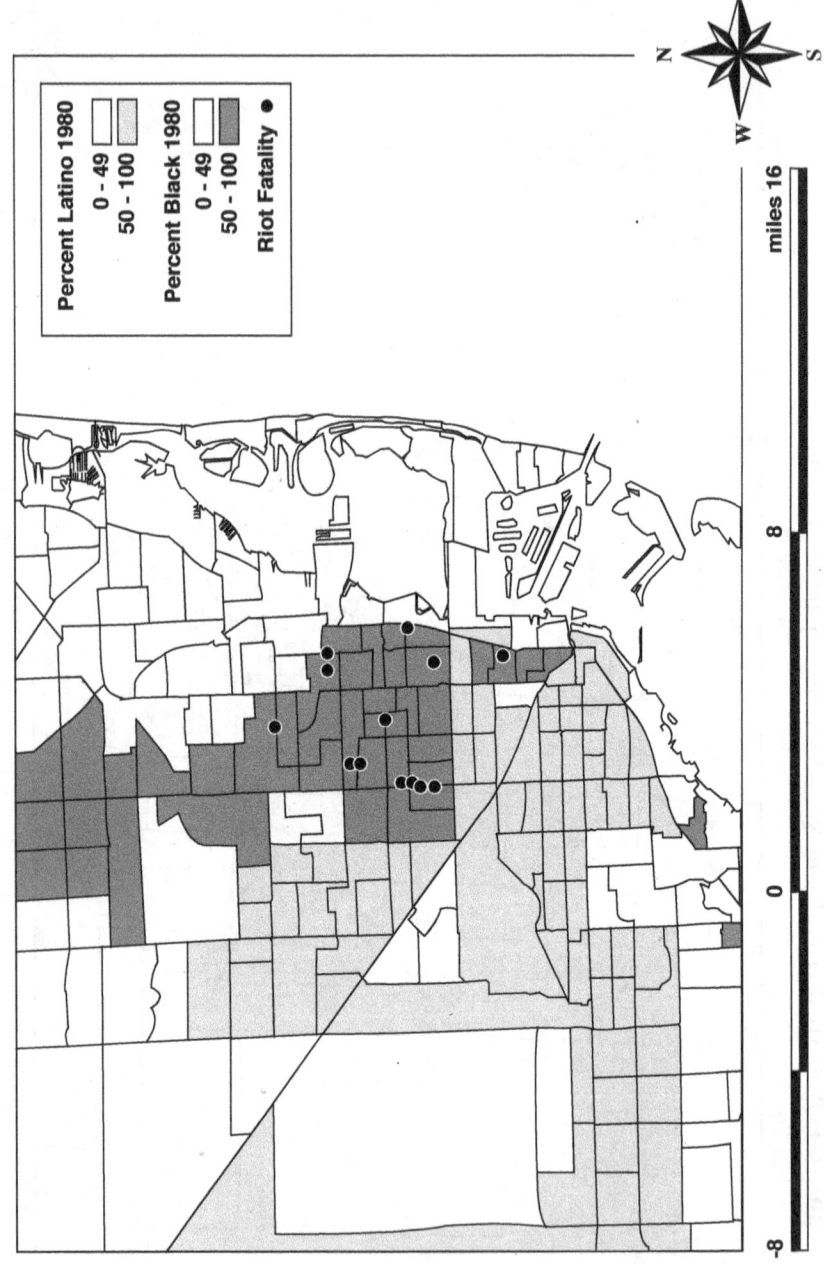

Figure 6.2 1980 Miami Riot Fatalities and Ethnic Compostion, 1980

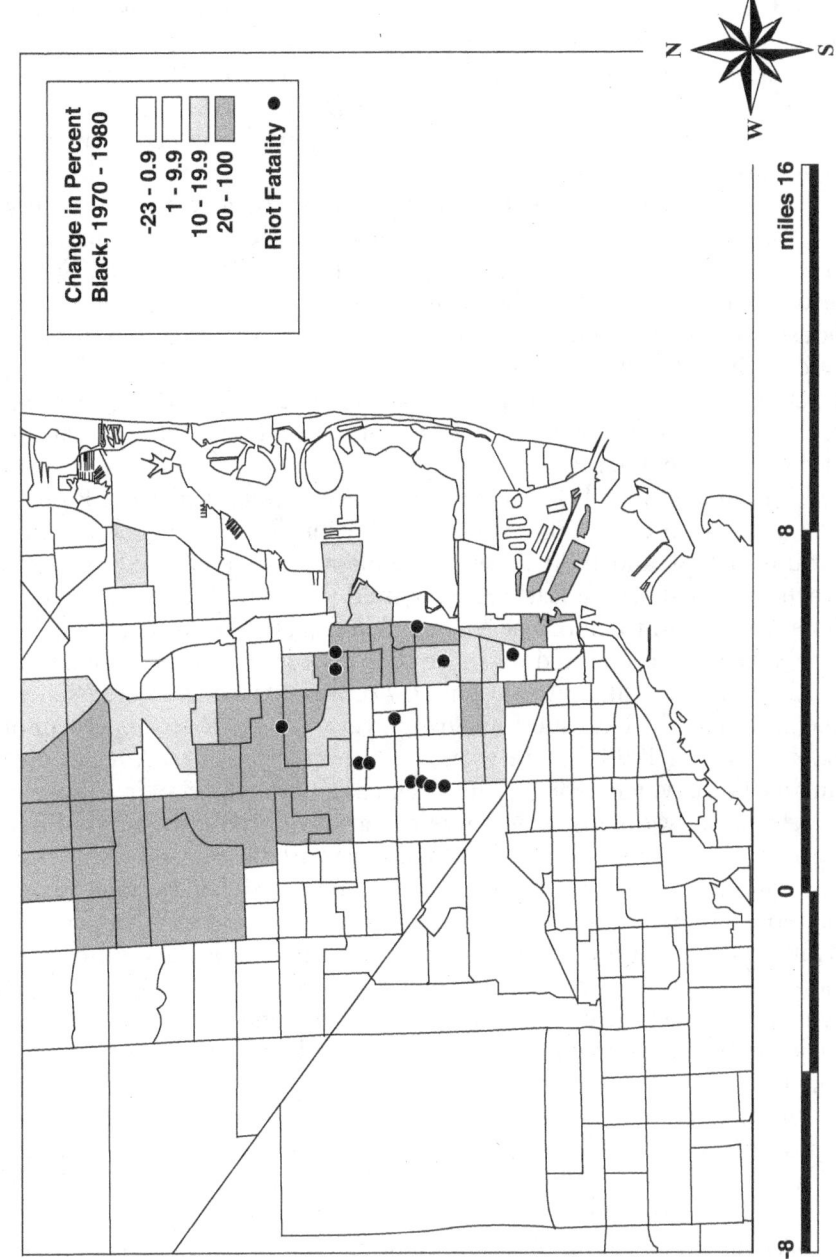

Figure 6.3 1980 Miami Riot Fatalities and Change in Percent Black, 1970-1980

As is shown in Figures 6.1 and 6.2, riot fatalities were located primarily within an area of concentrated black population known as Liberty City, a neighborhood whose racial composition had remained fundamentally unaltered during the ten years leading up to the riot. Whereas GIS analysis reveals little association between neighborhood ethnic/racial change and riot violence in Miami, it does lend support for an economic deprivation thesis.

As shown in Figure 6.4, there appears to be a relationship between the location of riot deaths and unemployment. Riot deaths cluster within tracts where the unemployment rate was 10 percent or greater. Figure 6.5 also reveals an association between riot violence and low levels of median household income. The vast majority of riot-related fatalities occurred in tracts where the median household income was under $10,000 per year. In short, based on these maps, it appears that economic deprivation and racial segregation, not ethnic succession, are more valid explanations for riot violence in Miami.

GIS analysis for Los Angeles presents a different picture. Figures 6.6 and 6.7 examine the population distribution for Los Angeles's minority groups in 1980 and 1990. As with the maps for Miami, the lighter shaded tracts are those where Latinos accounted for more than 50 percent of the population, and the more heavily shaded tracts were those in which African Americans accounted for more than 50 percent of the population.

Intermediate shading in Figure 6.7 represents tracts where Asians were the plurality (the largest ethnic group, yet with less than 50 percent of the population) in 1990. There were no such tracts in Los Angeles County during 1980, which explains the absence of percent Asian in Figure 6.6.

As these two maps show, there was a substantial movement of Latinos into South Central Los Angeles during the 1980s. Several tracts that had been 50 percent or more African American in 1980 had became 50 percent or more Hispanic in 1990. On the outskirts of the city proper, such as Monterey Park, a few tracts attained Asian pluralities. An ethnic succession process was clearly under way. As Figure 6.7 shows, there was also a tendency for riot deaths to line up along the zone of contact between the majority black and majority Latino areas, a likely indicator of competition for turf.

Figures 6.8 and 6.9 uncover a relationship between the changing racial/ethnic composition of neighborhoods and the location of riot deaths. Figure 6.8 looks at changes in the relative size of black population during the period 1980–1990.

As shown in Figure 6.8, a preponderance of riot deaths occurred in tracts located in South Central and Compton whose black population share had decreased by 20 percent or more during this period. Where blacks were moving out there appears to have been a clustering of fatal violence.

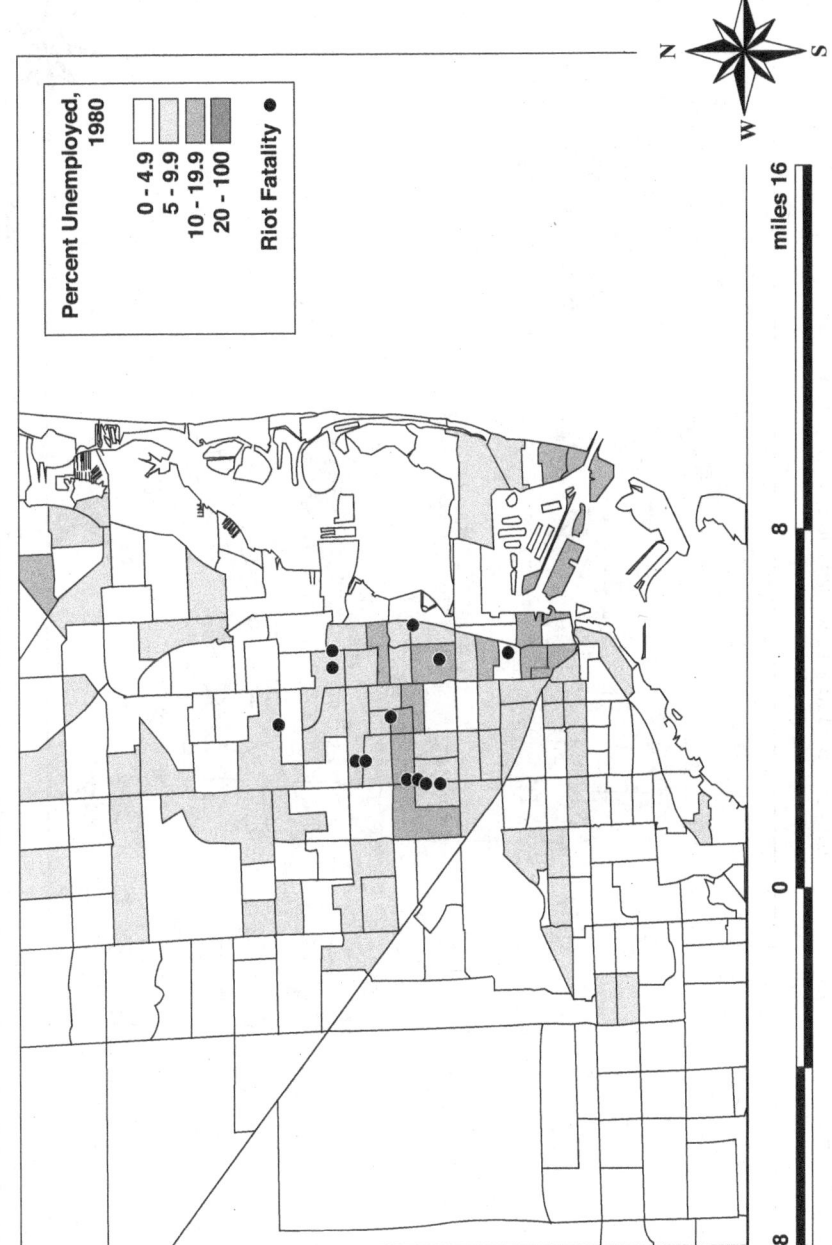

Figure 6.4 1980 Miami Riot Fatalities and Percent Unemployed

134 FIGHTING IN THE STREETS

Figure 6.5 1980 Miami Riot Fatalities and Median Household Income, 1980

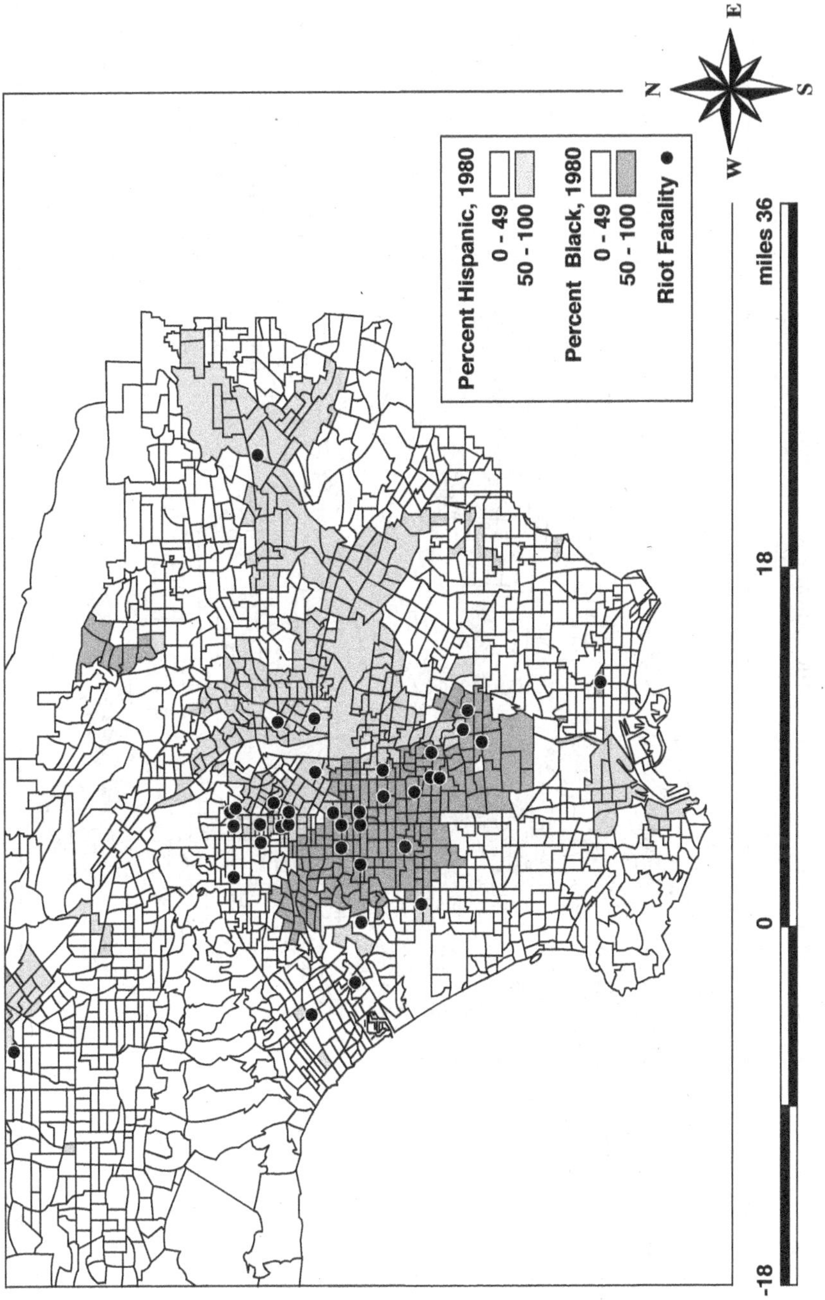

Figure 6.6 1992 Los Angeles Riot Fatalities and Ethnic Composition, 1980

136 FIGHTING IN THE STREETS

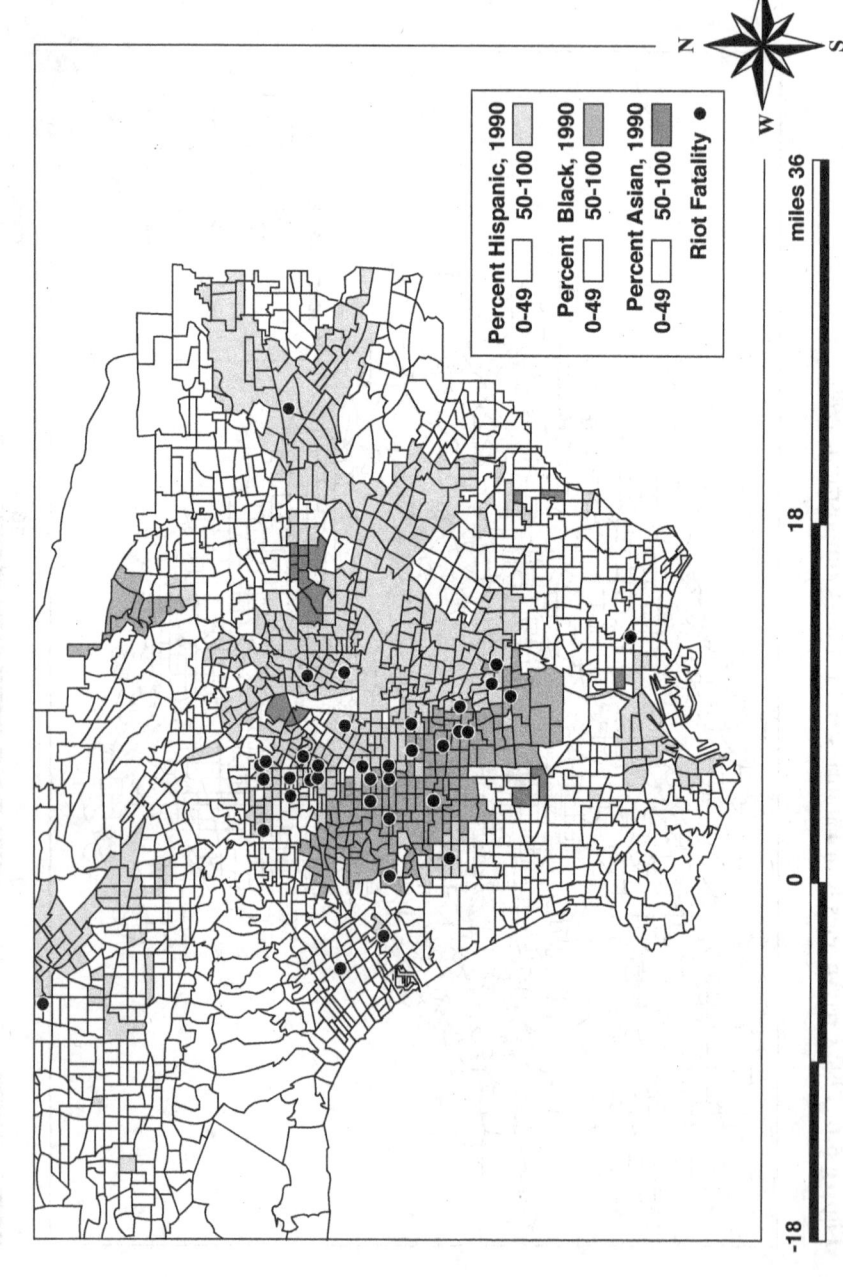

Figure 6.7 1992 Los Angeles Riot Fatalities and Ethic Composition, 1990

New Immigrants and Black Resentment 137

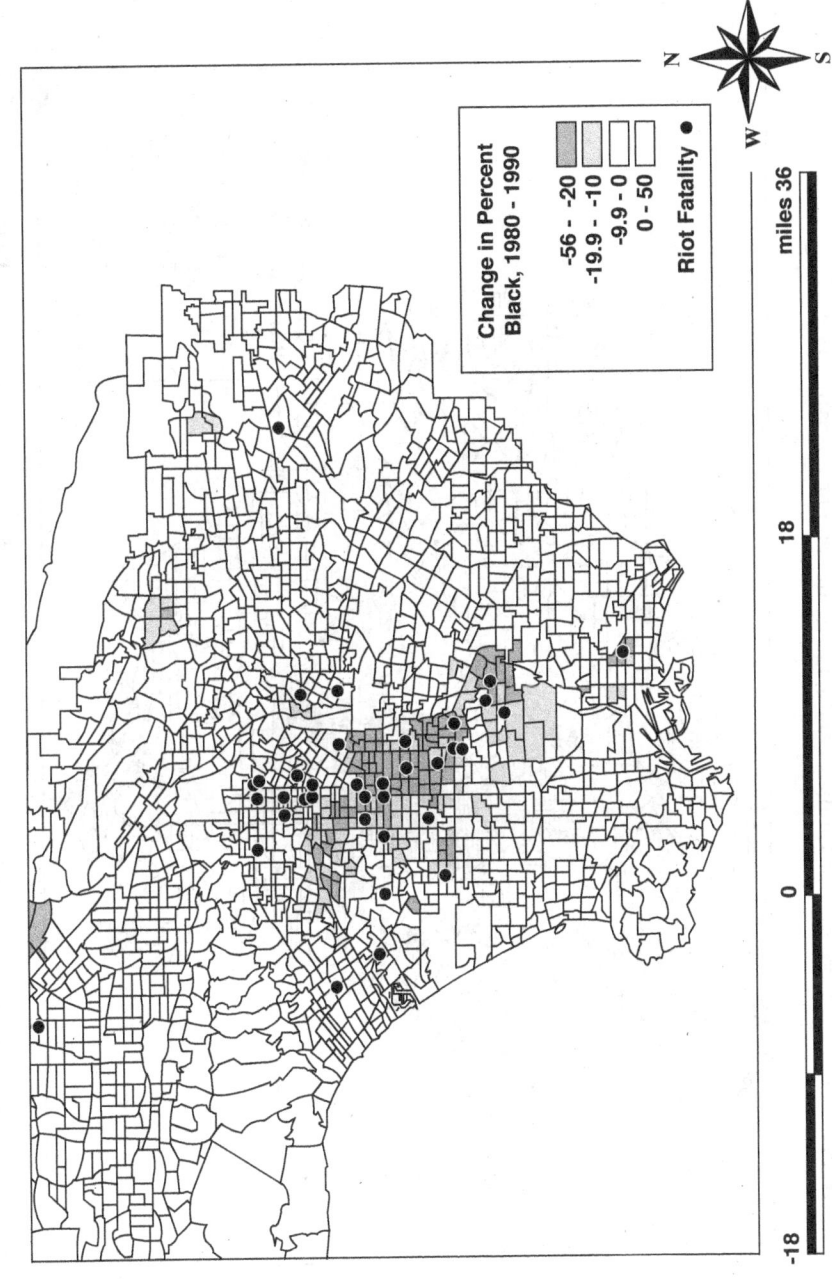

Figure 6.8 1992 Los Angeles Riot Fatalities and Change in Percent Black, 1980–1990

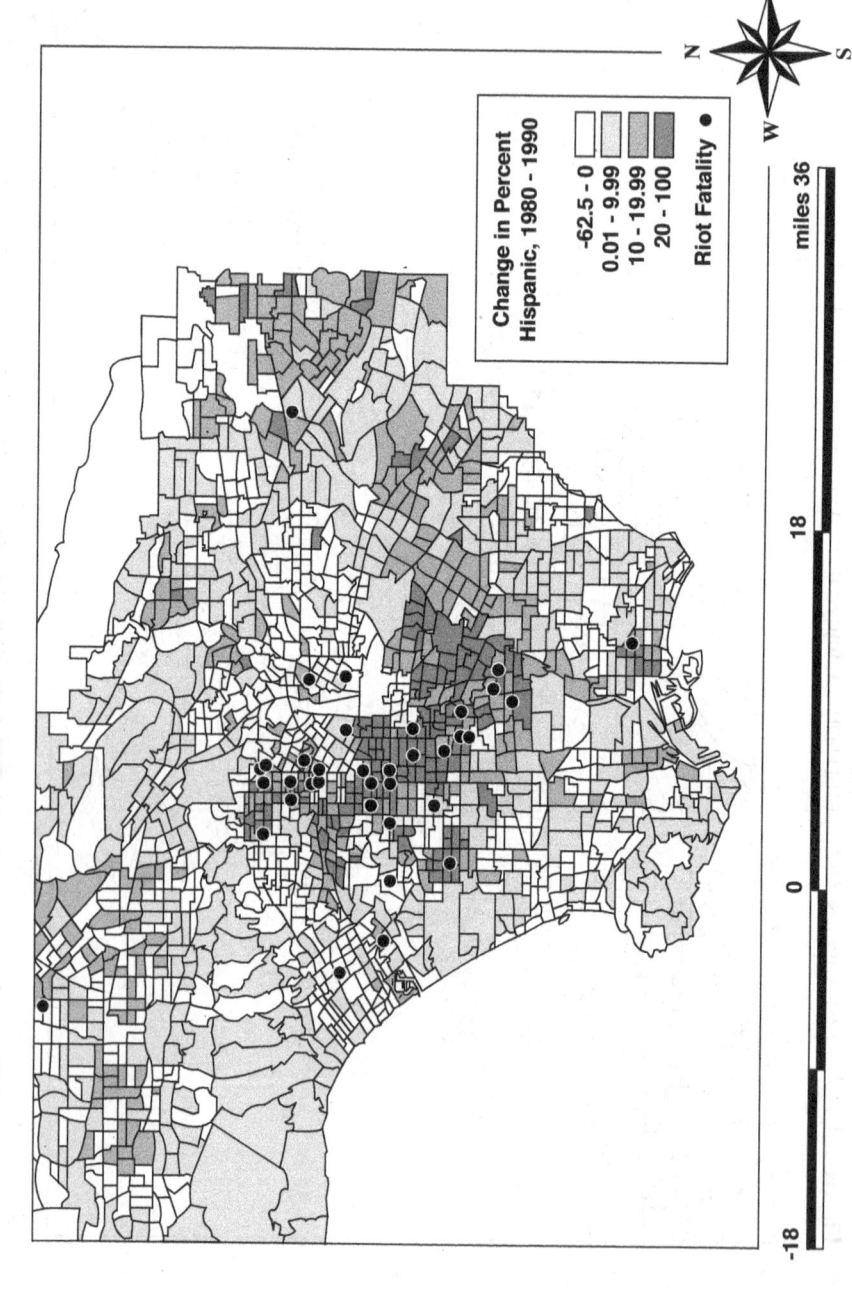

Figure 6.9 1992 Los Angeles Riot Fatalities and Change in Percent Hispanic, 1980–1990

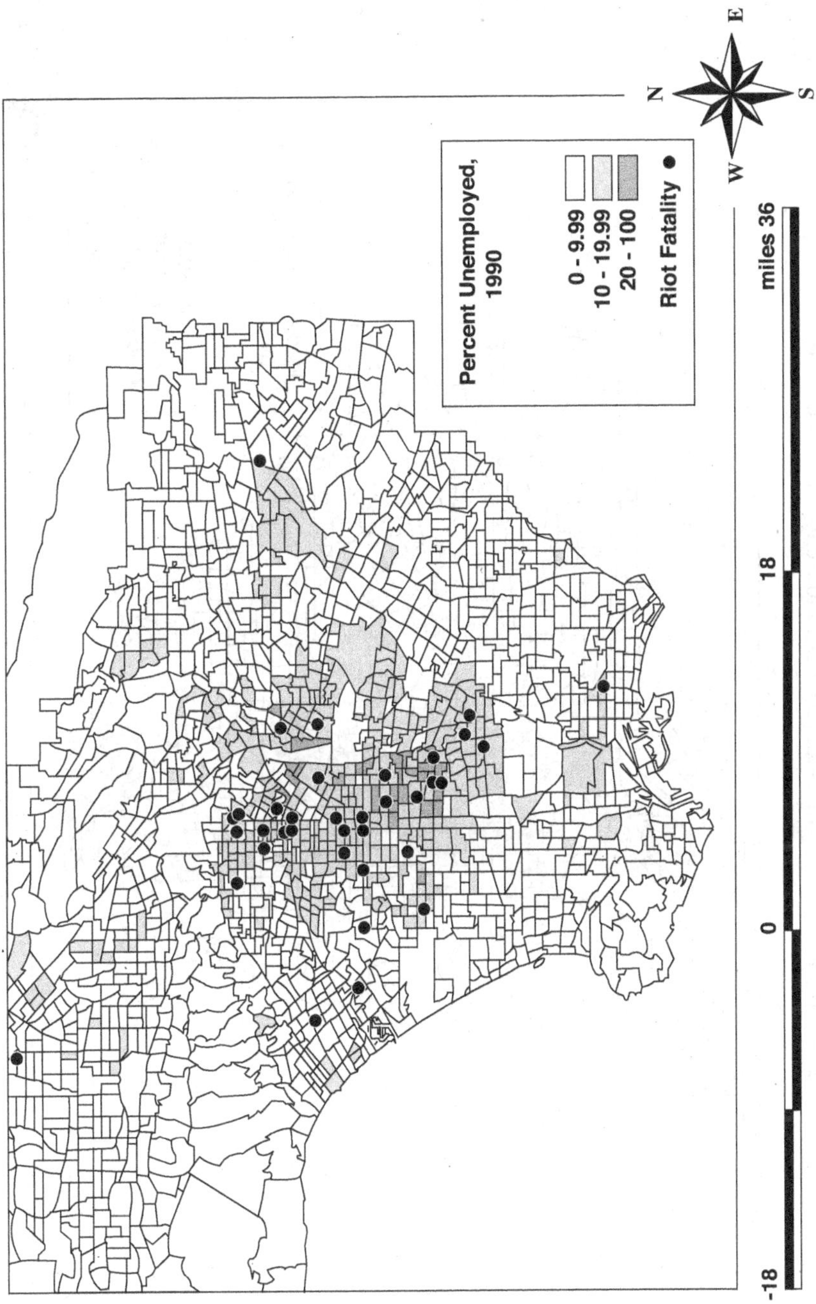

Figure 6.10 1992 Los Angeles Riot Fatalities and Percent Unemployed, 1990

140 FIGHTING IN THE STREETS

Figure 6.11 1992 Los Angeles Riot Fatalities and Median Household Income 1990

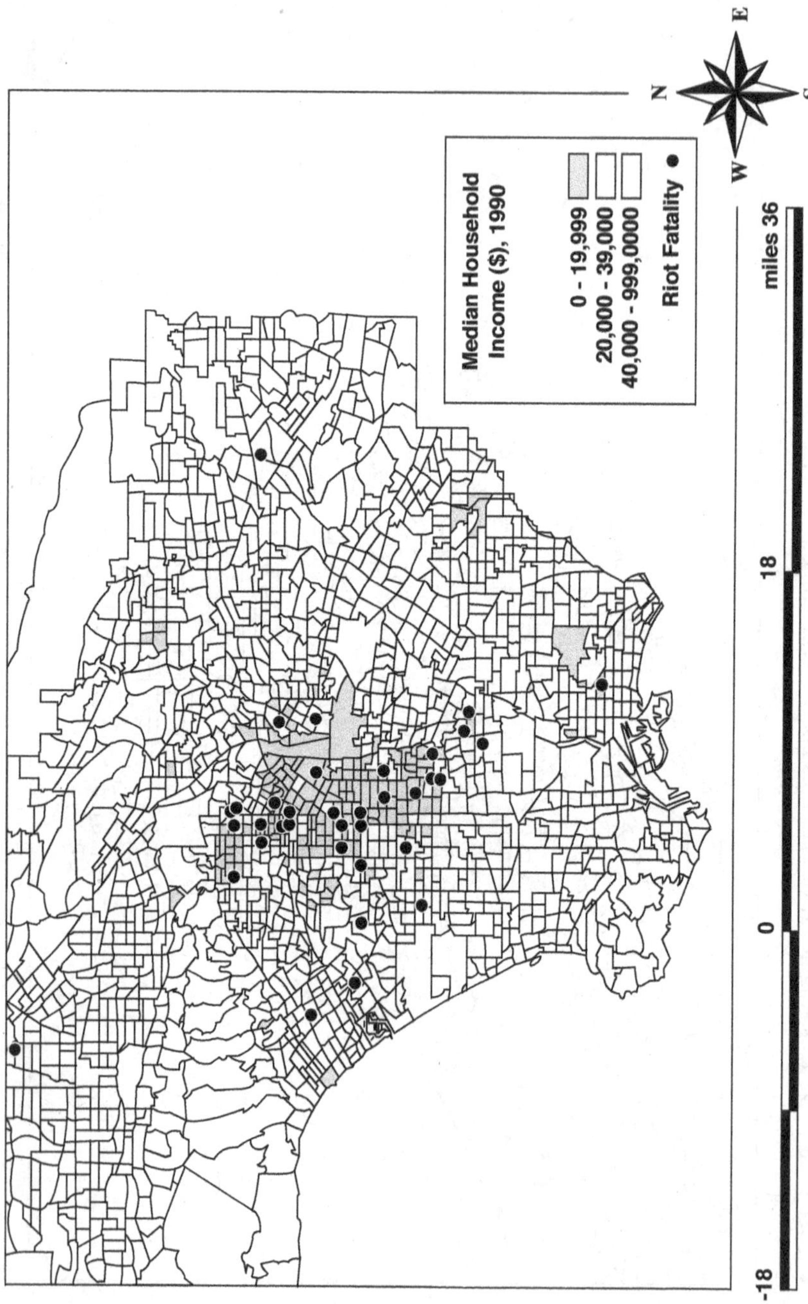

As Figure 6.9 illustrates, riot violence was also prevalent in tracts where Hispanic population share had increased 20 percent or more during the same period. If one were to overlay these two populations, it becomes clear that in South Central and Compton many of the tracts where the relative size of the black population rapidly *decreased* were the same tracts in which the population percent of Hispanics rapidly *increased*. Furthermore, as seen in Figure 6.9, in areas with little black population such as Koreatown and Pico-Union, sharp increases in percent Hispanic also correspond with the location of riot fatalities. GIS analysis thus suggests that for Los Angeles rapid changes in racial/ethnic composition were associated with the presence of riot violence. Such analysis provides preliminary support for the ethnic succession hypothesis.

GIS analysis also lends support for an economic deprivation account of riot violence in Los Angeles. As Figure 6.10 shows, the preponderance of deaths occurred in tracts where the unemployment rate was 10 percent or greater.

Figure 6.11 suggests a similar relationship between income levels and riot violence. The vast majority of deaths that occurred during the Los Angeles riot took place in census tracts where the median household income fell below $20,000 per year. In short, for Los Angeles there appeared to be strong relationships among changing racial composition, economic deprivation, and the presence of riot-related violence.

Difference of Means Test (T-Test)

Table 6.1 reports the results of a difference of means tests comparing tracts where deaths occurred to tracts in which no deaths took place. This test is designed to ascertain whether there are significant differences among tracts that contained riot fatalities versus tracts that were not touched by fatal violence.

For Miami, there were 16 census tracts that contained riot fatalities and 197 that did not. Difference of means tests reveal statistically significant differences among those tracts with and without riot fatalities. Change in percent black significantly distinguishes between these two sets of tracts. Tracts where deaths occurred had a greater mean rate of *increase* in black population than tracts without deaths. Since I had hypothesized that tracts where riot deaths took place would be characterized by a declining black population, this relationship runs counter to my expectations.

By contrast, tracts where deaths took place had, on average, a decreasing Hispanic share of the population. Furthermore, while the foreign-born population of tracts with deaths increased during 1970–1980, the mean increase in percent foreign born was greater in tracts where deaths did not occur. Therefore it seems unlikely that violence was generated at the tract level by an influx of Haitians or Cubans into formerly black neighborhoods. These findings casts doubt on residential ethnic succession

Table 6.1 Demographic Measures for Census Tracts with and without Riot Fatalities by City, Miami and Los Angeles

City	N	Percent Change			Mean Percent (End of Ten-Year Period)				
		Black	Foreign Born	Hispanic	Black	Foreign Born	Hispanic	Males Unemployed	Median Household Income
Miami 1970–1980									
Tracts with Fatalities	16	14.3*	4.1**	-1.5	73.6***	14.1***	8.8***	7.2**	$4,657***
Tracts without Fatalities	197	6.4	11.2		17.3	34.4	34.4	4.7	$5,697
Los Angeles 1980–1990		Black	Foreign Born	Hispanic	Black	Foreign Born	Hispanic	Males Unemployed	Median Household Income
Tracts with Fatalities	92	-11.7***	13.7	17.8***	31.5***	44.2***	53.6***	13.1***	$21,800***
Tracts without Fatalities	1514	-1.2	8.8	7.5	10.5	30.0	33.0	7.3	$39,090

*=p<.05 **=p<.01 ***=p<.001

Sources:
U.S Census of Population and Housing STF3a Miami–Dade County SMSA (1980, 1990).
U.S Census of Population and Housing STF3a Los Angeles–Long Beach SMSA (1980, 1990).

as a predictor of riot violence in Miami neighborhoods. Tracts that experienced fatalities had a significantly higher mean black population than tracts where deaths did not take place (73.6 percent to 17.3 percent). This suggests that rioting in Miami was associated with the size and concentration of the local black population. In this sense, riot violence may have been more a product of segregation than changes in racial/ethnic composition. Once again, the residential ethnic succession perspective is not supported by this analysis.

As for economic measures, there were significant differences in male unemployment and median household income among death and nondeath tracts. Tracts where deaths occurred had, on average, a male unemployment rate of 7.2 percent as opposed to 4.7 percent in tracts where no deaths occurred. Likewise, the median average household income for tracts where deaths took place was $9,106 compared with $15,863 for tracts where no deaths occurred. Such findings lend support for an economic deprivation explanation for rioting in Miami. To summarize the results for Miami, it appears that the location of riot violence is better predicted by segregation and economic deprivation than by residential change (ethnic succession).

In Los Angeles, there were significant differences in population change measures among tracts with and without violence. Unlike the case of Miami, such changes support an ethnic succession interpretation for riot violence. Tracts where deaths occurred had a significantly greater *decline*, on average, in black population share than tracts where no deaths occurred. Likewise, such tracts had a significantly larger *increase* in the percent Hispanic and percent foreignborn. Tracts where deaths occurred were characterized by a relative decline in black population and a relative increase in Hispanic and immigrant populations. Tracts where deaths occurred were, on average, 53.6 percent Hispanic and 31.5 percent black, underscoring a potential struggle for control of turf between two sizable "minority" groups. This supports an ethnic competition perspective for riot-related violence.

As with Miami, the difference of means tests for Los Angeles also provide support for the economic deprivation hypothesis. In tracts where deaths occurred, the male unemployment rate was, on average, double that of tracts where riot deaths did not take place. Likewise, tracts where riot deaths occurred had, on average, significantly lower household incomes ($21,800 vs. $39,090).

To summarize the results of these tests, difference of means analysis lends support to an ethnic succession account for riot violence in Los Angeles, but not for Miami. On the basis of this preliminary statistical evidence, I suggest that riot violence in Miami was primarily a result of segregation and economic deprivation whereas riot violence in Los Angeles was attributable to a combination of changing racial/ethnic composition (ethnic succession), niche overlap (ethnic competition), and economic hardship.

Poisson Regression Analysis

The conclusions reached thus far are based on visual association and a relatively simple statistical test. To confirm these results, more powerful statistical tests that simultaneously control for several variables are necessary. Thus, in this section, I describe the outcomes of Poisson regression analysis. In these models, I estimate the number of riots deaths that took place in census tracts according to their racial/ethnic composition and economic characteristics. The results of these tests are contained in Tables 6.2a–6.2b.

Testing for Nonlinear Effects of Minority Population

According to Blalock's "power threat" and "competition" formulations, we should expect to find nonlinear effects of percent minority on the number of deaths in a census tract. If power threat is operative, the relationship between percent Hispanic and riot-related deaths in a tract will be positive and ever increasing. This is indicated by a positive coefficient for percent Hispanic and a positive coefficient for percent Hispanic squared. If competition is operative, we should find a positive nonlinear relationship with a slope that decreases at the highest levels of percent Hispanic. This is evidenced by a positive coefficient for percent Hispanic and a negative coefficient for its squared term.

In Miami, when controlling for the effects of economic indicators (percent males unemployed and median household income), I did not find support for a curvilinear relationship between percent Hispanic and the number of riot fatalities in a tract (Table 6.2a, model 1). In separate analyses, neither the main effects for percent Hispanic or percent foreign born nor their respective squared terms attained statistical significance as predictors of riot intensity. For Miami, Blalock's power threat and competition formulations did not attain statistical significance.

In Los Angeles, controlling for the same economic indicators, I did find a nonlinear effect of percent Hispanic on the presence of riot fatalities (Table 6.2b, model 1). The main effect for percent Hispanic is positive and significant at the .01 level, single-tailed test. The corresponding squared term is negative and also significant at the .01 level. Together, these two terms indicate a positive relationship between percent Hispanic and the number of riot fatalities in a tract, a relationship that reverses direction at the highest levels of Hispanic population. In other words, the relationship between percent Hispanic and the number of riot deaths in a tract resembles an inverted U-shape curve. Such a result is consistent with Blalock's "competition" formulation, suggesting that where Hispanic population approached parity with non-Hispanic population, competition for resources such as jobs and housing was likely to be associated with the intensity of riot violence.

Testing for Effects of Changing Racial Composition: Ethnic Succession Theory

Table 6.2a (models 2 and 3) presents the results of Poisson regression analysis that estimates the effects of changing racial composition on the intensity of riot-related violence in Miami (Dade County) census tracts. Controlling for economic indicators (percent males unemployed and median household income) as well as percent Hispanic, the change in percent Hispanic is not significantly related to the number of deaths in Miami census tracts (model 2). Nor is change in percent black a significant predictor of riot intensity in Miami when controlling for relative black population size, unemployment, and median household income (Table 6.2a, model 3). In these respective models, however, the population percent of Latinos and African Americans are significantly associated with riot violence, albeit not in the hypothesized manner. Percent Hispanic is negative associated with the number of riot deaths in a tract, while percent black is positively associated with the number of riot fatalities. Apparently, riot intensity in Miami was greatest where black population was high and Latino population low, lending more support to Spilerman's assertion that riot violence is a function of black population.

Table 6.2b (models 2 and 3) presents the results for a comparable Poisson regression analysis for the effects of changing racial/ethnic composition on the number of riot fatalities in Los Angeles census tracts. For Los Angeles, unlike Miami, I found significant effects of changes in racial/ethnic composition on the intensity of riot violence. Controlling for the relative size of Hispanic population as well as economic indicators, change in percent Hispanic had a *positive* and significant effect on the number of riot-related deaths in Los Angeles census tracts (model 2). Increases in Hispanic population were associated with a higher number of fatalities. By contrast, controlling for the relative size of the local black population, change in percent black had a significant *negative* effect on the number of riot deaths in a tract (model 3). This suggests that the most intense riot violence in Los Angeles occurred in areas where African Americans were leaving. These models, taken together, lend support to the finding of the GIS analysis presented earlier. Looking back to Figures 6.8 and 6.9, the data suggests that the severity of riot violence was associated with the in-migration of Hispanics and the out-migration of blacks in neighborhoods like South Central and Compton. As with Miami, the relative size of the black population in Los Angeles census tracts was also predictive of riot violence. Once again Spilerman is correct. Riot violence in Los Angeles is associated with black population. However, for Los Angeles, unlike Miami, the intensity of riot violence was also associated with racial/ethnic population change. Contrary to Spilerman's hypothesis, riot violence in Los Angeles occurred where black population was decreasing. As with previous episodes of urban unrest that took place in Chicago and Detroit

Table 6.2a Poisson Regression Estimates of the Number of Riot Fatalities in Dade County (Miami) Census Tracts as a Function of Change in Racial/Ethnic Composition and Economic Characteristics,

Independent Variables	Dependent Variable: Number of Riot Fatalities						
	(1)	(2)	(3)	(4)	(5)	(6)	(7)
Racial/Ethnic Composition							
Percent Hispanic (1980)	-6.333 (6.737)	-9.172*** (2.554)	-----	-----	-----	-----	-----
Percent Hispanic Squared (1980)	-11.911 (23.791)	-----	-----	-----	-----	-----	-----
Change in Percent Hispanic (1970–1980)	-----	-2.627 (2.997)	-----	-9.342*** (2.614)	-7.291** (2.371)	-----	-----
Change in Percent Black (1970–1980)	-----	-----	-.2879 (1.043)	-----	-----	-----	-----
Percent Black 1980	-----	-----	4.816*** (.8110)	-----	-----	4.750*** (.8787)	4.419*** (.8641)
Change in Percent Hispanic (1970–1980) * Percent Males Unemployed (1980)	-----	-----	-----	84.903 (57.515)	-----	-----	-----
Change in Percent Hispanic (1970–1980)* Median Household Income (1980)	-----	-----	-----	-----	-1.357 (2.796)	-----	-----
Percent Black (1980) * Percent. Males Unemployed (1980)	-----	-----	-----	-----	-----	55.184** (25.239)	-----
Percent Black (1980)* Median Household Income (1980)	-----	-----	-----	-----	-----	-----	-1.615 (1.398)
Percent Males Unemployed (1980)	6.298 (6.143)	4.464 (6.227)	-5.195 (6.979)	17.507* (9.113)	6.872 (5.497)	-37.031*** (17.024)	-4.779 (7.212)
Median Household Income (1980)	-1.252** (.4171)	-1.167** (.3959)	-1.109** (.4637)	-1.070** (.3815)	-1.338*** (.3792)	-1.133** (.4747)	-.2508 (.9051)
Constant	10.619** (3.894)	10.064*** (3.788)	6.094 (4.527)	7.514* (3.799)	10.513** (3.699)	7.616* (4.623)	-1.954 (8.693)
Log Likelihood	-55.564	-55.358	-43.505	-68.218	-69.262	-41.041	-42.887
D.F.	207	207	207	207	207	207	207

* p < .05   ** p < .01   *** p< .001   One-tailed test.   Standard errors are in parenthesis.
Source: U.S. Census of Population and Housing, STF 3a (1970 paper volume, 1980 data tape).

Table 6.2b Poisson Regression Estimates of the Number of Riot Fatalities in Los Angeles County Census Tracts as a Function of Change in Racial/Ethnic Composition and Economic Characteristics

Independent Variables	Dependent Variable: Number of Riot Fatalities						
	(1)	(2)	(3)	(4)	(5)	(6)	(7)
Racial/Ethnic Composition							
Percent Hispanic (1990)	7.098*** (1.799)	.5947 (.3985)	-----	-----	-----	-----	-----
Percent Hispanic Squared (1990)	-5.795*** (1.643)	------	-----	-----	-----	-----	-----
Change in Percent Hispanic (1980-1990)	------	3.636*** (.7547)	-----	4.112*** (.9234)	3.445** (1.303)	-----	-----
Change in Percent Black (1980-1990)	------	-----	-3.205*** (.7238)	-----	-----		
Percent Black 1990	------	-----	1.452*** (.4181)	-----	-----	2.413*** (.3803)	2.855*** (.4022)
Change in Percent. Hispanic (1980-1990) * Percent Males Unemployed (1990)	------	-----	-----	-2.896 (8.927)	-----	----	-----
Change in Percent Hispanic (1980-1990)* log Median Household Income (1990)	------	-----	-----	-----	-.7763 (1.716)	-----	-----
Percent Black (1990) * Percent Males Unemployed (1990)	------	-----	-----	-----	-----	-11.253*** (4.820)	------
Percent Black (1990)* Median Household Income (1990)	------	-----	-----	-----	-----	-----	2.449*** (.7410)
Percent Males Unemployed (1990)	2.927* (1.476)	2.076 (1.437)	-1.063 (1.546)	1.923 (1.685)	1.445 (1.399)	4.905* (2.825)	2.251 (1.805)
Median Household Income (1990)	-1.834*** (.2970)	-1.841*** (.2974)	-1.866*** (.2790)	-1.895*** (.2887)	-1.918*** (.2816)	-1.784*** (.2810)	-2.186*** (.2473)
Constant	14.086*** (3.197)	15.131*** (3.156)	15.963*** (2.915)	15.931*** (3.058)	16.267*** (2.955)	14.611*** (3.023)	18.894*** (2.541)
Log Likelihood	331.001	-326.189	-316.676	-327.231	-327.179	-323.765	-321.469
D.F.	1603	1603	1603	1603	1603	1603	1603

* $p < .05$ ** $p < .01$ *** $p < .001$ One-tailed test. Standard errors are in parenthesis.
Source: U.S. Census of Population and Housing, STF 3a (1980 data tape, 1990 CD-ROM).

during the first half of the twentieth century, ethnic succession played a critical role in fomenting urban unrest in Los Angeles in the 1990s.

Testing for Ethnic Competition

Although change in ethnic composition (ethnic succession) was not associated with the number of deaths that occurred in Miami census tracts, this does not conclusively rule out an ethnic competition explanation for violence. Although Latino immigrants in Miami were not moving into the highly segregated black neighborhoods of Liberty City and Overtown, these groups still perceived each other as competitors for jobs, wealth, and housing. Indeed, several authors have noted that such perceptions played a role in the localized outbreaks of riot violence during the Miami riot (U.S. Commission on Civil Rights 1982; Porter and Dunn 1984; Portes and Stepick 1993). Furthermore, there are theoretical reasons to suggest that immigration may have strong effects on inducing competition in labor and housing markets (Olzak 1992, Olzak, Shanahan, and McEneany 1996).

To test Olzak's ethnic competition thesis for Miami riot deaths, I created interactions terms that multiplied change in percent Latino with percent males unemployed, median household income, and housing density (measured by the ratio of persons to dwellings). Models 4 through 6 of Table 6.2a present the results of this analysis. At the census tract level, neither job competition nor income competition are significantly related to the number of deaths in Miami census tracts (models 4 and 5). Competition for housing, however, was significantly associated with the intensity of violence. Higher densities of housing (persons per unit) interacted with increases in foreign-born population to produce higher levels of riot violence. Although Latinos were not moving into Miami's predominantly black neighborhoods in large numbers, the increased presence of immigrants (including Haitians who were classified by the Census Bureau as black) affected Miami's already congested housing market and played a significant role in generating riot violence.

In Los Angeles, where ethnic succession was statistically associated with the severity of riot violence, there was also a significant positive effect for the interaction of housing density and foreign-born migration on the number of deaths in a tract (Table 6.2b, model 6). This I found less surprising than the similar result obtained for Miami. Some of the Los Angeles neighborhoods where immigrants were moving in large numbers were also quite crowded, a factor that induced spillover of Latino population into the predominantly black neighborhoods of South Central, Compton, and Watts. In Los Angeles, unlike Miami, ethnic succession and competition for housing both had significant effects on the intensity of riot violence.

Economic competition indicators for Los Angeles census tracts provide mixed support for Olzak's hypotheses (Table 6.2b, models 4 and 5).

The interaction of male unemployment and change in percent foreign born was positive but failed to attain statistical significance (model 4). By contrast, the interaction of median household income and change in percent foreign born was negative and significant at the .01 level (model 5). As hypothesized, higher incomes ameliorate the effects of immigration on riot violence. This finding suggests that tracts with the highest levels of income were able to absorb more immigrants without violence than tracts with similar increases in immigrant population but lower income levels. Perhaps the immigrants moving into wealthier neighborhoods were themselves of relatively high socioeconomic status. This factor may explain why the presence of immigrants did not trigger such intense violence in more affluent communities. Alternatively, residents of wealthier neighborhoods may have responded less violently to an increased presence of immigrants because they felt more economically secure than those living in poorer areas. The next section examines the role that poverty and segregation may have played in these riot events.

Testing the Economic Deprivation Hypothesis

While it is intuitive to see the riots in Miami and Los Angeles as a response to widespread unemployment and poverty, the evidence for such an account is mixed. The percent of unemployed males is significantly associated with the number of deaths in Miami census tracts in only two of eight Poisson regression models. Furthermore, in one of these models, the relationship between unemployment and the number of riot-related fatalities is negative. For Los Angeles, there is a similar paucity of statistical support for an association between male unemployment and the intensity of riot violence. As with Miami, the relationship between male unemployment and riot violence is statistically significant in only two of eight Los Angeles Poisson regression models.

For both Miami and Los Angeles, median household income bears a stronger relation to the number of deaths in a census tract. In four of the eight Poisson regression models for Miami, median household income is significantly and negatively associated with the number of riot deaths. This finding suggests that rising levels of household income reduce the likelihood that multiple deaths will occur in a tract. In seven of eight Poisson regression models for Los Angeles there is a significant negative relationship between median household income and the number of deaths in a tract. Generally speaking, riot-related violence did not take place in the wealthier districts of Miami or Los Angeles. Riot violence in Los Angeles as well as Miami is spatially associated with lower levels of household income, lending support to an economic deprivation explanation based on income but not unemployment.

Urban sociologists like William Julius Wilson have argued that poverty and segregation combine to generate social pathologies in minority communities, e.g., high rates of crime. By interacting percent black with economic indicators (percent males unemployed, log median household income), I attempt to address whether the combination of poverty and segregation played a role in generating riot violence at the neighborhood level.

For Miami, I found a significant interaction effect of percent black and percent males unemployed on the number of riot-related fatalities in a tract. Controlling for the interaction of percent black and male unemployment, as well as median household income, the main effect of male unemployment on the number of deaths in a tract is negative (Table 6.2a, model 7). Yet, at higher levels of percent black the effect of male unemployment becomes positive. Unemployment exacerbates the effect of percent black on the number of riot deaths in a tract. By contrast, the interaction of median household income and percent black is not a statistically significant predictor of the intensity of violence in Miami (model 8).

For Los Angeles, a different picture emerges. There are significant interaction effects of male unemployment and median household income with percent black. These relationships are opposite of what we would expect according to economic deprivation theories. The coefficient for the interaction of male unemployment and percent black is negative, which reverses a positive main effect for male unemployment on the number of deaths in a tract (Table 6.2b, model 7). This finding counterintuitively suggests that unemployment decreases the intensity of violence in predominantly black communities. Equally interesting is the positive coefficient for the interaction of median household income and percent black (Table 6.2b, model 8). Taken together with the negative main effect for income, this finding implies that as percent black increases, higher income levels are associated with more violence. While this effect is not consistent with a segregation–economic deprivation perspective, it is consistent with what surveys of riot participants (Caplan and Page 1968; Singer, Osborn and Geschwender, 1970) have found. African Americans who participated in riots in Detroit and other cities were not the poorest of the poor but individuals from somewhat higher socioeconomic backgrounds whose aspirations for further mobility had been thwarted. As Olzak (1992) suggests, there is no conclusive relationship between poverty and ethnic collective action.

In his book *The Rage of a Privileged Class*, Ellis Cose (1993) suggests that middle-class blacks are more likely than poor blacks to overtly express resentment over racial injustices, such as the acquittal of the LAPD officers in the Rodney King case. African Americans who lived in communities with lower rates of unemployment and higher rates of income may have been more predisposed to violence than those who were downwardly mobile. On the other hand, it is also possible that wealthier black communities were targets of looters seeking spoils under the cover of civil unrest. More data are needed on the actual riot participants and their motivations. Nonetheless, the Los Angeles riot data confound the hypothesis that segregation and deprivation are linked to higher rates of violence. The violence that occurred in Miami fits better with a segregation-deprivation account. For both cities, however, there is statistical evidence that poverty played a role in determining where violence was most intense, independent of black population size. Nonetheless, for both Los Angeles and Miami there is a significant independent association of black population size and riot-related violence. Once again, this confirms Spilerman's hypothesis. Furthermore, for Los Angeles there is clear evidence that changes in the racial/ethnic composition of tracts (ethnic succession) were associated with riot violence.

Controlling for Spatial Autocorrelation

As discussed in Chapter 2, the presence of spatial autocorrelation raises questions about the reliability of regression estimators in models that employ geographic data. To test for the presence of spatial autocorrelation, I have reestimated the basic regression models that examine the effects changes in percent black and percent Hispanic on the presence or absence of deaths in a tract. These new models use the maximum likelihood technique and include a spatial autoregressive term. Table 6.3 presents the results of these models for Miami and Los Angeles.

For Miami, the reestimation of my regression models as maximum likelihood functions with a spatial autoregressive term challenges some of the results presented earlier. Such analysis strengthens the effect of black population size on riot deaths but eliminates the independent effects of change in percent Latino and of median household income on the presence of riot fatalities. As indicated in Table 6.3, neither the change in percent black nor the change in percent Hispanic are significant predictors of riot violence when controlling for their respective population percents in 1980, economic indicators, and spatial dependency.

Controlling for spatial autocorrelation, change in percent black no longer has a significant effect on fatalities in Miami. Surprisingly, when controlling for spatial autocorrelation, median household income also loses predictive power in Miami. The percent of black residents in 1980, however, remains a significant and positive predictor of where violence occurred. Controlling for spatial autocorrelation thereby yields results similar to what Spilerman found with respect to the 1960s riots. The proportionate size of a tract's black population-percent black remains the most consistent predictor of the severity of violence contained therein. Riot violence in Miami appears primarily to be a result of racial segregation.

In Los Angeles, controlling for spatial autocorrelation also alters the results of the previous regression analysis, weakening the effects of economic deprivation on the presence of riot deaths in a tract. When controlling for the effects of spatial autocorrelation, median household income is no longer associated with riot violence. However, controlling for spatial

Table 6.3 Linear Regression Estimates of the Number of Riot Fatalities in Miami and Los Angeles Census Tracts as a Function of Change in Racial/Ethnic Composition and Economic Characteristics (Controlling for Spatial Autocorrelation)

Independent Variables	Dependent Variable: Number of Riot Fatalities			
	Miami 1970-1980		Los Angeles 1980-1990	
	(1)	(2)	(3)	(4)
Racial/Ethnic Composition				
Change in Percent Black (Ten-Year Period)	.0613 (.1514)	------	-.3849*** (.0693)	-----
Percent Black (Beginning of Ten-Year period)	.4225*** (.0880)	------	.0659* (.0304)	-----
Change in Percent Hispanic (Ten-Year Period)	-------	-.0730 (.1969)	------	.1132* (.0511)
Percent Hispanic (Beginning of Ten-Year period)	-------	-.1723 (.1211)	------	.0036 (.0219)
Economic Indicators				
Percent Males Unemployed	-1.091* (.5700)	..0442 (.5457)	-.7479*** (.1257)	-.8713*** (.1197)
Median Household Income	-.0055 (.0173)	-.0000 (.0000)	-.0086 (.0056)	-.0056 (.0055)
Constant	.201 (.0737)	.1181 (.0817)	.0683 (.0617)	.0916 (.0605)
DF	213	213	1639	1639

* p < .05   ** p < .01   *** p < .001   One-tailed test.
Standard errors are in parenthesis.

Source: U.S. Census of Population and Housing, STF3a (1970 paper volume, 1980 data tape ICPSR, 1990 CD-ROM).

autocorrelation strengthens the effects of population change measures on the presence of riot deaths. Controlling for percent black as well as the economic indicators (male unemployment and median household income) and spatial dependency, the change in percent black is significantly and *negatively* associated with the presence of riot fatalities. Controlling for percent Hispanic as well as the economic indicators and spatial dependency, change in percent Hispanic is significantly and *positively* associated with the presence of riot deaths. Thus, taking spatial autocorrelation into account, the out-migration of blacks and the in-migration of Hispanics remain significant predictors of the outbreak of riot violence in Los Angeles neighborhoods. When taking spatial dependency into account, changes in the racial/ethnic composition of census tracts remain a key factor in predicting their susceptibility for riot violence. Thus, the ethnic succession hypothesis holds for Los Angeles.

SUMMARIZING THE RESULTS

Based on geographic information systems and statistical analysis, I draw the following conclusions regarding the origins of riot violence in Miami and Los Angeles.

Census tracts in Miami where fatal violence took place were characterized by high levels of unemployment, low levels of household income, and a sizable African-American population. Controlling simultaneously for the demographic and economic indicators, I found little support for a residential ethnic succession interpretation of riot-related violence in Miami.

Likewise, for Miami, I failed to find nonlinear effects of black population size on the intensity of riot violence. I, therefore, must reject both Blalock's "power threat" and "competition" formulations as they pertain to Miami. Rather, I found support in Miami for Spilerman's claim that riot severity is a function of black population size. In Miami I found a significant interaction of percent black and median household income. The data indicate that riot violence in Miami was most likely a joint function of segregation and economic deprivation. The rioting that took place in Miami seems to conform more closely to the classic 1960s model of urban riots during which aggrieved African Americans vented their frustration upon nonblacks, a category now expanded to include Latinos as well as Anglos.

In Los Angeles, the residential ethnic succession hypothesis received more statistical support. Census tracts with riot fatalities were marked by higher rates of black out-migration and higher rates of Hispanic and foreign-born in-migration. Tracts with riot fatalities in Los Angeles were also characterized by lower levels of median household income and higher levels of male unemployment than tracts without riot-related deaths. Controlling simultaneously for demographic and economic variables, the location and the intensity of riot violence was significantly related to the in-migration of Hispanics and the out-migration of blacks. This process occurred mainly in historically black sections of the city, e.g., South Central, Compton, and Watts. I also found a nonlinear effect of percent Hispanic and percent Hispanic squared on the number of deaths in Los Angeles County census tracts. Such a finding is consistent with Blalock's competition formulation. In this case, however, it is Hispanics who pose a competitive threat to blacks, rather than blacks presenting a competitive threat to whites.

By contrast, although the interaction of segregation and poverty was a statistically significant predictor of riot intensity in Los Angeles census tracts, the relationship was opposite to that which segregation-deprivation theorists posited. The intensity of riot violence was increased by lower rates of unemployment and higher median household incomes in black communities. This conforms less to a segregation-deprivation account for violence than a relative deprivation explanation that focuses on the frustration of a rising black middle class.

Finally, in both Miami and Los Angeles, statistical evidence suggests that housing competition was related to the intensity of violence. Although residential ethnic succession did not occur directly in Miami, the mass migration of Hispanic immigrants to Miami during the 1970s and early 1980s did increase competition for low-income housing outside of the black ghetto. In Miami, the housing preferences afforded to Hispanics had the effect of keeping blacks confined in segregated neighborhoods, generating resentment among blacks whose residential mobility was blocked. In Los Angeles, the increased presence of Hispanic immigrants put pressure on an already congested housing market. The increased competition for housing between Hispanic immigrants and black residents was positively related to the intensity of riot violence in both Miami and Los Angeles.

CONCLUSION

During the 1980s and 1990s respectively, Miami and Los Angeles experienced a new influx of immigrants from Latin America and Asia. Yet the impact of the new immigrants differed somewhat in these two cities. In the case of Miami, the Mariel boatlift brought over 100,000 new Cuban immigrants to the city. But these new Cuban immigrants, unlike previous waves of immigrants in other cities, did not compete directly for space with African Americans. Instead, this third wave of Cuban immigrants gravitated toward previously established Cuban enclaves where they could hope to obtain employment and housing. As the Cuban enclave in Miami grew, it expanded into surrounding neighborhoods that had been occupied by whites, not blacks. Whites who had lived in these neighborhoods offered little resistance. As a result, the residential transition in these areas was relatively peaceful. At the same time, a new wave of black immigrants from Haiti arrived in Miami. Yet, like the Cubans, they did not compete directly with native-born blacks for space. Rather, they choose to settle on the eastern fringe of the black community, establishing their own ethnic enclave adjacent to Liberty City. Thus, both historical and statistical analyses fail to support a residential ethnic succession interpretation of violence in Miami.

Yet, such evidence does not entirely discount an ethnic succession interpretation for riot violence in Miami. Although *residential* ethnic succession was not a key factor in the origins of unrest in Miami, succession in the *labor markets* and *politics* did appear to play a major part in explaining the outbreak of hostilities. Although the newest waves of Cuban and Haitian immigrants were not competing directly with native-born blacks for space, they were competing with African Americans for jobs and political power. As mentioned previously in this chapter, there is evidence that blacks lost out in competition for jobs in the hospitality (hotel and restaurant) industries to recent immigrants. There is also evidence that Cubans gained a virtual lock on construction jobs in the city. In terms of politics, Cuban immigrants took power in the city, promoting the election of Cuban mayors and city councilpersons, while black political representation in Miami declined.

Therefore, although immigrants did not displace blacks from their neighborhoods, they did displace black workers in several industries in Miami and from positions of power in city government. Ethnic succession in jobs and politics, played a key role in fomenting urban unrest in Miami, despite the absence of ethnic succession at the neighborhood level.

In Los Angeles, by contrast, a new wave of Hispanic immigration from Mexico and Central America did result in residential ethnic succession. Instead of moving into established Hispanic communities in East Los Angeles, these new immigrants moved into the traditional black enclaves of South Central and Compton. Within a decade, these once solidly black areas had become mixed black and Hispanic neighborhoods. As this demographic transition took place, tensions between newcomers and natives flared, leading to skirmishes between black and Hispanic youths on the streets and in the schools and local public housing projects. As GIS maps and statistical analyses indicate, a preponderance of riot-related deaths took place in neighborhoods like South Central and Compton where Hispanics were moving in and blacks were moving out. These neighborhoods undergoing ethnic succession were the flashpoints of urban unrest in Los Angeles.

As with Miami, however, riot violence in Los Angeles was also associated with ethnic succession in labor markets and politics. In Los Angeles, black workers had been displaced from jobs in the garment, janitorial, and hospitality industries by new immigrant workers. In the political sphere, Hispanics were flexing their new muscle by electing Hispanic representatives to the city council for the first time. Although at the time of the riot, an African American, Tom Bradley, was mayor of Los Angeles, it was clear that black political power in Los Angeles was on the wane. After the riots, with considerable help from the largely Catholic Hispanic community, an Irish Catholic mayor was elected, ending Mayor Bradley's twenty years in office. Given the demographic shifts, it is possible that there may never be another African-American mayor in Los Angeles. In short, both residential ethnic succession as well as ethnic succession in jobs and politics played a role in generating the potential for urban unrest in Los Angeles.

Comparing these two cases of urban unrest with previous ones in twentieth-century America, it is apparent that the rioting that swept Miami in the summer of 1980 bears more resemblance to episodes of unrest that occurred during the 1960s than do the events that took place in Los Angeles in 1992. Like the patterns of violence that characterized riots in Newark and Detroit during the 1960s, riot-related violence in Miami took place mostly within highly segregated black communities that were isolated from the centers of political and economic power. One could say that, despite the presence of new immigrants in surrounding communities, the 1980 Miami riot was principally a result of racial segregation and economic deprivation. By contrast, riot-related violence in Los Angeles took place in neighborhoods that were undergoing profound changes in their racial/ethnic composition as a result of the new immigration. In this respect, the rioting that took place in Los Angeles in 1992 seems to have more in common with episodes of urban unrest that occurred earlier in the century in Chicago (1919) and Detroit (1943) than with the more recent events in Miami. Only by extending the concept of ethnic succession to include labor markets and politics does Miami seem to fit an ethnic succession model. This raises the question of how well a general model of violence applies to all six cases of urban unrest examined in the larger study. This topic will be further explored in the following chapter.

CHAPTER SEVEN

Insights from the Past, Prescriptions for the Future

The twentieth century in America was marked by three major periods of urban unrest, each corresponding to a particular wave of domestic migration or international immigration. These waves of migration and immigration, I argue, dramatically altered the ethnic composition of city neighborhoods and urban labor markets, sowing the seeds for violent clashes between newcomers and natives.

The first period of urban unrest, which encompassed the two World Wars, was characterized by the large-scale migration of African Americans from the rural South to the industrial cities of the Midwest. This wave of black migration engendered resistance among first- and second-generation white immigrants who feared that Negro newcomers would "invade" their tight-knit ethnic enclaves and usurp their jobs. Violent clashes, such as those that took place in Chicago (1919) and Detroit (1943), often began at public recreational facilities, reflecting competition among white immigrants and black migrants over access to space.

The second major period of urban unrest, which took place during the mid- to late 1960s, was preceded by an exodus of white ethnics from their immigrant urban enclaves to surrounding suburban communities. This wave of "white flight" gave rise to the presence of new black residential majorities in the inner city. These new black majorities in places like Newark and Detroit sought access to political and economic power, but despite the changing demographics of the cities, institutional control remained in the hands of the whites. The disparity between the rising number of African Americans in the city and continuing white political and economic domination fostered mutual hostility among black customers and white merchants and led to overt clashes between black civilians and the police. In both Newark and Detroit, as well as other places such as Watts, the arrest and beating of black citizens by white police sparked several days of unrest marked by the destruction of white-owned property and the deaths of numerous black civilians at the hands of police and military personnel.

The third major period of urban unrest, which took place during the 1980s and 1990s, also corresponded to dramatic demographic changes. During this period there was a general shift in the U.S. population away from the "rustbelt" cities of the Midwest and Northeast to the "sunbelt" cities of the South and Southwest. This regional shift was accompanied by a new wave of immigrants from Latin America, Asia, and the Caribbean who settled in gateway cities such as Miami and Los Angeles. In those cities, residents of black communities that had become established in the 1950s and 1960s perceived the new immigrants as a threat to their fragile economic and political status. Industries that had once provided stable employment for many working-class blacks, such as hotels and restaurants, janitorial services, and garment manufacturing, were now increasingly occupied by foreign-born workers. Furthermore, as the recent immigrants became politically organized, they captured seats on city councils and other positions in city government, thereby reducing the power and influence of black voters. Ironically, African Americans, who at one time had been the targets of backlash violence at the hands of white immigrants, now sought to protect their hard-won gains against the most recent Latino and Asian immigrants. What began as protests against police abuse soon transformed into violent struggles between newcomers and natives.

Despite variation in the backgrounds of the principal combatants and the precipitating incidents that sparked individual episodes of urban unrest, a certain trend seems evident in all of the case studies presented earlier. In these six cases drawn from three distinct historical periods, riot-related violence appears to be associated with rapid changes in the ethnic composition of city neighborhoods. To test such a proposition, I will compare the results of analyses presented earlier as part of the preceding chapters. In drawing comparisons among these events from different places and time periods, I intend to lay the groundwork for a general explanatory model of urban ethnic violence. Before offering specific policy recommendations, I think it is imperative once more to address competing theoretical explanations for the origins of urban ethnic unrest. I will do so in light of the historical and statistical evidence presented in Chapters 3–5.

ECONOMIC DEPRIVATION AND RACIAL/ETHNIC SEGREGATION

As mentioned in Chapter 1, a common theoretical explanation for ethnic collective violence involves economic deprivation. Poverty and unemployment are hypothesized to give rise to frustration and resentment among those who are facing economic adversity. Such resentment then serves as a motivating factor for those who engage in rioting.

The statistical and historical analyses presented present mixed evidence for this perspective. In five of the six cases—Detroit (1943 and 1967), Newark (1967), Miami (1980), and Los Angeles (1992)—GIS mapping and difference of means statistical tests suggests that census tracts where violence took place had relatively high rates of male unemployment and low levels of median household income. Looking at Figures 3.8 and 3.9 (Detroit 1943), 4.4 and 4.5 (Newark 1967), 4.9 and 4.10 (Detroit 1967), 5.4 and 5.5 (Miami 1980), and 5.10 and 5.11 (Los Angeles 1992), it is clear that the many of the riot-related fatalities took place in neighborhoods where household incomes were low and rates of male unemployment were high. The one exception is Chicago (1919), where male unemployment was based on all males who were ten years of age or older, as opposed to age eighteen and above in all the other cases. Income measures were not available for census tracts in Chicago during that period. Yet when entered into multiple regression models (Poisson and spatial linear regression) that control for ethnic composition, the power of economic deprivation measures as predictors of the severity of violence is diminished in all six cases, although the effects of unemployment and income on riot violence seldom disappeared entirely.

Historical evidence offers more clear support for the economic deprivation hypothesis. In all six cases that I investigated, problems of overcrowded and dilapidated housing, poverty, and unemployment were present. In post–World War I Chicago, poverty and unemployment was concentrated among African Americans who lived in the black belt along south State Street and in the adjacent white ethnic neighborhoods "back of the yards." According to a myriad of historical studies, including Philpott (1978) and Grossman (1989), these neighborhoods suffered from both physical deterioration and social disorganization, which, in turn, gave rise to crime and delinquency. In Detroit's predominantly black Paradise Valley and in the adjacent white enclave on the other side of Woodward Avenue, black migrants and white immigrants alike lived in deplorable conditions, packed into tenement flats, some without heat or hot water. In these close quarters, illnesses like typhoid fever and tuberculosis spread rapidly among residents and infant mortality was common. With unemployment and poverty at high levels in the community, crime and vice were also prevalent. It is not surprising that both the Chicago riot of 1919 and the Detroit riot of 1943 erupted from such environs.

With the demolition of Paradise Valley in the 1950s and the subsequent construction of Interstate 75, black people in Detroit were displaced from east to west, moving several miles from Black Bottom to 12th Street. Twelfth Street, once a solidly Jewish middle-class neighborhood, experienced a rapid influx of poor blacks. With this influx came problems of gambling, alcoholism, and prostitution. In less than two decades, 12th Street had become a black slum. By 1967, the area seemed ripe for a riot. Similarly, in Newark's Central Ward, "urban renewal" combined with continuing black migration from the South to create a segregated and economically deprived community (Fullilove 2004). As chronicled in Nathan C. Heard's 1968 novel *Howard Street* and documented in George Sternlieb's study *The Tenement Landlord* (1969), Newark's Central Ward, like Detroit's 12th Street neighborhood, was beset by substandard housing, unemployment, and social disorder. When rioting broke out in July 1967, the Central Ward became the epicenter of unrest.

Years later, when civil disorders erupted in Miami and Los Angeles, once again rioting originated in the respective cities' most impoverished communities, Liberty City and South Central. During the 1950s, Miami's Liberty City neighborhood was advertised as a peaceful haven for prospective black homeowners. Over time, however, middle-class blacks, like whites before them, relocated to the suburbs. This community then began a long decline into poverty and despair, which resulted in rioting during the summer of 1968. By 1980, little had changed, with one notable exception. An island of concentrated black poverty, Liberty City found itself surrounded by more economically mobile immigrants—Haitians to the east and Cubans to the south. In May 1980, a group of white and Latino police officers were acquitted in the murder of a black insurance salesman. This acquittal set the stage for another riot, once again centered in Liberty City.

By 1992, one could describe the South Central and Compton neighborhoods of Los Angeles in similar terms. Middle-class flight and deindustrialization that had begun in the early 1960s reduced South Central to a shadow of its 1940s and 1950s glory days. As with Liberty City, South Central directly experienced the effects of urban unrest during the 1960s, which led to accelerating disinvestment in the community. When Latino immigrants arrived in large numbers during the 1980s, their presence exacerbated conditions of unemployment and overcrowding in the neighborhoods. This, in turn, gave rise to escalating rates of violent crime. Gangs, organized along ethnic lines, fought against one another for control of territory as the drug trade provided a means of employment for many young black and Latino men. Operation Hammer, a police operation that involved nighttime raids on the homes of suspected drug dealers, led to accusations of police brutality, fostering mutual mistrust between the police and local residents. In this cauldron of despair, on the corner of Florence and Normandie Avenues, rioting broke out on April 28, 1992. Once more, riot violence originated in a city's poorest neighborhood.

The combination of statistical, geographical, and historical evidence presented above suggests a link between economic deprivation and urban unrest that took place in American cities during the twentieth century. Yet, statistically speaking, the power of economic indicators is outweighed by measures of racial/ethnic composition and change.

It is apparent that racial segregation also played a critical role in the origins of urban unrest. In Chicago's black belt, Detroit's Paradise Valley and 12 Street, Newark's Central Ward, Miami's Liberty City, and South Central Los Angeles it is evident that economic deprivation and the concentration of minority population went hand in hand. The impoverished neighborhoods where riots occurred during the turbulent twentieth century were mostly inhabited by black people. These neighborhoods not only concentrated African Americans within their borders, but denied blacks access to better jobs, housing, and schooling opportunities in adjacent white communities. As Massey and Denton state in their book *American Apartheid* (1993), such segregation has negative consequences for the health, education, and economic status of African Americans:

> Deleterious neighborhood conditions are built into the structure of the black community. They occur because segregation concentrates poverty to build a set of mutually reinforcing and self-feeding spirals of decline into black neighborhoods. When economic dislocations deprive a segregated group of employment and increase its rate of poverty, socio-economic deprivation inevitably becomes more concentrated in neighborhoods where that group lives. The damaging social consequences that follow from increased poverty are spatially concentrated as well, creating uniquely disadvantaged environments that become progressively isolated—geographically, socially, and economically-from the rest of society. (1993:2)

It is the contention of scholars like Peterson and Krivo (1993) that high levels of black/white segregation leads to increased rates of homicidal violence in spatially and socially isolated black communities. Exclusion from opportunities for economic and social advancement may have fostered resentment that set the stage for both routine and riot-related violence in the highly segregated black neighborhoods of Chicago, Detroit, Newark, Los Angeles, and Miami.

Statisticians and demographers may note that it is nearly impossible to compute measures of segregation at a neighborhood or census tract level. Standard measures of segregation such as the Index of Dissimilarity or Isolation Index are compiled at the city or MSA level by aggregating census tract level data. Nonetheless, for purposes of the present study, I feel that the percentage of black residents in a census tract is a good proxy for racial segregation. A neighborhood where more than 80 percent of the residents are black is obviously segregated and subject to the pernicious effects of racial isolation. Therefore I am not hesitant to use percent black as a measure of segregation at the tract level.

Looking across all six cases of urban unrest, Chicago (1919), Detroit (1943), Detroit (1967), Newark (1967), Miami (1980), and Los Angeles (1992), the presence of riot-related violence in a census tract was strongly correlated with the relative size of its black population (percent black).

This relationship remained statistically significant when controlling for economic factors such as male unemployment and median household income. This relationship also held for the absolute number of black residents in a tract. The analysis therefore confirms Spilerman's (1970, 1971) claim that a significant amount of the variation in riot violence from one place to the next is explained by the size of the local black population.

The GIS maps presented in Figures 3.2 (Chicago 1919), 3.6 (Detroit 1943), 4.2 (Newark 1967), 4.7 (Detroit 1967), 5.2 (Miami 1980), and 5.6 (Los Angeles 1992) all show a clear visual correspondence between the location of riot fatalities and high levels of black population. Segregation, it seems, is a critical factor in the explaining the origins and locus of urban racial unrest.

Taken together, racial segregation and economic deprivation appear to have had a profound impact on increasing the potential for ethnic collective violence. Rather than treating each factor separately, I decided to look at the interaction of these two variables on the presence of riot violence/fatalities. For both Chicago (1919) and Miami (1980), the interaction of male unemployment and percent black was positive and significant. This indicates that increased levels of unemployment exacerbated the effect of racial segregation in these two cities. Similar results, however, were not obtained for the other four cities. This may be a result of multicollinearity, a statistical problem commonly encountered in regression models where several variables within the model are correlated with one another. This is particularly problematic when working with smaller-scale units of analysis such as census tracts where demographic factors and economic factors such as percent black and unemployment are often intertwined.

In the four remaining cases, Detroit (1943, 1967), Newark (1967), and Los Angeles (1992), the census tract level measures of percent black and unemployment were so strongly related to one another that it is hard to gauge their interactive effects. While both segregation and unemployment increased the likelihood of violence in neighborhoods within these cities, both variables, when included in a multiple regression model at the tract level, seem to be capturing the same underlying construct. Racial segregation and economic deprivation in these cities are thus inextricably linked and their effects on neighborhood-based ethnic violence are thus inseparable. A spatial overlay using GIS mapping software indicates that tracts both heavily black in composition and characterized by low levels of median household income contained a clear majority of the riot-related fatalities in at least five of the six cases studied. I therefore conclude that both segregation and economic deprivation increase the likelihood of a neighborhood to be touched by violence if a riot breaks out in the city. Poor, highly segregated neighborhoods are more susceptible than other kinds of neighborhoods to violence associated with urban rioting.

As noted previously, Spilerman (1970, 1971) found that only the size of the black population had a significant impact on the frequency and severity of riot activity. Faced with the problem of multicolinearity in our regression models, we should not be so quick to rule out the impact of variables besides percent black on the presence or intensity of riot violence. Furthermore, although there is a general association between the size of a tract's black population and the presence of riot fatalities, we should not assume that this association is tantamount to causation. Spilerman argues that all that is necessary for rioting to occur is a critical mass of aggrieved blacks. I find such an explanation inherently unsatisfying. To understand the origins of urban unrest, we must go beyond static measures of population and examine the dynamic processes by which population change influences riot related violence.

DEMOGRAPHIC CHANGE AND ETHNIC SUCCESSION

Over the course of the twentieth century, population change has had a profound impact on the relationship among different racial/ethnic groups in American cities and urban neighborhoods. During the period 1900–1910, a record number of immigrants entered the U.S., mostly from Central and Eastern Europe, as well as a large number from Ireland. After processing at entry points like Ellis Island, many of these immigrants boarded trains bound for the industrial centers of the Midwest. Factories were booming and jobs were plentiful. For industrial capitalists, immigration was a ready source of inexpensive labor. Having arrived in places like Chicago and Detroit, the new immigrants linked up with their countrymen and built ethnic enclaves anchored by churches, synagogues, and saloons. The following decade, during World War I, immigration from abroad was curtailed and employers began to look elsewhere for sources of cheap labor. They looked to the South, encouraging Southern blacks to move northward and take jobs in the factories. Thus began the Great Migration, which brought nearly two million African-American migrants from the South to the North within a span of twenty years. From 1920 to 1940, the black population of cities like Chicago, Detroit, and Newark more than doubled. Black migrants were, at first, largely confined to segregated "black belt" neighborhoods, but as their population increased, they began to spill over the borders of these districts. With immigration from abroad and migration from the South, the population of these cities swelled. Chicago, Detroit, and Newark all reached their peak population levels in the 1930s and 1940s. The combination of white immigrants and black migrants, while good for big business, soon became a recipe for conflict. Shortages of affordable housing and period layoffs in the factories pitted white immigrants and black migrants against one another in a battle for housing, jobs, and space.

From a statistical standpoint, in Chicago (1919) and Detroit (1943), the changing proportional size of the black population was a significant factor in predicting where riot violence occurred. Census tracts that had a proportionately greater increase in the size of their black population relative to other tracts/neighborhoods were more likely to be touched by riot-related violence. In these riots, violence at the neighborhood level was clearly associated with black in-migration and white out-migration. The observation of such effects persists when controlling for the relative size of the black population in these cities' neighborhoods. As black population moved from highly segregated ghetto neighborhoods into surrounding white immigrant communities, whites sought to hold the line against this perceived invasion, employing violence as a means of preventing further residential change. The GIS maps displayed in Figures 3.1–3.3 and 3.5–3.7 show how the expansion of black population into nearby white enclaves was associated with the location of riot violence in both Chicago and Detroit. The preponderance of riot fatalities took place in neighborhoods where the black population had increased by 20 percent or more between 1910 and 1920 in Chicago and between 1940 and 1950 in Detroit.

By the 1950s, when a second wave of black migrants arrived from the South, white resistance to racial integration began to take another form. Rather than attempting to "hold the line" against black in-migration through violence and intimidation, whites began to flee from their old ethnic enclaves. Taking advantage of federally subsidized mortgages and newly constructed highways, they sought to put geographic distance between themselves and the rising population of African Americans in the cities. As a result, for the first time, Northern cities like Newark and Detroit attained a black majority of residents.

Yet, despite this massive demographic shift, African Americans still lacked access to political and economic power in these cities. While entire neighborhoods like Detroit's 12th Street and Newark's Central Ward shifted from white to black residential majorities, business ownership remained in the hands of Jewish merchants and political power resided largely with predominantly Irish and Italian political officials and police. This incomplete succession set off another wave of urban unrest in American cities. Unrest in Newark and Detroit that took place during the summer of 1967, like the episodes of civil disorder that had occurred decades earlier, was centered in neighborhoods that had undergone rapid demographic transition. Statistically and geographically speaking, the greater the change in the racial/ethnic composition of census tracts in Newark and Detroit, the greater the likelihood was for violence to occur in those neighborhoods. As the GIS maps displayed in Figures 4.1–4.3 and 4.6–4.8 indicate, the majority of deaths attributed to the rioting in Newark and Detroit during the summer of 1967, like the fatalities associated with the Chicago and Detroit riots earlier in the century, occurred in neighborhoods where the black population had increased and the white population had decreased by 20 percent or more over the preceding decades. According to this analysis, the riots that took place during the 1960s and riots that occurred during and immediately after the World Wars share a common feature. During both of these historical periods, the process of ethnic succession played a key role in predicting the location of riot-related violence within the cities that had experience unrest.

During the 1970s, these cities elected black mayors and city councilpersons. Black businessmen then began to make inroads to economic power. The ethnic succession process involving the replacement of white elites by African-American elites had come full circle. Yet by the 1980s, a new demographic trend emerged. People began moving from the rustbelt cities of the Northeast and Midwest to the sunbelt cities of the South and Southwest. Cities such as Miami and Los Angeles attracted large waves of migrants from other U.S. regions as well as immigrants from abroad. With this demographic shift, the locus of rioting moved to these new destinations.

At the neighborhood level, the arrival of immigrants, primarily from Latin America (Miami and Los Angeles) and Asia (Los Angeles), was accompanied by the out-migration of native-born whites (Miami) and native-born blacks (Los Angeles). In Miami, by 1980, new Latino immigrants had already established their own enclaves in neighborhoods previously inhabited by Anglos. In 1980, when it became known that a new wave of Cuban immigrants would be arriving shortly, black Miamians began to fear that these new Cuban immigrants would "invade" their neighborhoods. Meanwhile, in Los Angeles, between 1980 and 1990, a new wave of Mexican and Central American immigrants entered the city. These immigrants gravitated toward previously African American enclaves in South Central Los Angeles, Compton, and Watts. As noted in Chapter 5, within just one decade South Central was transformed from a predominantly black neighborhood to a mixed Latino and black neighborhood. Niche overlap in housing and job markets led to overt tensions between blacks and Latinos competing for jobs and space. Ethnic competition and succession theories would suggest that competitive pressures resulting from rapid demographic change gave rise to ethnic violence that took place during the 1992 Los Angeles riot and the 1980 Miami riot.

Statistical and GIS analysis supports the claim that ethnic succession was associated with riot violence in Los Angeles. A preponderance of the riot-related deaths and property damage occurred in the neighborhoods where the black and Hispanic populations overlapped. Increases of more than 20 percent in Latino population and decreases of more than 20 percent in the black population of census tracts were associated with an increased potential for violence at the neighborhood level. These statistical associations remained significant when controlling for economic indicators (percent males unemployed and median household income) as well as percent black. In Miami, the statistical evidence was less supportive of the ethnic succession hypothesis. Neither the change in percent Latino or the change in percent black was associated with riot violence at the tract level.

As I suggested in Chapter 5, this finding reflects the fact that Cuban immigrants were not moving into black neighborhoods in Miami. Nonetheless, survey data collected in Miami suggests that blacks feared that the new wave of immigrants would compete with them for the scarce supply of affordable housing (U.S Commission on Civil Rights 1982:23). As Ladner et al. (1982) indicate, the perception of competition for housing was a powerful factor in provoking black Miamians to engage in violence again the new Latino immigrants.

DEMOGRAPHIC CHANGE AND ETHNIC COMPETITION

Olzak hypothesizes that riots are most likely to occur during periods of job scarcity combined with increased immigration/migration. To test this notion, I computed a statistic that measured the interaction of male unemployment and change in percent black (for periods when black migration was occurring) or change in percent foreign born (for periods when immigration was taking place) on the presence of riot violence. I also computed a similar statistic that measured the interaction of housing density (persons/dwellings) and change in percent black or change in percent foreign born.

In four of the six cases there were significant interaction effects of change in percent black or change in percent foreign-born with unemployment and housing density. For both Chicago (1919) and Detroit (1943), the interaction of change in percent black and percent unemployed increased the effect of percent black on the severity of riot violence. In those cities higher unemployment rates at the tract level increased the effect of changing racial composition in fostering riot violence. By contrast, for Miami (1980) and Los Angeles (1992) the interaction of change in percent black and unemployment was not statistically significant. However, in these two cities, the interaction of change in percent black and housing density did significantly enhance the effect of racial/ethnic change on the likelihood of violence taking place at the tract level. This implies that the riots that took place earlier in the century were spurred by competition for jobs and that the episodes of urban unrest that occurred toward the end of the century were fueled primarily by competition for housing. The historical evidence, however, suggests that both housing and job competition were key factors leading to interethnic violence during all three historical periods (1916–1919/1941–1945, 1964–1968, and 1980–1992).

At the turn of the century, white immigrants working in the steel, meatpacking, automotive, and defense industries battled black migrants whom they saw as a potent threat to their relatively privileged economic position. In many cases, black workers were categorically banned from union membership. White union members sought to exclude black workers from the factories on the assumption that the presence of black workers would depress their wages. Labor strikes in Chicago and Detroit therefore took on racial overtones, especially when black workers were employed as strikebreakers. During the first half of the century, strikes often served as precursors to large-scale rioting.

By mid-century, white-dominated labor unions reluctantly admitted blacks as members in several manufacturing industries, including the automobile and steel industries. This change occurred in part as a precondition of government recognition of the right to collective bargaining. Yet some trades, such as the construction industry, remained highly segregated. Due to seniority rules and blatant discrimination, relatively few black rose to the top positions within the "integrated" defense and automobile industries. Nonetheless, as a result of industrial expansion, African Americans seemed to benefit from their concentration in the manufacturing sector. By the 1960s, however, the manufacturing sector had begun to decline. As the industrial labor market contracted and manufacturing jobs were exported overseas, labor competition once again heated up. The continued relocation of black migrants in search of industrial employment to cities such as Newark and Detroit intensified this competition. As shown statistically, the interaction of continued black migration and unemployment (due to industrial decline) had a significant effect on the level of collective ethnic violence in Newark and Detroit neighborhoods. Higher unemployment rates increased the effect of black in-migration on the propensity for riot activity to occur.

In Newark and Detroit, there is also evidence that political competition contributed to violence. In Newark, Mayor Hugh Addonizio's administration excluded African Americans from top leadership positions, for example by passing over a qualified black applicant for school board secretary and instead appointing a political crony with a high school education. In Detroit, despite the promotion of several African Americans to positions within Mayor Jerome Cavanagh's administration, blacks were still underrepresented in the city council. In fact, before the 1965 election, there were no black council members (Fine 1989:22). Surveys taken in both Newark and Detroit suggest that blacks in those cities found city government unresponsive to their needs (*Detroit Free Press* 1968; Governor's Select Commission on Civil Disorders 1968:55).

Ethnic competition for economic status and political power also played a key role in the Miami and Los Angeles riots in the latter part of the century. As mentioned in Chapter 5, the entry of immigrant workers into particular occupation niches, such as the janitorial and garments industries (Los Angeles) or the hotel/restaurant industry (Miami), was associated with a decline in the number of black employees in these industries. It is clear that ethnic succession occurred in these occupations and that such changes fostered resentment among African Americans toward their Latino counterparts (Portes and Stepick 1993; Piatt 1997; U.S Commission on Civil Rights 1982).

Over the past three decades, Latinos in Miami and Los Angeles made remarkable political gains, electing a Cuban mayor in Miami and Latino city councilperson in Los Angeles. Given the continued growth of the Latino population in Los Angeles, which has surpassed that of the local black population, one might expect more political contention to result in the near future as Latinos become a more organized political force (Piatt 1997). Political competition, as well as competition for jobs and housing, played a central role in fomenting urban unrest in both Miami and Los Angeles during the latter decades of the twentieth century as well as the episodes of collective violence that took place during the 1960s.

SUMMARIZING THE FINDINGS

Looking comparatively at all six cases of urban unrest in this study, it is evident that demographic change or the prospect of demographic change played a critical role in creating the conditions under which violence flourished. To be more specific, waves of black migration and Latino immigration led to the rapid turnover of the population of neighborhoods in at least five of the six cases, which caused tensions to flourish between newcomers and natives. In all six cases, this neighborhood-level change was accompanied by competition among racial/ethnic groups for jobs and political power at both the neighborhood and city level. It is more than the mere presence of black people or other ethnic minorities that predicts where riot violence is most likely to occur. Rather, it is the combination of changes in the racial/ethnic composition of neighborhoods and competition for jobs and political power at the city level that gave rise to deadly ethnic violence in American cities throughout the twentieth century.

As the present study shows, when urban unrest does occur in a city, riot activity tends to cluster in particular places rather than spread uniformly throughout the city. Despite the presence of some job competition and political contention at the city level, it is at the neighborhood level, where the deadly ethnic violence is manifested. As Katznelson (1981) argued, race and class conflict may be generated in the workplace or at the polls, but is ultimately expressed in the "city trenches" of local neighborhoods. Therefore, if we aspire to reduce the potential for future outbreaks of ethnic violence, we should focus our attention on the demographic and economic characteristics of neighborhoods. Some neighborhoods are clearly more susceptible to urban unrest than others based on their demographic and economic profile.

A PROFILE OF THE RIOT PRONE NEIGHBORHOOD

In recent years, due to abuses of police authority, particularly involving traffic stops, the term "profiling" has taken on a negative connotation. Typically preceded by the word "racial," profiling has come to be associated with the violation of minorities' civil rights by police. Racially biased police practices, such as routinely stopping black motorists on suspicion of drug trafficking, have generated legitimate criticism of and lawsuits against police in several states and cities. Yet the concept of profiling itself, applying selective attention to people or places that are statistically associated with certain kinds of crimes, is a widely accepted practice and is a fundamental part of policing. In recent years, stung by accusations of racial profiling, police have begun to pay more attention to matters of place rather than targeting particular kinds of people. Geographic Information Systems (GIS) analysis has enabled police commanders to "geocode" or map the addresses of crimes over a particular time period and plan policing strategies accordingly. Rather than driving around randomly, they are able to target their efforts toward locations where a preponderance of crimes have occurred and thereby disrupt the "routine activities" of criminals. Programs like CompStat have made a significant difference in reducing crime in cities such as New York and Newark. Sensitivity to issues of place, I believe, may play a similar role in helping to curtail rioting or at least moderating riot intensity.

The theoretical insights and new methodological techniques examined in the present study, including the use of GIS software, can and should be applied to the task of generating a profile of the riot-prone neighborhood. Having reviewed the statistical and historical data for these six cases of urban unrest, it is apparent that riot violence cannot be reduced to one factor alone, but is a product of multiple factors that interact with one another and are thus difficult to disentangle. Chief among these factors in robustness are black population size and changes in the relative size of in-migrant and out-migrant groups. Like Spilerman (1970, 1971), I predict that predominantly black neighborhoods are most at risk.

Yet one should not stop there. While there is a statistically significant relationship between the size of a tract's black population and its potential for unrest, there are other factors that are equally worthy of consideration, such as population change. As is evident from the case studies presented in this volume, riot violence is associated with communities undergoing racial change. For example, during the 1992 Los Angeles riot, violence did not take place to any significant extent in stable black and Latino neighborhoods. East Los Angeles, a predominantly Latino enclave, was largely untouched by violence. Rather, riot-related activity was most likely to take place in the transitional neighborhoods such as South Central Los Angeles and Compton, where as a result of recent Latino immigration, neither blacks nor Latinos had a clear majority (Bergesen and Herman 1998).

To be certain, these neighborhoods where riot violence was concentrated did have significantly higher black populations than some other nonriot neighborhoods, but they were also in the midst of demographic flux. African Americans were moving out and Latinos were moving in.

With the exception of Miami (1980), the most riot-prone neighborhoods in the cities under investigation were those that had both significant black populations and had experienced fundamental changes in racial composition in the years preceding the riot event. Such neighborhoods, as noted in the preceding section on economic deprivation, also tended to be characterized by poverty and/or high rates of unemployment. Thus, in seeking to generate a profile of the riot-prone neighborhoods in a city, I argue that we should look for the signature combination of a sizable black population, rapid demographic change, and economic despair. Putting these three factors (segregation, poverty, and ethnic succession) together suggests that we can focus our efforts to avert rioting toward neighborhoods with sizable African American populations that are experiencing an influx of immigrants or migrants under conditions of poverty and high unemployment.

CULTURE AND COMMUNITY

Although I have attempted to specify a profile of the riot-prone neighborhood, I have not yet addressed how riot violence can be averted. Thus far I have only explored the relationship among several variables that are associated with riot violence. I have not provided an explanatory mechanism to determine why some places with similar demographic profiles have been marked by violence and others have not. I will thereby add a corollary proposition to my previous claims. Rioting is most likely to occur when there is a strong sense of cultural difference among newcomers and natives. Given the presence of rapid demographic change, conflict is particularly acute when ethnic/racial groups establish claims to territory on the basis of cultural difference and are later challenged by the arrival of new groups.

During the first half of the twentieth century in Chicago and Detroit, the Irish, Italians, Poles, and Eastern European Jews all engaged in the construction of communities by building community institutions: churches, synagogues, saloons, beer gardens, barber and beauty shops, etc. These were the places where gossip was exchanged, deals were brokered, and jobs proffered. These institutions, like the neighborhoods they were located in, were distinctly ethnic. Parish boundaries divided the enclaves into separate but contiguous social worlds. The movement of African Americans into these neighborhoods was seen as a threat, triggering fears that the communal culture of the area would change along with its inhabitants (McGreavey 1996). To the extent that these white ethnics saw black migrants as culturally alien and inferior to themselves, their resistance to neighborhood change stiffened and competition among these groups for space and jobs took on a more violent aspect.

During the 1950s and 1960s, as whites fled from the inner-city neighborhoods of Newark and Detroit, blacks continued to build their own businesses, churches, and social clubs. Imbued with the rhetoric of the Civil Rights Movement as well as the militant black power movement's call for black self-determination, they sought to take charge of their own communities, demanding access to political power and community control of schools. Through the use of Community Action Program (CAP) grants, the federal government encouraged such efforts to empower black residents. Yet, despite the support of the federal government for local efforts in participatory democracy, the growing empowerment of African Americans was resisted by the largely white membership of the local teacher's unions and by city officials who felt that such programs would create an oppositional power base. Furthermore, some local African-American leaders, such as Albert Cleage in Detroit and LeRoi Jones in Newark, did not want to share power with whites. For them, the term "community control," first coined by the Ford Foundation to refer to power-sharing arrangements between school boards and local communities, meant total control of all institutions in the black community by black people. Thus, each group, rather than sharing power, mobilized their own constituents. Such polarization, I argue, was both a cause and, later, a symptom of rioting. At the time, few crosscutting social ties existed among white and black citizens to prevent interethnic conflict from transforming into violence.

During the 1980s and 1990s, a similar lack of communication and cooperation among different racial/ethnic groups was evident in Miami and Los Angeles. Both cities had recently experienced a new wave of immigration, and many of these new arrivals found themselves embroiled in conflicts with their African American and white neighbors. In South Central Los Angeles and Liberty City, Miami, African Americans worked hard to establish a sense of community power, yet in both places recent immigrants from Latin America and Asia began to assert their own claims to economic and political power. As Mexicans moved into the formerly black enclave of South Central and Cubans moved into downtown Miami, these immigrants brought with them their own language, politics, and religion. For African American in these places, the neighborhoods were no longer exclusively "theirs," and in the face of the new immigration, blacks felt that once again they would have to fight for respect. For their part, many Latino immigrants readily absorbed American racism and in the process of interacting with African American came to view them as their chief competitors.

The mechanisms by which ethnic succession leads to ethnic collective violence must therefore be more clearly delineated. Ethnic succession generates the potential for riot violence when members of one group that has dominated a neighborhood and built its own community institutions feels threatened by the arrival of members of new group members who are equally intent on building their own institutions that reflect their culture. This is not simply a matter of objective competition for resources, because ethnic competition is itself socially constructed. Competition is a product of a particular kind of interaction among groups. For groups to compete with one another, they must first come to see one another as culturally different. This suggests that groups need not perceive one another as competitors but may work together cooperatively if they are provided with common goals and/or interdependent interests.

BUILDING COMMUNITY TO PREEMPT VIOLENCE

Given the potential for rapid demographic change to create competition and conflict among difference racial/ethnic groups, we need to investigate the cultural basis of conflict and realize how building community institutions may alleviate notions of cultural difference. Borrowing from the recent work of Ashutosh Varshney (2002), I propose that in order to alleviate the potential for future episodes of unrest in our cities we must attempt to bridge the cultural differences among natives and newcomers. According to Varshney, the most effective means of bridging cultural difference is to create crosscutting associational ties among members of the two groups.

As Varshney suggests, when members of two or more competing groups share institutional or associational ties, for example, as members of the same business association, labor union, or neighborhood association, such ties may foster intergroup dialogue and prevent cultural misunderstandings that lead to violence. With these ties comes mutual interdependence, raising the stakes to the point where violence would be equally destructive to the interests of all parties. Varshney makes this case with respect to Hindus and Muslims in India, finding that where Muslims and Hindus share civic ties the likelihood of mass ethnic violence diminishes. Cities such as Ahmedabad, which experienced multiple riots of great intensity, lacked institutional mechanisms to bridge ethnic/religious group membership. By contrast, cities such as Surat, where Muslims and Hindus built strong associational ties (e.g., multiethnic trade unions and neighborhood peace committees), remained relatively quiet during the peak days of Hindu-Muslim conflict following the destruction of the mosque at Ayodha.

> Hindu and Muslim businessmen who had worked together for years were able to call on each other's time, contacts and goodwill. They took it upon themselves to quash rumors. They would investigate quickly whether a temple or mosque had indeed been attacked, women assaulted or raped, houses or shops burned. They would tell communities in their neighborhoods how false the rumors were and would also inform the local administration of the likely trouble spots and potential trouble makers. Many of the Hindu businessmen involved in

such peace committees were sympathizers of Hindu nationalism but they were unwilling to break their age-old business connections for the sake of a political benefit. For some, the issue of protecting the life of neighbors or colleagues was moral. For others, the concerns were more mundane but equally effective. They were simply not ready to risk disruptions in business. Hindus and Muslims are too tightly integrated into the city's economic life. (Varshney 2002:259)

Applying these insights from India to the American context, I argue that we need to forge such crosscutting associational ties in urban neighborhoods at greatest risk for future violence. Using statistical modeling and GIS mapping, these neighborhoods can be readily identified. Having identified neighborhoods that meet the profile of those prone to ethnic conflict (neighborhoods with significant black population and poverty that are undergoing rapid demographic change), government, nonprofit, and corporate organizations should proactively intervene in these areas, creating programs that foster dialogue and economic interdependence among members of different racial/ethnic groups. To avoid future episodes of urban unrest we must build community. Only then can we hope to end the fighting in the streets.

REFERENCES

Abbot, Andrew. 1997. "Of Time and Space: The Contemporary Relevance of the Chicago School." *Social Forces* 75 (4):1149–1182.
Abu-Lughod, Janet. 1997. "Race Riots in Los Angeles, Chicago and New York." Unpublished Conference Paper. Annual Meeting of The American Sociological Association. Toronto, Canada
Abelmann, Nancy and John Lie. 1995. *Blue Dreams: Korean Americans and the Los Angeles Riots*. Cambridge, MA: Harvard University Press.
Abrahamson, Mark. 1996. *Urban Enclaves: Identity and Place in America*. New York: St. Martin's Press.
Agresti, Alan. 1996. *An Introduction to Categorical Data Analysis*. New York: John Wiley Publishers
Aldrich, John H. and Forrest D. Nelson. 1984. *Linear Probability, Logit and Probit Models*. Newbury Park, CA: Sage Publications.
Anselin, Luc. 1995. *SpaceStat Tutorial: A Workbook for Using SpaceStat in the Analysis of Spatial Data*. NCGIA, University of California, Santa Barbara, and Regional Research Institute, West Virginia University.
Baldassare, Mark., ed. 1994. *The Los Angeles Riots: Lessens for the Urban Future*. Boulder, CO: Westview Press.
Balkwell, James W. 1990. "Ethnic Inequality and the Rate of Homicide." *Social Forces* 69:53–70.
Banton, Michael P. 1983. *Racial and Ethnic Competition*. Cambridge, UK, and New York: Cambridge University Press.
Baron, Harold. 1969. "The Web of Urban Racism." In Louis L. Knowles and Kenneth Prewitt, eds., *Institutional Racism in America*. Englewood Cliffs, NJ: Prentice-Hall.
Barth, Frederik. 1969. *Ethnic Groups and Boundaries*. Boston: Little Brown.
Barth, Frederik. 1981. *Process and Form in Social Life*. Boston: Routledge.

Beck, E.M. and Stewart Tolnay. 1990. "The Killing Fields of the Deep South: The Market for Cotton and the Lynching of Blacks, 1882–1930." *American Sociological Review* 55:526–539.

Bergesen, Albert. 1980. "Official Violence during the Watts, Newark, and Detroit Race Riots of the 1960s." In Pat Lauderdale, ed., *A Political Analysis of Deviance*. Minneapolis: University of Minnesota Press.

Bergesen, Albert. 1982. "Race Riots of 1967: An Analysis of Police Violence in Detroit and Newark." *Journal of Black Studies* 12 (March):261–274.

Bergesen, Albert and Max A. Herman. 1998. "Immigration, Race, and Riot: The 1992 Los Angeles Uprising." *American Sociological Review* 63:39–54.

Blalock, Hubert M. 1967. *Towards a Theory of Minority-Group Relations*. New York: Capricorn Books.

Blau, Judith R. and Peter M. Blau. 1982. "The Cost of Inequality: Metropolitan Structure and Violent Crime." *American Sociological Review* 47:114–129.

Blauner, Robert. 1972. *Racial Oppression in America*. New York: Harper & Row.

Blumer, Herbert. 1955 "Race Prejudice as a Sense of Group Position." *Pacific Sociological Review* 1 (1):3–7.

Bonacich, Edna. 1972. "A Theory of Ethnic Antagonism: The Split Labor Market." *American Sociological Review* 37:547–559.

Bonacich, Edna. 1973. "A Theory of Middleman Minorities." *American Sociological Review* 38:583–594.

Bonacich, Edna. 1976. "Advanced Capitalism and Black/White Relations." *American Sociological Review* 41:31–51.

Botifol, Luis J. 1985. "How Miami's New Image Was Created." Occasional paper no. 1985-1, Institute for Inter-American Studies, University of Miami, Florida.

Burgess, Ernest W. 1932. *Census Data for the City of Chicago, 1920*. Chicago: University of Chicago Press.

Capeci, Dominic. 1984. *Race Relations in Wartime Detroit*. Philadelphia: Temple University Press.

Capeci, Dominic. 1985. "Black-Jewish Relations in Wartime Detroit: The Marsh, Loving, Wolf Surveys and the Race Riot of 1943." *Jewish Social Studies* 47:221–241.

Capeci, Dominic and Martha Wilkerson. 1991. *Layered Violence: The Detroit Rioters of 1943*. Jackson: University of Mississippi Press.

Caplan, Nathan S. and Jeffrey Paige. 1968 "A Study of Ghetto Rioters." *Scientific American*. 219: 15-21

Carmichael, Tom. Personal interview, June 21, 2002.

Chang, Edward T. and Russell Leong. 1993. *Los Angeles: Struggles toward Multi-Ethnic Community: Asian American, African American, and Latino Perspectives*. Seattle: University of Washington Press.

REFERENCES

Chernick, J., B. Indik, and George Sternlieb. 1967. *New Jersey Population and Labor Force Characteristics, Spring 1967.* Newark, NJ: Graduate School of Business, Rutgers University.

Chicago Commission on Race Relations. 1922, 1968. *The Negro in Chicago: A Study of Race Relations and a Race Riot in 1919.* Chicago: University of Chicago Press (1922). New York: Arno Press and The New York Times (1968).

Clark, Kenneth B. 1965. *Dark Ghetto: Dilemmas of Social Power.* New York: Harper Torchbooks.

Corzine, Jay, James Creech, and Lin Huff-Corzine. 1983. "Black Concentration and Lynchings in the South: Testing Blalock's Power-Threat Hypothesis." *Social Forces* 61 (3):775–796.

Corzine, Jay, Lin Huff-Corzine, and James Creech. 1988. "The Tenant Labor Market and Lynching in the South: A Test of the Split Labor Market Theory". *Sociological Quarterly* (58):261-278.

Cose, Ellis. 1993. *The Rage of a Privileged Class.* New York: Harper Collins.

Creech, James, Jay Corzine, and Lin Huff-Corzine. 1989. "Theory Testing and Lynching: Another Look at the Power Threat Hypothesis." *Social Forces* 67 (3):627–640.

Croucher, Sheila L. 1997. *Imagining Miami: Ethnic Politics in a Postmodern World.* Charlottesville: University of Virginia Press.

Darden, Joe T., Richard Hill, June Thomas, and Richard Thomas. 1987. *Detroit: Race and Uneven Development.* Philadelphia: Temple University Press.

Davies, James C. 1971. *When Men Revolt and Why: A Reader in Political Violence and Revolution.* New York: The Free Press.

Davis, Mike. 1993a. "Who Killed Los Angeles? Part Two: The Verdict is Given." *New Left Review* 199 (May–June):29–54.

Davis, Mike. 1993b. "Uprising and Repression in L.A.: An Interview with Mike Davis by the *CovertAction* Information Bulletin." In Robert Gooding-Williams, ed., *Reading Rodney King, Reading Urban Uprising.* New York: Routledge.

Detroit Free Press. 1968. "Return to 12th Street: A Follow-Up Survey of Attitudes of Detroit Negroes." October 7.

Deveare-Smith, Ann. 1993. *Fires in the Mirror: Crown Heights Brooklyn and Other Identities.* New York: Anchor Doubleday.

Dollard, John. 1949, 1957. *Caste and Class in a Southern Town.* Garden City, NY: Doubleday.

Domanick, Joe. 1996. "The Browning of Black L.A." *Los Angeles Magazine* May:74–79, 172.

Downes, Bryan T. 1968. "Social and Political Characteristics of Riot Cities: A Comparative Study." *Social Science Quarterly* 49 (December):504–520.

REFERENCES

Drinkard, Gerald. Personal interview, October 5, 2001.

Duncan, Otis Dudley and Beverly Duncan. 1957. *The Negro Population of Chicago: A Study of Residential Succession.* Chicago: University of Chicago Press.

Dunn, Marvin and Alex Stepick III. 1992. "Blacks in Miami." In Guillermo Grenier and Alex Stepick III, eds., *Miami Now!: Immigration, Ethnicity, and Social Change.* Gainseville: University Press of Florida.

Eisenman, Russell. 1995. "Is There Bias in the U.S. Law Enforcement?" *Journal of Social, Political and Economic Studies* 20 (2):229–240.

Eui-Young, Yu, ed. 1994. *Black-Korean Encounter: Toward Understanding and Alliance.* Claremont, CA: Regina Books.

Farley, Reynolds, Sheldon Danziger, and Harry J. Holzer. 2000. *Detroit Divided.* New York: Russell Sage.

Farrell, James T. 1938. *Studs Lonigan: A Trilogy.* New York: Modern Library.

Feagin, Joe R. and Harlen Hahn. 1973. *Ghetto Revolts; The Politics of Violence in American Cities.* New York: Macmillan.

Fine, Sidney. 1989. *Violence in the Model City.* Ann Arbor: University of Michigan Press.

Fogelson, Robert M. 1971. *Violence as Protest; A Study of Riots and Ghettos.* Garden City, NY: Doubleday.

Forbes, H. D. 1997. *Ethnic Conflict: Commerce, Culture, and the Contact Hypothesis.* New Haven, CT: Yale University Press.

Fullilove, Mindy Thompson. 2004. *Root Shock: How Tearing Up City Neighborhoods Hurts America and What Can We Do About It.* New York: Ballantine Books.

Governor's Dade County Citizens Commission 1980: The Report of the Governor's Dade County Citizens Commitee.

Governor's Select Commission on Civil Disorders. 1968. *Report for Action: An Investigation into the Causes and Events of the 1967 Newark Race Riots.* New York: Lemma Publishing.

Grant, David M., Melvin L. Oliver, and Angela D. James. 1996. "African Americans: Social and Economic Bifurcation." In Roger Waldinger and Mehdi Bozorgmehr, eds., *Ethnic Los Angeles.* New York: Russell Sage.

Grenier, Guillermo and Alex Stepick, eds. 1992. *Miami Now!: Immigration, Ethnicity, and Social Change.* Gainesville: University Press of Florida.

Grimshaw, Allen. 1969. "Urban Racial Violence in the United States: Changing Ecological Considerations." In Allen Grimshaw, ed., *Racial Violence in the United States.* Chicago: Aldine Publishing.

Grossman, James R. 1989, 1991. *Land of Hope: Chicago, Black Southerners and the Great Migration.* Chicago: University of Chicago Press.

Gurr, Ted Robert. 1970. Why Men Rebel. Princeton, NJ: Princeton University Press.

REFERENCES

Hahn, H. and Joe Feagin. 1970. "Riot Precipitating Police Practices." *Phylon* 31:183.

Halpern, Rick. 1997. *Down of the Killing Floor: Black and White Workers in Chicago's Packinghouses, 1904–54*. Chicago: University of Illinois Press.

Hanushek, Eric A. and John E. Jackson. 1977. *Statistical Methods for Social Scientists*. San Diego, CA: Academic Press.

Hayden, Tom. 1968 *Rebellion in Newark: Official Violence and Ghetto Response*. New York: Vintage Books.

Heard, Nathan C. 1968. *Howard Street: A Novel*. New York. Dial Press.

Hechter, Michael. 1975. *Internal Colonialism : The Celtic Fringe in British National Development, 1536–1966*. Berkeley: University of California Press.

Helmreich, William B. 1998. *The Enduring Community: The Jews of Newark and Metrowest*. New Bruswick, NJ: Transaction Publishers.

Herman, Max A. 1999. *Fighting in the Streets: Ethnic Succession and Urban Unrest in 20th Century America*. Doctoral dissertation, University of Arizona. Available from University Microfilms.

Hewitt, Ron. Personal interview, June 19, 2001.

Hirsch, Arnold. 1988. *Making the Second Ghetto: Race and Housing in Chicago*. Chicago: University of Chicago Press.

Hirschi, Travis. 1969. *Causes of Delinquency*. Berkeley, CA: University of California Press

Hofstadter, Richard and Michael Wallace, eds. 1970. *American Violence: A Documentary History*. New York: Alfred A. Knopf.

Hurt, Roosevelt. Personal interview, June 15, 2001.

Jaccard, James, Robert Turrisi, and Choi K. Wan. 1990. *Interaction Effects in Multiple Regression*. Newbury Park, CA: Sage Publications.

Jackson, Kenneth T. 1967. *The Ku Klux Klan in the City 1915–1930*. New York: Oxford University Press.

Janowitz, Morris. 1969 "Patterns of Collective Racial Violence." In Hugh Davis Graham and Tedd Robert Gurr, eds. *Violence in America: Historical and Comparative Perspectives*. New York: Signet Books.

Jiobu, Robert M. 1971. "City Characteristics, Differential Stratification, and the Occurrence of Interracial Violence." *Social Science Quarterly* 52 (3):508–520.

Kapsis, Robert. 1976. "Continuities in Delinquency and Riot Patterns in Black Residential Areas." *Social Problems* 23 (5):567–580.

Kapsis, Robert. 1978. "Residential Succession and Delinquency: A Test of Shaw and McKay's Theory of Cultural Transmission." *Criminology* 15 (4):459–486.

Kapsis, Robert, Jim Smith, Bruce Saunders, Paul Takagi, and Oscar Williams. 1970. *Reconstruction of a Riot: A Case Study of Community Tensions and Civil Disorder*. Waltham, MA: Brandeis University Press.

Katznelson, Ira. 1981. *City Trenches: Urban Politics and the Patterning of Class in the United States.* New York: Pantheon Books.

Kwong, Peter. 1992. "The First Multicultural Riots." In Don Hazen, ed. *Inside the L.A. Riots.* New York: Institute for Alternative Journalism.

Ladner, Robert A., Barry J. Schwartz, Sandra J. Roker, and Loretta S. Titterud. 1981. "The Miami Riots of 1980: Antecedent Conditions, Community Responses and Participant Characteristics." *Research in Social Movements, Conflict and Change* 4:171-214.

Land, Kenneth C. and Glenn Deane. 1992. "On the Large-Sample Estimation of Regression Models with Spatial- or Network-Effects Terms: A Two-Stage Least Squares Approach." *Sociological Methodology* 22:221-248.

Lee, Alfred McClung and Norman Daymond Humphrey. 1943. *Race Riot.* New York: Dryden Press.

Lemann, Nicholas. 1992. *The Promised Land: The Great Black Migration and How It Changed America.* New York: Vintage Books.

Lieberson, Stanley. 1980. *A Piece of the Pie: Blacks and White Immigrants Since 1880.* Berkeley: University of California Press.

Lieberson, Stanley and A. R. Silverman. 1965. "The Precipitants and Underlying Conditions of Race Riots." *American Sociological Review* 30:887-898.

Locke, Hubert G. 1969. *The Detroit Riot of 1967.* Detroit, MI: Wayne State University Press.

Lupsha, Peter A. 1968. "On Theories of Urban Violence." Paper presented at the 1968 Meeting of the American Political Science Association, Washington, D.C., September 2-7.

Massey, Douglas S. and Nancy A. Denton. 1993. *American Apartheid: Segregation and the Making of the Underclass.* Cambridge, MA: Harvard University Press.

McAdam, Doug. 1982. *Political Process and the Development of Black Insurgency, 1930-1970.* Chicago: University of Chicago Press.

McGreavey, John T. 1996. *Parish Boundaries: The Catholic Encounter with Race in the Twentieth Century Urban North.* Chicago: University of Chicago Press.

Miles, Jack. 1992. "Blacks vs. Browns: Immigration and the New American Dilemma." *The Atlantic* 270 (4/October):41-68.

Mohl, Raymond A. 1996. "Making the Second Ghetto in Metropolitan Miami 1940-1960." In Kenneth Goings, and Raymond Mohl, eds., *The New African American Urban History.* Thousand Oaks, CA: Sage Publications.

Moore, Charity and Jan Probst. "Not All Regressions are Linear or Logistic: Analysis of Count Data". Powerpoint Presentation Prepared for The South Carolina Health Research Center. Http://rhr.sph.sc.edu/Not%20all%20regressions%2010_20v3.ppt

Morenoff, Jeffrey D. and Robert J. Sampson. 1997. "Violent Crime and the Spatial Dynamics of Neighborhood Transition: Chicago 1970–1990." *Social Forces* 76 (1): 31–64.

Morrison, Peter A. and Ira S. Lowry. 1994. "A Riot of Color: The Demographic Setting." In Mark Baldassare, ed., *The Los Angeles Riots: Lessens for the Urban Future.* Boulder, CO: Westview Press.

Myers, Daniel J. 1997. "Race Rioting in the 1960s: An Event History Analysis of Local Conditions." *American Sociological Review* 62:94–112.

National Advisory Commission on Civil Disorders. 1968. Report of the National Advisory Commission on Civil Disorders.

National Commission on the Causes and Prevention of Violence. 1969. *Violence in America: Historical and Comparative Perspectives.* New York: Signet Books

Norman, Alex. 1994. "Resolving Inter-ethnic Conflicts between Non-Whites: The Search for a New Construct." In Eui-Young Yu, ed., *Black-Korean Encounter: Toward Understanding and Alliance.* Claremont, CA: Regina Books.

Odland, John. 1988. *Spatial Autocorrelation.* Newbury Park, CA: Sage Publications.

Oliver, Melvin, James H. Johnson Jr., and Walter C. Farrell Jr. 1993. "Anatomy of a Rebellion." In Robert Gooding-Williams, ed., *Reading Rodney King, Reading Urban Uprising.* New York: Routledge.

Olzak, Susan. 1992. *The Dynamics of Ethnic Competition and Conflict.* Stanford, CA: Stanford University Press.

Olzak, Susan and Joane Nagel, eds. 1986. *Competitive Ethnic Relations.* Orlando, FL: Academic Press.

Olzak, Susan and Shanahan, Suzanne. 1996. "Deprivation and Race Riots: An Extension of Spilerman's Analysis." *Social Forces* 74 (3):931–961.

Olzak, Susan, Suzanne Shanahan, and Elizabeth H. McEneany. 1996. "Poverty, Segregation, and Race Riots: 1960–1993." *American Sociological Review* 61:590–613.

Ong, Paul and Abel Valenzuela Jr. 1996. "The Labor Market: Immigrant Effects and Racial Disparities." In Roger Waldinger and Mehdi Bozorgmehr, eds., *Ethnic Los Angeles.* New York: Russell Sage.

Park, Robert Ezra. 1949. *Race and Culture.* Glencoe, IL: Free Press.

Park, Robert Ezra. 1952. *Human Communities: The City and Human Ecology.* Glencoe, IL: Free Press.

Pastor, Manuel Jr. 1993. "Latinos and the Los Angeles Uprising: The Economic Context." Pamphlet. Claremont, CA: Tomas Rivera Center, Occidental College.

Peterson, Ruth D. and Lauren J. Krivo. 1993. "Racial Segregation and Black Urban Homicide." *Social Forces* 71 (4):1001–1026.

Philpott, Thomas. 1978, 1991. *The Slum and the Ghetto: Neighborhood Deterioration and Middle-Class Reform, Chicago, 1880.* New York: Oxford University Press and Wadsworth.

Piatt, Bill. 1997. *Black and Brown in America: The Case for Cooperation.* New York: New York University Press.

Porambo, Ron. 1971. *No Cause for Indictment: An Autopsy of Newark.* New York: Holt, Rinehart, and Winston.

Porter, Bruce and Marvin Dunn. 1984. *The Miami Riot of 1980: Crossing the Bounds.* Lexington, KY: Lexington Books.

Portes, Alejandro and Alex Stepick. 1993. *City on the Edge: The Transformation of Miami.* Berkeley: University of California Press.

Quillian, Lincoln. 1995. "Prejudice as a Response to Perceived Group Threat: Population Composition and Anti-Immigrant and Racial Prejudice in Europe." *American Sociological Review* 60:586–611.

Reed, John Shelton. 1972. "Percent Black and Lynching: A Test of Blalock's Theory." *Social Forces* 50:356–360.

Rieder, Jonathan. 1985. *Canarsie: The Jews and Italians of Brooklyn against Liberalism.* Cambridge, MA: Harvard University Press.

Roncek, Dennis W. and Andrew Montgomery. 1984. "Spatial Autocorrelation Diagnoses and Remedies for Large Samples." Paper presented at the Annual Meetings of the Midwest Sociological Society.

Sauter, Van Gordon and Burleigh Hines. 1968. *Nightmare in Detroit; A Rebellion and Its Victims.* Chicago: Regnery.

Shaw, Clifford and Henry D. McKay. 1929. *Delinquency Areas: A Study of the Geographic Distribution of School Truants, Juvenile Delinquents, and Adult Offenders in Chicago.* Chicago: University of Chicago Press.

Shogan, Robert and Tom Craig. 1964. *The Detroit Race Riot: A Study in Violence.* New York: Chilton Books.

Sigelman, Lee and Susan Welch. 1993. "The Contact Hypothesis Revisited: Black-White Interaction and Positive Racial Attitudes." *Social Forces* 71 (3):781–795.

Singer, Benjamin D., Richard W. Osborn, and James A. Geschwender. 1970. *Black Rioters: A Study of Social Factors and Communication in the Detroit Riot.* Lexington, MA: Heath Lexington Books.

Soule, Sarah A. 1992. "Populism and Black Lynching in Georgia, 1890–1900." *Social Forces* 71 (12):431–449.

Spear, Allan. 1967. *Black Chicago: The Making of a Negro Ghetto, 1890–1920.* Chicago: University of Chicago Press.

Spilerman, Seymour. 1970. "The Causes of Racial Disturbances: A Comparison of Alternative Explanations." *American Sociological Review* 35:627–649.

Spilerman, Seymour. 1971. "The Causes of Racial Disturbances: Tests of an Explanation." *American Sociological Review* 36:427–442.

Steinberg, Stephen. 1995. *Turning Back: The Retreat from Racial Justice in America*. Boston: Beacon Press.
Sternlieb, George. 1969. *The Tenement Landlord*. New Brunswick, NJ: Urban Studies Center, Rutgers University.
Sternlieb, George and Mildred Barry. 1967. "Social Needs and Social Resources Newark 1967." Research pamphlet. Graduate School of Business, Rutgers University–Newark.
Sugrue, Thomas J. 1996. *The Origins of the Urban Crisis: Race and Inequality in Postwar Detroit*. Princeton, NJ: Princeton University Press.
Suro, Roberto. 1998. *Strangers among Us: How Latino Immigration Is Transforming America*. New York: Alfred A. Knopf.
Suttles, Gerald D. 1968. *The Social Order of the Slum: Ethnicity and Territory in the Inner City*. Chicago: University of Chicago Press.
Suttles, Gerald D. 1972. *The Social Construction of Communities*. Chicago: University of Chicago Press.
Taeuber, Karl E. and Alma F. Taeuber. 1965. *Negroes in Cities; Residential Segregation and Neighborhood Change*. Chicago: Aldine Publishing.
Thomas, June Manning. 1997. *Redevelopment and Race: Planning a Finer City in Postwar Detroit*. Baltimore: Johns Hopkins University Press.
Tierney, Kathleen. 1994. "Property Damage and Violence: A Collective Behavior Analysis." In Mark Baldassare, ed., *The Los Angeles Riots: Lessons for the Urban Future*. Boulder, CO: Westview Press.
Tilly, Charles. 1969. "Collective Violence in European Perspective." In Hugh Davis Graham and Robert Ted Gurr, eds., *Violence in America: Historical and Comparative Perspectives*. New York: Signet Books.
Tolnay, Stewart E. and E. M. Beck. 1995. *A Festival of Violence: An Analysis of Southern Lynchings, 1882–1930*. Urbana: University of Illinois Press.
Tolnay, Stewart E., E. M. Beck, and James L. Massey. 1993. "Black Lynchings: The Power Threat Hypothesis Revisited." *Social Forces* 67 (3):605–623.
Tuttle, William M. Jr. 1975. *Race Riot: Chicago in the Red Summer of 1919*. New York: Atheneum.
United States Bureau of the Census. 1940. Census of Population. Census Tracts, Detroit (microfilm).
United States Bureau of the Census. 1950. Census of Population. Census Tracts. Vol 3. Pt. 1, Detroit.
United States Bureau of the Census. 1970. Census of Population and Housing, Census Tracts, Miami SMSA.
United States Bureau of the Census. 1980. Census of Population and Housing STF 3a, Data Tape Distributed by the International Consortium for Political and Social Research, Ann Arbor, MI.
United States Bureau of the Census. 1990. Census of Population and Housing STF 3a, CD-ROM. Distributed by the Census Bureau.

United States Commission on Civil Rights. 1982. *Confronting Racial Isolation in Miami.* Washington, DC: U.S. Commission on Civil Rights.

United States Department of Commerce News. 1992. "Information Release on Selected Los Angles Population and Economic Characteristics." CB92-145. May 11, 1992.

Upton, James M. 1981, 1989. *Urban Riots in the 20th Century: A Social History.* Bristol, IN: Wyndham Hall Press.

Useem, Bert. 1997. "The State and Collective Disorders: The Los Angeles Riot/Protest of April, 1992." *Social Forces* 76 (2):357–377.

U.S. News and World Report. 1993. "The Untold Story of the LA Riot." May 31:35–59.

Varshney, Ashutosh. 2002. *Ethnic Conflict and Civic Life: Hindus and Muslims in India.* New Haven, CT: Yale University Press.

Waldinger, Roger. 1986. "Who Makes the Beds. Who Washes the Dishes? Black/Immigrant Competition Re-assessed." In Harriet O. Dulup and Phanidra V. Wannara, eds. *Immigrants and Immigration Policy: Individual Skills, Family Ties, and Group Identities.* Greenwich, CT: JAI Press.

Waldinger, Roger. 1996. *Still the Promised City?: African Americans and New Immigrants in Post-Industrial New York.* Cambridge, MA: Harvard University Press.

Waldinger, Roger. 1997. "Black/Immigrant Competition Re-Assessed: New Evidence from Los Angeles." *Sociological Perspectives* 40 (3):365–386.

Waldinger, Roger and Mehdi Bozorgmehr. 1996. *Ethnic Los Angeles.* New York: Russell Sage.

Webster, William H., ed. 1992. *The City in Crisis: A Report by the Special Advisor to the Board of Police Commissioners on the Civil Disorder in Los Angeles.* Los Angeles: Special Advisory Study.

Widick, B. J. 1972. *Detroit: City of Race and Class Violence.* Chicago: Quadrangle Books.

Wilson, William Julius. 1987. *The Truly Disadvantaged: The Inner City, the Underclass, and Public Policy.* Chicago: University of Chicago Press.

Winters, Stanley, ed. 1979. *From Riot to Recovery: Newark after Ten Years.* Washington, DC: University Press of America.

Wright, Nathan, Jr. 1968. *Ready to Riot.* New York: Holt, Rinehart, and Winston.